Student Study Guide With IBM® SPSS® Workbook for Research Methods, Statistics, and Applications

Second Edition

Sara Miller McCune founded SAGE Publishing in 1965 to support the dissemination of usable knowledge and educate a global community. SAGE publishes more than 1000 journals and over 800 new books each year, spanning a wide range of subject areas. Our growing selection of library products includes archives, data, case studies and video. SAGE remains majority owned by our founder and after her lifetime will become owned by a charitable trust that secures the company's continued independence.

Los Angeles | London | New Delhi | Singapore | Washington DC | Melbourne

Student Study Guide With IBM® SPSS® Workbook for Research Methods, Statistics, and Applications

Second Edition

Kathrynn A. Adams

Guilford College

Eva K. Lawrence

Guilford College

Los Angeles | London | New Delhi
Singapore | Washington DC | Melbourne

FOR INFORMATION:

SAGE Publications, Inc.
2455 Teller Road
Thousand Oaks, California 91320
E-mail: order@sagepub.com

SAGE Publications Ltd.
1 Oliver's Yard
55 City Road
London, EC1Y 1SP
United Kingdom

SAGE Publications India Pvt. Ltd.
B 1/I 1 Mohan Cooperative Industrial Area
Mathura Road, New Delhi 110 044
India

SAGE Publications Asia-Pacific Pte. Ltd.
3 Church Street
#10–04 Samsung Hub
Singapore 049483

Printed in the United States of America

ISBN: 978-1-5443-1867-7

Acquisitions Editor: Leah Fargotstein
Content Development Editor: Chelsea Neve
Editorial Assistant: Elizabeth Wells
Marketing Manager: Shari Countryman
Production Editor: Veronica Stapleton Hooper
Copy Editor: Diana Breti
Typesetter: Hurix Digital
Proofreader: Dennis W. Webb
Cover Designer: Glenn Vogel

This book is printed on acid-free paper.

Certified Sourcing
www.sfiprogram.org
SFI-00453

SFI label applies to text stock

18 19 20 21 22 10 9 8 7 6 5 4 3 2 1

Contents

PREFACE   vii

PUBLISHER'S ACKNOWLEDGMENTS   ix

ABOUT THE AUTHORS   x

CHAPTER 1   Thinking Like a Researcher   1

CHAPTER 2   Building a Solid Foundation for Your Study Based on Past Research   11

CHAPTER 3   The Cornerstones of Good Research: Reliability and Validity   23

CHAPTER 4   Basics of Research Design: Description, Measurement, and Sampling   47

CHAPTER 5   Describing Your Sample   63

CHAPTER 6   Beyond Descriptives: Making Inferences Based on Your Sample   87

CHAPTER 7   Comparing Your Sample to a Known or Expected Score   103

CHAPTER 8   Examining Relationships Among Your Variables: Correlational Design   115

CHAPTER 9   Examining Causality   141

CHAPTER 10   Independent-Groups Designs   149

CHAPTER 11   Dependent-Groups Designs   191

CHAPTER 12   Factorial Designs   229

CHAPTER 13   Nonparametric Statistics   251

CHAPTER 14 Focusing on the Individual:
Case Studies and Single *N* Designs   267

CHAPTER 15 How to Decide? Choosing a Research
Design and Selecting the Correct Analysis   277

**ANSWERS TO ODD-NUMBERED QUESTIONS AND
DATA ANALYSIS PRACTICES**   **285**

Preface

The *Student Study Guide and IBM® SPSS® Workbook* is a companion for the textbook *Research Methods, Statistics, and Applications*. Students can use the study guide and workbook as a self-guided tool to reinforce and apply concepts from the textbook, or it can be used as an in-class or in-lab workbook, or both. Professors also may wish to assign exercises from the study guide and workbook as homework.

In the textbook, we included in-chapter practice and applications. Students can also test their knowledge via multiple-choice quizzes available on the student website. The study guide and workbook provides students with additional opportunities to review, practice, and apply essential knowledge and skills related to research methods and statistics.

Whereas many study guides repeat information from the textbook, we designed the study guide and workbook to supplement, rather than supplant, the textbook, and therefore we keep chapter summaries very brief. Additionally, the study guide and workbook goes beyond the textbook by including step-by-step directions for using the data analysis program, IBM® SPSS®, interpreting output, and writing up results. In the textbook, we consistently integrate research methods and statistics so that students understand how the research process requires a combination of these elements. Likewise, information about IBM® SPSS® is integrated within the relevant chapters of the study guide and workbook.

Many study guides focus on recognition and recall of material, and we acknowledge that gaining basic knowledge is an essential initial step in the learning process. We provide students with recognition activities via the online quizzes, but we wanted the study guide to require deeper processing. Consequently, the review exercises in the study guide require students to recall, rather than merely recognize, key terms.

A unique feature of this study guide and workbook is that it encourages students to build on their foundational knowledge. The majority of the exercises require students to think critically and actively engage with the material. These application exercises require more effort and involvement than recognition or recall tasks. Such exercises encourage students to make meaningful connections and are more likely to have enduring effects on their understanding and retention of research processes. Additionally, each chapter of the study guide includes a "Your Research" exercise so that students can apply key terms and concepts to their own research projects.

Each chapter in the *Student Study Guide and IBM® SPSS® Workbook* contains the following sections:

- Chapter Summary

- Learning Outcomes

- Review and Application of Key Concepts

- Your Research

- IBM® SPSS® Data Analysis and Interpretation

The **Chapter Summary** provides students with a very brief overview of the material covered in the textbook chapter. The summary is designed to reorient the students to the textbook chapter.

Learning Outcomes are listed in both the textbook and the study guide and workbook. Like the chapter summary, the learning outcomes are designed to help students reorient to the textbook chapter. Moreover, a reminder of the learning outcomes encourages students to consider what they have learned and what areas require additional review.

The **Review and Application of Key Concepts** section is divided into several short exercises. The exercises designated as "Review" require students to fill in the blank with a correct word or phrase in order to help the students solidify and distinguish key terms. The exercises designated as "Application" go beyond simple definitions and require students to apply key terms and concepts. These application exercises lend themselves particularly well to in-class or in-lab activities and discussion, especially when students are required to complete the fill-in-the blank sections prior to class or lab.

Students: Answers to odd-numbered questions are provided at the end of this book so that you can obtain quick feedback on these questions. Instructors have access to the complete answer keys.

Instructors: You can download the complete answer keys via the Instructor's Resource page on the textbook website, and then share with your students as you see fit. You may wish to grade the even-numbered questions and not share those answers with students, or you may wish to make all the answers immediately available so that students can guide their own study. In our own research methods and analysis course, we have found assigning exercises from the study guide as ungraded homework (checked simply as complete or incomplete) helps to ensure students come to class prepared and with good questions about the material. We then share the answers after class.

In the **Your Research** section, students apply key concepts and skills from the chapter to a research topic of their choice. We have found that encouraging students to think about and develop their own area of research promotes deeper understanding and integration of the material. The exercises in this section may be used as homework assignments, and they are especially useful in classes that require a semester- or year-long research project. Having students consider how different concepts apply to a topic of their choosing can also be useful in the absence of such a requirement. The questions about the research project are worded to apply to a great range of topics that might be selected by students or professors. In addition, the format allows students to compare their responses when working as a group on a research project.

Step-by-step directions for **IBM® SPSS® Data Analysis and Interpretation** are included in relevant chapters. Practice exercises are provided to help students gain competence using the program as well as interpreting and writing up results. As with the review and application questions, answers to odd-numbered practice exercises are at the end of this book, and instructors have online access to all the practice exercise answer keys.

We provide small example datasets in the workbook to enable students to practice data entry. Many exercises use larger datasets based on real studies. These larger datasets are provided on the textbook website (edge.sagepub.com/adams2e), along with links to other datasets that are available for download.

Publisher's Acknowledgments

SAGE wishes to acknowledge the valuable contributions of the following reviewers.

Derrick Michael Bryan, Morehouse College
Ben Denkinger, Augsburg University
Erin M. Fekete, University of Indianapolis
John D. Foshay, Central Connecticut State University
Charles Fountaine, University of Minnesota Duluth
David Han, University of Texas at San Antonio
John Hazy, Youngstown State University
Erin Henshaw, Denison University

About the Authors

Kathrynn (Kathy) A. Adams earned her PhD in general experimental psychology from the University of Alabama in 1977. She was a Charles A. Dana Professor of Psychology at Guilford College when she retired in 2017 after 37 years of teaching. Her professional interests include gender issues, relationships, and teaching pedagogy. She worked with the Preparing Future Faculty Program for 20 years and helped establish the Early College at Guilford, a nationally ranked high school. In her spare time, she spends as much time as possible outdoors, practices yoga, and bakes chocolate desserts.

Eva K. Lawrence earned her PhD in clinical psychology from Virginia Commonwealth University in 2002. She is a Professor of Psychology at Guilford College, where she has taught since 2003. Her research interests include environmental psychology and computer-mediated communication. Eva enjoys walking, yoga, and bike riding, and she loves to listen to live music.

Thinking Like a Researcher

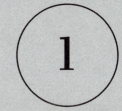

CHAPTER SUMMARY

Students in the social and behavioral sciences are often curious about personal and social phenomena, and learning about research methods and statistics will give you the tools necessary to engage your curiosity on a deeper level. Critical thinking is key to research, and this theme is carried out in the discussion of ethics. The chapter provides a brief history of ethical violations that led to the development of current ethics codes. Key ethical principles and standards are discussed, and you are encouraged to consider how ethical standards help to uphold broader ethical principles.

The remaining part of the chapter focuses on the scientific approach and, more specifically, the scientific method. You are encouraged to consider why the scientific approach is important and to consider the scientific method as a process rather than a list of steps that must be followed in order. A complete overview of the research process from start to finish is included in this chapter. The goal is to introduce you to key concepts in the context of the scientific approach, and later chapters detail the steps and concepts in more depth. The chapter ends with a discussion of proof and progress in science, debunking the notion that any single study leads to proof and, instead, encouraging you to consider how multiple studies move the field forward.

REVIEW AND APPLICATION OF KEY CONCEPTS FROM CHAPTER 1

Exercise 1.1: Critical Thinking (Application)

Think critically about the information you have received about this research methods course, and consider how you might gather new evidence to evaluate such information.

LEARNING OUTCOMES

After reading and reviewing Chapter 1, you should understand

- The connection between thinking critically and thinking like a researcher
- How to think critically about research ethics, including understanding and applying the ethical principles and standards of your discipline
- How to take a scientific approach and apply the steps in the scientific process
- Basic research terms that we will expound on in later chapters

1. What have you heard about this class?

   _____

   _____

2. How might this information impact your attitude or behaviors in the class?

   _____

   _____

3. Who are the sources of this information?

   _____

   _____

4. What biases might these sources have?

   _____

   _____

5. What evidence is available to support or refute the information?

   _____

   _____

   _____

   _____

   _____

6. What additional evidence would help you evaluate the information, and how might you go about gathering this evidence?

   _____

   _____

   _____

   _____

   _____

Exercise 1.2: Thinking Critically About Ethics (Review)

1. "Do no harm" is best represented by the ethical principle of
   _____.

2. "Do good" is best represented by the ethical principle of
   _____.

3. If you ensure your participants' _____ _____,
   that means that only the participants can identify their own responses.

4. _____ indicates that the participants'
   responses are kept private, but the researcher may be able to link
   participants to their responses.

5. _____ occurs prior to participation in a
   research study and _____ occurs after participation.
   Both are designed to inform participants about the nature of the study.

6. Participants have the right to _____, or
   stop participation without penalty.

7. _____ occurs when a researcher misleads participants
   and, if used, must be followed by a thorough _____
   to explain the true nature of the study.

8. In the 1960s, Stanley Milgram conducted several studies on obedience.
   In all cases, an experimenter ordered participants to administer increasingly
   powerful shocks to a "learner" whenever he gave an incorrect answer.
   In actuality, the "learner" never received any shocks because he was a
   confederate who was working with the experimenter. However, the
   participants believed they were causing harm to someone else.

   a. The experimenter used _____, in that he
      misled participants.

   b. At the end of each session, participants were told the real nature of the
      study and were assured that they had not actually shocked the "learner."
      In other words, the participants were _____.

   c. Still, this study is often used as an example of an unethical experiment
      because the participants experienced significant emotional distress. This
      violates the ethical principle of _____.

   d. Additionally, when participants asked to stop, the experimenter ordered
      them to continue. This violates the ethical standard of the right to
      _____.

Exercise 1.3: Thinking Critically About Ethics (Application)

1. In the Stanford prison experiment (Zimbardo, 1972), some participants assigned to be guards acted cruelly toward the participants assigned to be prisoners. Some of those assigned to be prisoners became depressed and withdrawn. What ethical principles did this experiment violate? Explain.

    _____

    _____

    _____

    _____

    _____

2. A classmate interviews someone for a sociology class and then tells you how "stupid" some of the interviewee's answers were. When you tell your classmate that you have some ethical concerns with how she is treating the interviewee, she retorts by saying that she has done nothing wrong because she is not revealing the interviewee's name or other identifying information. How might you respond? Consider not only ethical standards but also ethical principles that serve as guidelines for ethical decision making.

    _____

    _____

    _____

    _____

    _____

3. A researcher wants to observe interactions in a social media group. The group members are anonymous and the group is open, in that anyone can log on and view conversations. If you were a member of the Institutional Review Board, what questions might you have for the researcher before deciding whether or not to approve the study?

    _____

    _____

    _____

    _____

_____

_____

4. A researcher wants to investigate the relationship between depression and exposure to neighborhood violence, which includes hearing gunshots, witnessing verbal abuse, witnessing a physical assault, or witnessing a murder. The researcher plans on recruiting adult participants at various community meetings and then asking them to complete a questionnaire. If you were a member of the Institutional Review Board, what questions might you have for the researcher before deciding whether or not to approve the study?

_____

_____

_____

_____

_____

_____

5. A woman researcher proposes a study to examine how men support each other, but she does not want to rely on self-report that she believes might be biased. She would like to disguise herself as a man in order to infiltrate a men's therapy group, pretend to be a client, and covertly observe the sessions.

a. What ethical issues are raised by this study?

_____

_____

_____

_____

_____

_____

b. Do you think an IRB would approve this study? Explain.

_____

c. How would your evaluation of the ethics change if the researcher instead proposed disguising herself as a man to unobtrusively observe a public sporting event?

_____

_____

Exercise 1.4: The Scientific Approach (Review)

1. The steps in the scientific method are

   Step 1: _____

   Step 2: _____

   Step 3: _____

   Step 4: _____

   Step 5: _____

   Step 6: _____

   Step 7: _____

2. True or false? The steps must be followed in the exact order listed above.

   _____

3. A(n) _____ study is the only type of study that can demonstrate causation.

4. A(n) _____ study is used to describe one or more variables.

5. A(n) _____ study examines relationships among variables and can be used for prediction but not to demonstrate causality.

6. A(n) _____ is a prediction based on past research or theory that can be disproven.

7. In an experiment, the _____ variable is manipulated, participants/subjects are randomly _____, and then the _____ variable is measured.

Exercise 1.5: Choose a Research Design (Application)

1. Which of the following questions can be examined with an experiment?

   a. Do student athletes study more or less than nonathletes?

   b. Can political campaigns raise more money using negative campaign ads?

   c. Are attractive people perceived as more or less intelligent than not-so-attractive people?

   d. How do individuals perceive their local police department?

   e. Does exposure to violence increase risk of heart disease?

f. Do people high in the personality trait narcissism take more "selfies" than those low in this trait?

g. Is humanity becoming more or less violent?

h. Can daily statements of gratitude improve one's well-being?

2. For those questions you identified in question 1 that *could* be examined with an experiment, identify the independent and dependent variable.

_____

_____

_____

_____

_____

_____

3. For those questions you identified in question 1 that could *not* be examined with an experiment, identify the most appropriate research study to help answer the question.

_____

_____

_____

_____

_____

_____

Exercise 1.6: Identifying and Avoiding Plagiarism (Application)

The following excerpt was taken directly from Cash and Whittingham (2010, p. 180):

> We found that Nonjudge, the ability to refrain from judging one's own cognitions, emotions, and bodily sensations, predicted lower levels of depression, anxiety, and stress. Furthermore, Act-aware, the ability to maintain awareness of daily activities, predicted lower levels of depression.

Imagine that four students summarized this excerpt. Consider whether each student plagiarized Cash and Whittingham (2010) and explain your answer.

Student 1

Cash and Whittingham (2010) found that Nonjudge, the ability to refrain from judging one's own cognitions, emotions, and bodily sensations, predicted lower levels of depression, anxiety, and stress. Furthermore, Act-aware, the ability to maintain awareness of daily activities, predicted lower levels of depression.

_____ plagiarism or _____ not plagiarism

because _____.

Student 2

Cash and Whittingham (2010) found that participants who were most aware during their daily activities and most accepting of their own thoughts, feelings, and sensations tended to report the fewest depressive and anxious symptoms.

_____ plagiarism or _____ not plagiarism

because _____.

Student 3

"Nonjudge, the ability to refrain from judging one's own cognitions, emotions, and bodily sensations" and "Act-aware, the ability to maintain awareness of daily activities" are linked to improved mood.

_____ plagiarism or _____ not plagiarism

because _____.

Student 4

The ability to refrain from judging one's own thoughts, feelings, and physical sensations and the ability to maintain awareness of activities each day are linked to lower levels of depression, anxiety, and stress (Cash & Whittingham, 2010).

_____ plagiarism or _____ not plagiarism

because _____.

Exercise 1.7: The Big Picture: Proof and Progress in Science (Application)

1. A study found that mindfulness training was effective in reducing stress. Does this prove that mindfulness is an effective stress-reduction strategy? Explain.

_____

_____

2. Research consistently demonstrates the effectiveness of mindfulness in reducing stress. Does this body of research prove that mindfulness is an effective stress-reduction strategy? Explain.

_____

_____

3. Research consistently demonstrates the effectiveness of mindfulness in reducing stress. What might we conclude?

_____

_____

_____

4. What might be some of the next steps we take to examine the relationship between mindfulness training and stress?

_____

_____

_____

_____

5. If someone asked you how science helps us understand something, how might you answer?

_____

_____

_____

_____

YOUR RESEARCH

Taking a Scientific Approach in Identifying a Research Topic

1. Identify a topic that interests you: _____
2. Think about what you have learned about this topic from textbooks, research articles, or research summaries. Focus on scientific sources, not personal opinions or stories.

3. Come up with a list of 7–10 questions on this topic. Try to have some that build from what you have learned from scientific sources (see question 2), but you can also include questions based on observations or experiences.

a. _____

b. _____

c. _____

d. _____

e. _____

f. _____

g. _____

h. _____

i. _____

j. _____

4. Now evaluate your list and cross out or modify any that

- are biased, in that you think you already know the answer.

- are not testable (you cannot disprove them).

- necessitate equipment or a population to which you do not have easy access.

- do not fit the criteria, if any, laid out by your professor (e.g., your professor may require you to do an experiment, and not all questions can be experimental).

5. What questions remain? These might serve as a good starting point. Keep in mind that your research question will change as you read more research in this area.

Building a Solid Foundation for Your Study Based on Past Research

2

CHAPTER SUMMARY

Chapter 2 focuses on finding and evaluating past research on a topic. The chapter is designed to help you discern different sources, including the difference between primary and secondary sources, the difference between scholarly and popular sources, and the various types of scholarly work that you might find in an academic journal (i.e., primary research articles, literature reviews, and commentaries) as well as other scholarly sources (conference papers and posters, unpublished manuscripts, books, theses and dissertations, etc.). You will also learn the various ways to search for relevant research.

How to read and evaluate primary research articles is another major focus of this chapter. The key sections of a primary research article are outlined and their purpose discussed. An article on the topic of academic achievement is used to illustrate the different parts of a research article, and finding and referring to this article will greatly enhance your understanding of key concepts. Toward the end of the chapter, you will find suggestions for how to build on past research. The chapter ends with an ethics tip on how to avoid plagiarism and specific APA-style guidelines for citing and referencing sources.

LEARNING OUTCOMES

After reading and reviewing Chapter 2, you should understand

- The difference between a primary and secondary research source
- How to identify scholarly works
- How to find different types of scholarly works
- The parts of a primary research article
- Ways to build on past research to develop your research study
- The basics of APA format

REVIEW AND APPLICATION OF KEY CONCEPTS FROM CHAPTER 2

Exercise 2.1: Types of Sources (Review)

1. A _____ source is one that was written by an expert in a field and is designed to advance knowledge in that field.

2. A _____ source may have been written by an expert or by a layperson and is designed to educate or entertain.

3. A review of past research without a report of new, original research is a _____ research source.

4. An article in a newspaper, such as the *New York Times,* is a _____ source, but it may be either a primary or secondary research source depending on what the article covers.

5. An article reporting results of an original research study is a _____ research source, and it would also be considered _____ if it was written by and for experts in the field.

Exercise 2.2: Types of Scholarly Works (Review)

1. True or false? An article in an academic journal is a scholarly source, but it may be either a primary or secondary research source depending on what the article covers. _____

2. Literature reviews, meta analyses, and commentaries are examples of _____ research sources.

3. Most academic journals include a _____, in which work is reviewed by experts in the field.

4. The best type of source for a high-quality report of original research is the _____.

5. _____ and _____ tend to be more recent works than primary research articles, although they may not undergo as rigorous a peer review process.

Exercise 2.3: Types of Sources (Application)

1. The comedian Aziz Ansari wrote a book called *Modern Romance.* In addition to sharing personal anecdotes, he reports results of interviews and focus groups that he and his research partner conducted.

   a. Is this a popular or scholarly source?

   _____

   b. Are the reports of interviews and focus groups a primary or secondary research source? _____

2. Paul Eastwick, PhD, and his colleagues conducted a meta-analysis examining the role of physical attractiveness in dating preferences and actual

dating behaviors. Their findings were published in 2014 in the academic journal *Psychological Bulletin*.

    a. Is this a popular or scholarly source?

    _____

    b. Is their article a primary or secondary research source?

    _____

3. Günter Hitsch, PhD, and his colleagues conducted a study examining online dating behavior. Their findings were published in 2010 in the academic journal *Quantitative Marketing and Economics*.

    a. Is this a popular or scholarly source?

    _____

    b. Is their article a primary or secondary research source?

    _____

4. "Dating: One Key Determinant of Who Winds up Together" is an article on the website ScienceofRelationships.com. The author of the article, Gary Lewandowski, PhD, summarizes the results of two different research studies (neither of which he conducted) and explains what the results mean to the average person.

    a. Is this a popular or scholarly source?

    _____

    b. Is this article a primary or secondary research source?

    _____

5. Use Figure 2.1 in the textbook to help you answer the following questions.

    a. Which of the sources from questions 1 to 4 above might you use to generate ideas for a research topic but not include in your written report?

    _____

    b. Which of the sources from questions 1 to 4 above might you use to identify patterns and gaps in past research and to help you identify original research sources?

    _____

    c. Which of the sources from questions 1 to 4 above represents the type of source that should make up the majority of your sources for a research project?

    _____

6. Imagine you were using the online search engine Google (likely against your professor's recommendations) and you came across a report of original research.

a. How would you determine whether or not the source was a scholarly one?

_____

_____

b. Suppose that you determine the source is, in fact, scholarly. How else should you evaluate it to determine whether it is appropriate to use as a source for a research project?

_____

_____

_____

Exercise 2.4: Strategies to Identify and Find Past Research (Application)

Use the Database PsycINFO to answer these questions:

1. Do a search for the article "Honesty and Heroes: A Positive Psychology View of Heroism and Academic Honesty."

a. Who are the authors of this article? _____

b. What is the publication year? _____

c. Which journal published the article? _____

d. What is the volume number? _____

e. What are the page numbers? _____

f. Is this a primary or secondary research source? _____

2. Use the thesaurus function to identify narrower terms for *interpersonal relationships:*

_____

3. Do a keyword search for "interpersonal attraction," limiting the search to peer-reviewed articles published in academic journals between 2010 and 2015. How many search results are there? _____

4. What is the name of the article by Valerie Foster that was published in 2013 in the journal *Science?*

_____

5. How many references are cited in the article about interpersonal attraction by Tidwell, Eastwick, and Finkel (2013)? _____

Exercise 2.5: Reading and Evaluating Primary Research Articles (Review)

1. List, in order, the key parts of a primary research article:

    a. _____

    b. _____

    c. _____

    d. _____

    e. _____

    f. _____

    g. _____

    h. _____

2. A review of the research appears in the _____.

3. Details about the participants and the procedures for the study are found in the _____ section.

4. The _____ is a brief description of the purpose, method, and results.

5. Detailed results are found in the _____ section, and a summary of the results and their implications are found in the _____ section.

6. The hypothesis(es) of the study is usually found at the end of the _____.

7. An explanation of whether or not the results supported the hypothesis(es) is usually found near the beginning of the _____.

8. Limitations of the current study are explained in the _____.

9. Limitations of or gaps in past research are explained in the _____.

10. The _____ section lists all the sources cited in the paper.

Exercise 2.6: Reading and Evaluating a Primary Research Article (Application)

Look at the example published article in Appendix B in the textbook.

1. What is the title of the article? _____

2. Who are the authors? _____

3. Is this a primary or secondary research source? _____

4. Can you tell from reading the abstract whether or not the authors conducted an experiment? Why or why not?

_____

_____

_____

5. Summarize, in your own words, the key point of the first paragraph of the Introduction.

_____

_____

6. Summarize, in your own words, the key point of the second paragraph of the Introduction.

_____

_____

7. What is the purpose of the last paragraph in the Introduction?

_____

_____

8. In your own words, summarize the method of the study.

_____

_____

_____

9. In your own words, summarize the results of the study.

_____

_____

_____

10. What is the first limitation noted by the authors? How might a future research study address that limitation?

_____

_____

_____

Exercise 2.7: APA Format for References (Application)

1. Fill in the blanks:

First citation in text	Later citations
a. _____	Foster (2013)
(Estow, Lawrence, & Adams, 2011)	b. (_____)
c. _____	Kurzban and Weeden (2005)
Li et al. (2013)	d. _____
e. (_____)	(Buss & Schmitt, 1993)

2. Write an APA-style reference for the example published article in Appendix B in the textbook.

   _____

   _____

3. Find and correct the five APA-format citation errors in the paragraph:

   Many of us like to believe that "beauty comes from within" and that that inner beauty is more important than physical beauty. However, research suggests that physical attractiveness is the single most important factor that impacts our desire to date someone (Kurzban & Weeden, 2005; Li et al., 2013). An early cross cultural survey conducted by Buss & Schmitt found that across the world physical attractiveness of one's partner was more important for men than it was for women (1993). A more recent meta-analysis found that gender differences only occur in ratings of ideal romantic partners and ratings of hypothetical targets. Both men and women generally find physical attractiveness equally important in actual face-to-face interactions (Eastwick, Luchies, Finkel & Hunt, 2014). Moreover, although we might all desire an attractive partner, we tend to wind up with someone who matches our level of physical attractiveness (Miller, 2012). Thus our stated preferences do not fully predict our actual dating behaviors (Eastwick, Luchies, Finkel, & Hunt, 2014).

4. Find and correct the five APA-format errors in the references.

References

Miller, R. S. (2012). *Intimate relationships* (7th ed.). New York: McGraw-Hill.

Buss, D. M., and Schmitt, D. P. (1993). Sexual strategies theory: An evolutionary perspective on human mating. *Psychological Review, 100,* 204–232. doi:10.1037/0033-295X.100.2.204

Eastwick, P. W., Luchies, L. B., Finkel, E. J., & Hunt, L. L. (2014). The predictive validity of ideal partner preferences: A review and meta-analysis. *Psychological Bulletin, 140*(3), 623–665. doi:10.1037/a0032432

Kurzban, R., & Weeden, J. (2005). HurryDate: Mate Preferences in Action. *Evolution and Human Behavior, 26,* 227-244. doi:10.1016/j.evolhumbehav.2004.08.012

Li, N. P., Yong, J. C., Tov, W., Sng, O., Fletcher, G. J. O., Valentine, K. A...Balliet, D. (2013). Mate preferences do predict attraction and choices in the early stages of mate selection. *Journal of Personality and Social Psychology, 105,* 757–776. doi:10.1037/a0033777

Exercise 2.8: The Big Picture: Use the Past to Inform the Present (Application)

1. Why is it important for you to know how to find, read, and evaluate past research on a topic?

    _____

    _____

    _____

    _____

2. How does a specific formatting style for references, such as APA format, help make the process of finding past research easier?

    _____

    _____

    _____

    _____

    _____

Find Research on Your Topic

1. What database is most commonly used in your discipline?

   _____

2. Using that database, conduct a search for relevant and recent research articles on your topic. Doing this search will help you identify appropriate articles as well as help you refine and revise your research topic. It should take several hours if you do it correctly!

   a. What key words and phrases were most useful for finding relevant articles?

      _____

      _____

   b. What key words and phrases were least useful?

      _____

      _____

   c. What other search strategies were helpful for finding articles (e.g., searching by author, looking at references of articles)?

      _____

      _____

   d. Identify a few of the most relevant and interesting articles. Find the full text of these articles.

Read, Evaluate, and Reference a Primary Research Article on Your Topic

1. Identify and find the full text of a primary research on your topic (or revised topic) that you might model (in other words, you might use a similar method).

2. Write the reference list entry for the article in APA format:

   _____

   _____

   _____

3. Answer the following based on the article, using your own words (do not copy sentences or phrases directly from the article).

a. Briefly, what is the rationale for the study? (Hint: Look in the Introduction.)

_____

_____

_____

_____

_____

_____

b. Identify one hypothesis from the article that most interests you. (Hint: Hypotheses are usually toward the end of the Introduction section.)

_____

_____

_____

c. Outline the method used to test the hypothesis you identified. Include information about the participants, procedure, design, and measures. (Hint: Look in the Method section.)

_____

_____

_____

_____

_____

_____

d. Did the results support the hypothesis you identified? Explain. (Hint: Look in the Results and Discussion sections.)

_____

_____

_____

_____

_____

_____

4. Consider ways to build on the study:

   a. Identify one suggestion for future research that the author(s) identified in the Discussion section of the article and that you think you might be able to do.

   _____

   _____

   _____

   _____

   b. Review the section "Develop Study Ideas Based on Past Research" in Chapter 2 of the textbook. Which one of the four ways to build on past research does your answer to question 4a best fit under?

   _____

   c. Identify one other way that you might build on this study.

   _____

   _____

   _____

The Cornerstones of Good Research

RELIABILITY AND VALIDITY

3

CHAPTER SUMMARY

Reliability indicates consistency and *validity* indicates accuracy. Chapter 3 introduces these concepts and then explains how these terms relate to measurement.

In order to assess the reliability and validity of a measure, one must first clearly identify the constructs of interest and how these constructs will be operationally defined (or measured). It is also important to identify the scale of measurement (nominal, ordinal, interval, ratio). There are several ways to calculate the reliability of a scale, including internal consistency (coefficient alpha and split-half), test-retest, alternative forms, and interrater. Likewise, there are different ways to assess validity, and these can be conceptualized as face validity versus construct validity. Construct validity can be assessed by examining content validity, convergent validity, divergent validity, and criterion validity (either concurrent or predictive).

Next, reliability and validity at the study level are discussed. Reliability of a study indicates that results have been replicated in other studies, and validity of a study refers to both internal validity (the amount of control) and external validity (the generalizability of findings).

LEARNING OUTCOMES

After reading and reviewing Chapter 3, you should understand

- The definition of reliability and validity
- How to operationally define constructs with qualitative and quantitative measures
- How to identify different scales of measurement
- Different types of measures, including questionnaires, unobtrusive, and physiological measures
- How to assess the reliability and validity of measures
- How to evaluate the reliability and validity of a study

REVIEW AND APPLICATION OF KEY CONCEPTS FROM CHAPTER 3

Exercise 3.1: Broad Definitions of Reliability and Validity (Review and Application)

Fill in the blank with either the term *reliability* or *validity*.

1. Consistency = _____

2. Accuracy = _____

3. If you were to weigh yourself every day for a week using the same weight scale, and every day the scale gave you about the same result, that weight scale would have good _____ _____.

4. If you stood on a weight scale and it indicated that you weighed two pounds (an impossible weight for an adult), that weight scale would not have good _____.

5. Imagine that a friend wants to use a stretchy string as a measurement tool to determine whether a desk will fit in her bedroom. You tell her this is not a good idea because the stretchiness of the string might lead to different results each time she measures, and therefore her chosen measurement tool has questionable _____.

6. Your friend decides instead to use a stick to measure the space and the desk. Based on her measurements, she determines that the desk will fit. She checks several times and gets the same result. However, when she tries to put the desk in the space, the desk will not fit. Her measurement tool had good _____, but not good _____.

7. Imagine that your friend tells you that spinach tastes bad but admits she has never tried it. You might question the _____ of her conclusion about spinach.

8. In order for a measure or study to have _____, it must first have _____.

Exercise 3.2: Constructs, Operational Definitions (Review)

1. Love is a _____, or a concept that cannot be directly measured.

2. If you wanted to conduct a research study about love, you would need to decide what your _____ of love will be in your study. In other words, you would need to decide how to measure love (acknowledging that it will not be a perfect, direct measure of love).

3. If you decided to ask people to rate how much they love their partner on a scale from 1 to 10, you would be operationally defining love using a _____ measure because it is numerical.

4. The scale of measurement for a 1 to 10 rating scale is _____.

5. A 1 to 10 rating scale could just as easily be a 0 to 10 rating scale, or a −5 to +5 rating scale, for that matter. This demonstrates that on such scales, zero is not a fixed point in that it does not always have the same value. In other words, such rating scales do not have a(n) _____.

6. Fill in the table:

Property	Scales of Measurement With the Property
_____: Each number on the scale has a unique meaning.	
_____: Numbers on a scale are ordered.	
_____: The distance between numbers on a scale is equal.	
_____: The scale has a fixed zero.	

7. Weight is a _____ scale of measurement because the weight of 0 is a fixed point.

8. A rating scale from 1 = *Strongly Disagree* to 5 = *Strongly Agree* is a _____- type scale that represents a _____ scale of measurement.

9. Rankings (1st place, 2nd place, etc.) represent the _____ scale of measurement.

10. Marital status is often divided into categories, such as married or single, and therefore represents the _____ scale of measurement.

Exercise 3.3: Types of Measures (Review)

1. Social scientists often ask participants to respond to a series of questions about some characteristic or attitude. This is called a _____.

   a. Questions consist of a prompt called a _____ and an answer called a _____.

   b. The total computed for a series of items assessing a single construct is called a _____ _____.

   c. The two types of response formats are _____ and _____.

   d. A questionnaire examining consumerism asks, "Do you shop for clothing? Explain your answer." This is an example of a(n) _____ _____ response format.

e. Another question on the consumerism questionnaire asks for a rating on a 10-point scale (1 = *Not at All*; 5 = *Very Much*) in response to "Do you enjoy shopping for clothing?". This is an example of a(n) _____ _____ response format.

f. Suppose the question "Do you enjoy shopping for clothing?" used the response format of "Yes or No." What type of response format is this? _____

g. Because scoring is more difficult for the _____ response format, questionnaires most often employ the _____ response format.

h. Write an open-ended item assessing time spent one's cell phone.

i. Write a closed-ended item assessing the most common use of one's cell phone.

j. In the table below, summarize the advantages and limitations of the open-ended format and the closed-ended format.

Format	Advantages	Limitations
Open-ended format		
Closed-ended format		

2. _____ measures consist of recording the behavior or gestures of people, often outside the lab.

a. An observational measure should have a clear _____ and observers must be trained so that their assessments are _____ and _____.

b. A major reason to collect observational measures is _____.

c. Suggest an observational measure of student study habits.

_____

_____

d. Is your answer to question 2c an unobtrusive measure? How do you know?

_____

_____

3. Measures that assess bodily functions or physical reactions are called

_____.

a. _____ is an example of a physiological measure.

b. Students just learning how to conduct research often do not use physiological measures in their studies because _____

_____

Exercise 3.4: Assessing the Reliability of Measures (Review)

1. Two observers record whether people avert their gaze when a uniformed police officer enters the room. The consistency between the two observers' scores is the _____.

2. The consistency of a measure over time is _____.

3. _____ is used to assess internal consistency and involves examining the correlations among all items from a measure.

4. Fifty students complete two versions of an implicit bias scale and their scores are correlated. This is an example of _____ reliability.

5. In split-half reliability, the _____ items and the _____ items on a scale are correlated.

6. Suppose you find for your newly developed scale of kindness that Cronbach's alpha = .85. What does this finding imply about your scale?

_____

_____

7. You have the same group of people from question 6 take your kindness scale three weeks later, and then you correlate the scores for the first administration with the second administration. This is a measure of _____ reliability.

Exercise 3.5: Assessing the Validity of Measures (Review)

1. A relatively superficial judgment of the validity of a measure is _____, whereas a more thorough analysis would assess a measure's _____.

2. If a researcher creates a brief intelligence (IQ) test that shows results similar to established IQ tests, she could say her brief intelligence test has good

_____ .

3. If an IQ test shows different results than established tests of academic motivation (which is not part of IQ), the test has good _____

_____ .

4. You find that students' scores on a test of implicit bias are correlated with their willingness to partner with a person of another ethnicity for a problem-solving activity immediately following completion of the test. This is an example of _____ and is a subtype of _____ validity.

5. You also find that students' scores on the test of implicit bias are correlated with their willingness to partner at the end of the semester with a person of another ethnicity in a class presentation. This is an example of

_____ .

6. In developing a new kindness scale, you search relevant scholarly sources for ideas about what to include in your scale. You are concerned with

_____ .

7. In the table below, outline the specific types of measurement reliability and measurement validity.

Measurement Reliability	Measurement Validity
I.	I.
A.	II.
B.	A.
II.	B.
III.	C.
IV.	D.
	i.
	ii.

Exercise 3.6: Assessing Reliability and Validity of Measures (Application)

1. A political scientist wants to test the measurement reliability of this single item: "On a scale from 1 to 7, with 7 = *very likely*, how likely are you to vote in a political election?" Identify the type of measurement reliability she should assess and explain how she should assess it.

_____

_____

2. The political scientist from question 1 followed up with participants to determine whether or not they voted in the election. She compared their self-report to their subsequent voting behavior.

    a. Is she assessing the reliability or the validity of the self-report?

      _____

    b. Specifically, this is an example of _____.

    c. Identify a different type of measurement validity the researcher might use to evaluate the self-report question. Explain how she would evaluate this type of validity.

      _____

      _____

3. A mental health researcher wants to examine the reliability and validity of a five-item measure of state (or current) anxiety.

    a. What type of measurement reliability would you recommend he assess, and how would he do it?

      _____

      _____

    b. What type of measurement validity would you recommend he assess, and how would he do it?

      _____

      _____

4. A professor is interested in developing an academic confidence scale. How might she go about establishing the content validity of the new scale?

    _____

    _____

    a. The professor has students complete an academic confidence scale after the first week of the semester and again in the next class period in the second week. He is examining the _____ of the measure of academic confidence.

    b. The academic confidence scale has 10 items which are scored on a 5-point Likert-type scale ranging from 1 = *Strongly disagree* to 5 = *Strongly agree*. The professor finds that Cronbach's alpha = .80 in the administration during the first week. What would you say about the internal consistency of the scale?

      _____

      _____

c. What if the professor had found Cronbach's alpha = .40. What would you then say about the scale?

_____   _____

_____

d. How else could the professor measure the internal consistency of the confidence scale?

_____

_____

e. Suppose the professor finds that students' scores on the academic confidence scale in the first week are positively correlated with their end-of-semester grades. Is this a measure of validity or reliability? _____ What type? _____

f. Suppose the professor finds that students' scores on the academic confidence scale in the third week are positively correlated with the number of hours they reported studying that week. What type of validity or reliability has the professor assessed? _____

Exercise 3.7: Reliability and Validity at the Study Level (Review)

1. Replication helps determine the _____ of a study.

2. If replications of studies show similar results, we can say that the study is _____, but we cannot be certain of the study's _____.

3. There are two ways to evaluate the validity of a study: _____ _____ and _____.

4. _____ validity is especially important in an experiment.

5. Having a tightly controlled study improves its _____ _____ but likely impairs its _____.

6. A study that takes place in a natural setting and does not involve any manipulation by researchers has better _____ than _____.

7. _____ is how well results generalize.

8. Researchers should always be aware of the balance between _____ and _____ for their study.

Exercise 3.8: Reliability and Validity at the Study Level (Application)

1. A researcher finds that using content-related humor in her class presentations for one section of a course results in more engagement by students (as measured by attendance and number of student questions) than in her other section where she did not include humor. The researcher isn't sure that her results were due to the humor she included, and she repeats the process in her two sessions of a course the next semester. This is an example of _____replication.

2. A colleague in another discipline then decides to try telling jokes in one section of his course and not in the other. He finds the same result of increased student engagement. This is an example of _____replication.

3. These studies (in questions 1 and 2) demonstrate _____ reliability.

4. Suppose another colleague who tells jokes in one section of his course found no difference in engagement by the students in the joke vs. no joke course sections. In their end-of-semester feedback, however, students in both sections reported that the professor sang and danced in all his classes, and the students in both sections rated him equally funny. _____validity is in question here.

5. A professor tells jokes in an Introduction to Criminal Justice class and the students report that the professor is funny. The same professor tells the same jokes in an upper-level criminal justice class and the students report that the professor is not funny. _____ validity is in question here.

Exercise 3.9: The Big Picture: Consistency and Accuracy (Application)

1. If a measure of self-esteem was found to be consistent, we would say that the _____ was good.

2. The next step in assessing the measure would be to assess its _____ _____.

3. If studies using reliable and valid measures consistently found similar results, we would say that the results are _____.

4. If studies using reliable and valid measures consistently found similar results, we could then look at the _____ of the results.

YOUR RESEARCH

Find a primary research article on your topic. Choose one variable from the article and answer the following questions.

1. How was the variable operationally defined (or measured)?

   _____

   _____

2. What scale of measurement (nominal, ordinal, interval, or ratio) was used to operationally define the variable?

   _____

   _____

3. What evidence, if any, is provided about the measure's reliability?

   _____

   _____

4. What evidence, if any, is provided about the measure's validity?

   _____

   _____

Find an article you have recently read that described an experiment (it might be the study you considered in questions 1 to 4).

5. Can you describe how the authors of the article addressed internal and external validity?

   _____

   _____

6. What trade-offs did they make in order to achieve an acceptable balance between internal and external validity?

   _____

   _____

IBM® SPSS®* DATA ANALYSIS AND INTERPRETATION

Before you begin, you should first carefully review your raw data (raw data are the original measures your participants completed, the observation checklists your observers

*IBM® SPSS® Statistics / SPSS is a registered trademark of International Business Machines Corporation·

filled out, etc.). Review the section "Using Data Analysis Programs" in Chapter 3 for some hints on reviewing your raw data. Then, give each of your variables a unique name.

- If you are entering data for a class research project, be sure you use the variable names your professor tells you to use.

- If this is your own data set, you can name the variables anything you want as long as there are *no spaces or symbols* and the name begins with a *letter* (not a number).

For example, your variable names for the questionnaire below might be as follows:

ID, learnexp, afraid, lookforward, love, gender, age

Research Methods Questionnaire

ID#_____
Rate how much you agree or disagree with each statement:

1. Research Methods is a good learning experience.	Strongly Disagree	Disagree	Agree	Strongly Agree
2. I am afraid of Research Methods.	Strongly Disagree	Disagree	Agree	Strongly Agree
3. I look forward to Research Methods.	Strongly Disagree	Disagree	Agree	Strongly Agree
4. I love Research Methods.	Strongly Disagree	Disagree	Agree	Strongly Agree

Gender: _____ Male _____ Female _____ Non-binary Age: _____

Set up Your Data Set

1. Open SPSS® and go to "Variable View."

Go to "Variable View" by clicking the tab at the bottom of the screen.

2. List the names of your variables in the "Name" column.

Enter the variable names in the Name column.
Be sure each variable name is unique, there are no spaces or symbols, and the name does not begin with a number.

	Name					Values	Missing				Role
1	ID	Numeric	8	2		None	None	8	Right	Unknown	Input
2	learnexp	Numeric	8	2		None	None	8	Right	Unknown	Input
3	afraid	Numeric	8	2		None	None	8	Right	Unknown	Input
4	lookforward	Numeric	8	2		None	None	8	Right	Unknown	Input
5	love	Numeric	8	2		None	None	8	Right	Unknown	Input
6	gender	Numeric	8	2		None	None	8	Right	Unknown	Input
7	age	Numeric	8	2		None	None	8	Right	Unknown	Input

3. Be sure "Type" is Numeric for all your quantitative variables (numbers).

Untitled2 [DataSet2] - IBM SPSS Statistics Data Editor

	Name	Type	Width	Decimals	Label	Values	Missing	Columns	Align	Measure	Role
1	ID	Numeric	8	2		None	None	8	Right	Unknown	Input
2	learnexp	Numeric	8	2		None	None	8	Right	Unknown	Input
3	afraid	Numeric	8	2		None	None	8	Right	Unknown	Input
4	lookforward	Numeric	8	2		None	None	8	Right	Unknown	Input
5	love	Numeric	8	2		None	None	8	Right	Unknown	Input
6	gender	Numeric	8	2		None	None	8	Right	Unknown	Input
7	age	Numeric	8	2		None	None	8	Right	Unknown	Input

4. In the "Label" column, you can provide more information about what each variable measures.

Adding a label serves as a reminder for you, but you can skip this step if you have a small data set and the variable names provide enough of a reminder.

The label allows you to add more detail about each variable.

	Name	Type	Width	Decimals	Label	Values	Missing	Columns	Align	
1	ID	Numeric	8	2	ID	None	None	8	Right	Unl
2	learnexp	Numeric	8	2	RM good learning experience	None	None	8	Right	Unl
3	afraid	Numeric	8	2	afraid of RM	None	None	8	Right	Unl
4	lookforward	Numeric	8	2	look forward to RM	None	None	8	Right	Unl
5	love	Numeric	8	2	love RM	None	None	8	Right	Unl
6	gender	Numeric	8	2	participant's gender	None	None	8	Right	Unl
7	age	Numeric	8	2	participant's age	None	None	8	Right	Unl

5. The "Values" column serves as a reminder for how your nominal, ordinal, and interval variables are coded. You do not have to enter value labels, but it is a good idea so that you can easily access data codes without having to return to your raw data or code sheets.

Untitled2 [DataSet2] - IBM SPSS Statistics Data Editor

	Name	Type	Width	Decimals	Label	Values	Missing	Columns	Align	
1	ID	Numeric	8	2	ID	None	None	8	Right	U
2	learnexp	Numeric	8	2	RM good learning experience	None ···	None	8	Right	U
3	afraid	Numeric	8	1	afraid of RM	None	None	8	Right	U
4	lookforward	Numeric	8	2	look forward to RM	None	None	8	Right	U
5	love	Numeric	8	2	love RM	None	None	8	Right	U
6	gender	Numeric	8	2	participant's gender	None	None	8	Right	U
7	age	Numeric	8	2	participant's age	None	None	8	Right	U

Value Labels

Value Labels

Value: 4   Spelling...

Label: strongly agree

[Add]   1.00 = "strongly disagree"
           2.00 = "disagree"
[Change]   3.00 = "agree"

[Remove]

[Help]   [Cancel]   [OK]

Enter the value labels one at a time, clicking "add" after each.
Click **OK** after you have entered all the value labels.

6. The example above is for the first question on our Research Methods questionnaire (named "learningexp"). We had already entered value labels for the values 1 through 3 and are in the process of finishing our last value label.

Value → **1** Value Label → **strongly disagree; Add**

Value → **2** Value Label → **disagree; Add**

Value → **3** Value Label → **agree; Add**

Value → **4** Value Label → **strongly agree; Add**

When you have finished adding all the value labels, you click **OK**.

Hints:

- You do not need value labels for ratio data.

- Your value labels will depend on how your variables are coded.

  o For nominal variables (such as gender, in our example), you will decide how to code the categories. We decided to code male as 1 and female as 2 in our example, but we could have reversed that or used different numbers.

- Some interval scales might not have value labels for every score, and you can just enter the lowest and/or highest value labels. For example, if we asked participants to rate how happy they are on a scale from 1 to 10, with 10 being extremely happy, we might just enter the value label for the value 10 (extremely happy).

- If you have multiple variables with the same value labels, you can **copy and paste**.

Enter Data

1. Go to the "Data View" screen.

Click on the "Data View" tab on the bottom of the screen.

2. Enter your participants' scores.

Each row represents the data from one participant (*in this example, there are 10 participants*).

If you have missing data, leave the cell blank ('.').

ID	learnexp	afraid	lookforward	love	gender	age
1.00	4.00	2.00	3.00	3.00	1.00	21.00
2.00	3.00	2.00	3.00	3.00	2.00	19.00
3.00	3.00	2.00	2.00	2.00	1.00	31.00
4.00	2.00	4.00	1.00	1.00	1.00	28.00
5.00	3.00	2.00	2.00	2.00	2.00	29.00
6.00	4.00	1.00	3.00	3.00	1.00	32.00
7.00	4.00	2.00	3.00	3.00	2.00	23.00
8.00	3.00	2.00	3.00	3.00	1.00	25.00
9.00	2.00	3.00	1.00	4.00	2.00	30.00
10.00	2.00	3.00	3.00	4.00	2.00	58.00

Be sure to SAVE your data often! Data files are .sav files.

On the Menu bar, click **File → Save**

- At this point, you do not need to save the output file (.spo). But the output will be important once you have run analyses, and you will want to save it then.

Checking for Data Entry Errors Using SPSS

On the Menu Bar, click **Analyze → Descriptive Statistics → Frequencies**

The "Frequencies" box will open:

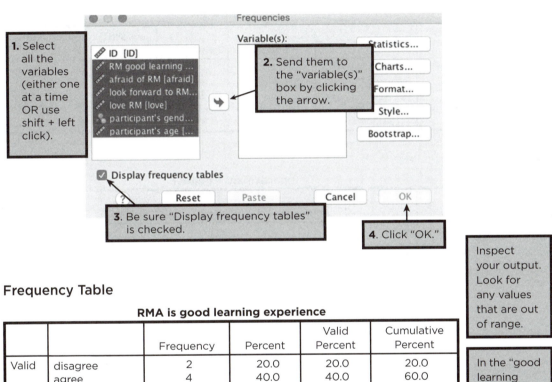

1. Select all the variables (either one at a time OR use shift + left click).

2. Send them to the "variable(s)" box by clicking the arrow.

3. Be sure "Display frequency tables" is checked.

4. Click "OK."

Inspect your output. Look for any values that are out of range.

In the "good learning experience" example, the value '9' is out of range.

Frequency Table

RMA is good learning experience

		Frequency	Percent	Valid Percent	Cumulative Percent
Valid	disagree	2	20.0	20.0	20.0
	agree	4	40.0	40.0	60.0
	strongly agree	3	30.0	30.0	90.0
	9.00	1	10.0	10.0	100.0
	Total	10	100.0	100.0	

afraid of RMA

		Frequency	Percent	Valid Percent	Cumulative Percent
Valid	strongly disagree	1	10.0	10.0	10.0
	disagree	6	60.0	60.0	70.0
	agree	2	20.0	20.0	90.0
	strongly agree	1	10.0	10.0	100.0
	Total	10	100.0	100.0	

look forward of RMA

		Frequency	Percent	Valid Percent	Cumulative Percent
Valid	strongly disagree	2	20.0	20.0	20.0
	disagree	2	20.0	20.0	40.0
	agree	6	60.0	60.0	100.0
	Total	10	100.0	100.0	

love RMA

		Frequency	Percent	Valid Percent	Cumulative Percent
Valid	strongly disagree	1	10.0	10.0	10.0
	disagree	2	20.0	20.0	30.0
	agree	5	50.0	50.0	80.0
	strongly agree	2	20.0	20.0	100.0
	Total	10	100.0	100.0	

participant's gender

		Frequency	Percent	Valid Percent	Cumulative Percent
Valid	male	5	50.0	50.0	50.0
	female	4	40.0	40.0	90.0
	30.00	1	10.0	10.0	100.0
	Total	10	100.0	100.0	

In the "gender of participant" example, the value '30' is out of range.

Create Scale Scores

Remember that some constructs are operationally defined with multiple items, in which case you will need to create a scale score. To do so, you will follow these steps:

- Make sure that all items are coded in the same direction, and recode variables if necessary.

- Check that the scale has good internal consistency (a type of measurement reliability).

- Compute a scale score.

(Note: If the measure has separate subscales, follow these directions for each subscale.)

1. Make sure that all the items are coded in the same direction. Recode any that are coded in the opposite direction.

For example, the four items below are part of the "Attitudes Toward Research Methods" measurement scale.

1. Research Methods is a good learning experience	Strongly Disagree	Disagree	Agree	Strongly Agree
2. I am afraid of Research Methods	Strongly Disagree	Disagree	Agree	Strongly Agree
3. I look forward to Research Methods	Strongly Disagree	Disagree	Agree	Strongly Agree
4. I love Research Methods	Strongly Disagree	Disagree	Agree	Strongly Agree

- A higher score on questions 1, 3, and 4 indicates a positive attitude.

- However, a higher score on question 2 indicates a negative attitude.

- We want a higher score on our "Attitudes Toward Research Methods" scale to indicate more positive attitudes, and we therefore will need to recode question 2 (named "afraid" in our example data set) so that it is coded in the same direction as the other variables.

It is best to use "Recode into Different Variable" so that you can keep track of changes you have made to your data set.

- When you recode into a different variable, you create a brand new variable in your data set. An easy strategy for naming your recoded variables is to add an "R" to the end of the original name (in our example, we will recode "afraid" into "afraidR").

- After recoding, the new recoded variable will show up at the end of your data set. The original variable will remain in your data set.

Recoding Variables

On the Menu Bar, click **Transform → Recode → into different variables**

The "Recode" box will open:

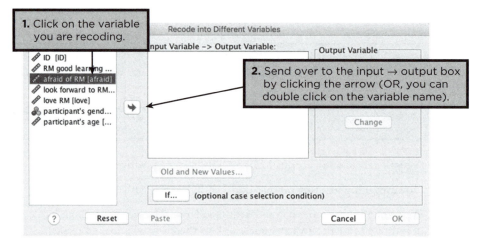

1. Click on the variable you are recoding.

2. Send over to the input → output box by clicking the arrow (OR, you can double click on the variable name).

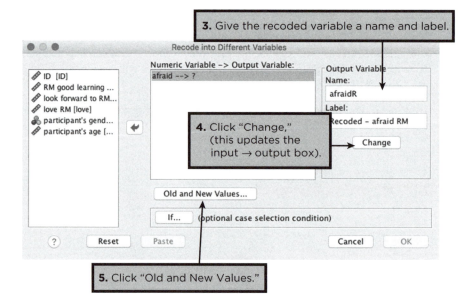

3. Give the recoded variable a name and label.

4. Click "Change," (this updates the input → output box).

5. Click "Old and New Values."

A new box will open:

Enter the Old and New Values, clicking "Add" after each.

When you are done with all the values, click "Continue."

You will return to the 1st Recode box, then click "OK."

In our example dataset, the original variable was coded on a 4-point scale. To recode, we need to reverse the codes so that a higher score indicates more positive attitudes:

$1 \rightarrow 4$

$2 \rightarrow 3$

$3 \rightarrow 2$

$4 \rightarrow 1$

Hints:

- Your old and new values will depend on how your original variable was coded.

- You need to enter new values for ALL your old values. Even if the old and new values are the same number, you need to enter it (i.e., $3 \rightarrow 3$).

- You can recode multiple variables at the same time as long as the old and new values are the same for all the variables.

- Your recoded variable will show up at the end of your dataset. If you like, you can click and drag it to a different position in your dataset.

- You can check that you did the recoding correctly by looking at the recoded variable in data view. Select a few participants and compare the original value to the recoded value.

- Recoding can be used for other transformations as well. For example, you could convert a 4-point scale to two categories (low vs. high).

2. Check that the scale has good internal consistency (a type of measurement reliability). Here we will show you how to calculate Cronbach's alpha to test the internal consistency of a scale.

Reliability Analysis (Cronbach's Alpha)

On the Menu bar, click **Analyze → Scale → Reliability Analysis**

The "Reliability Analysis" box will appear:

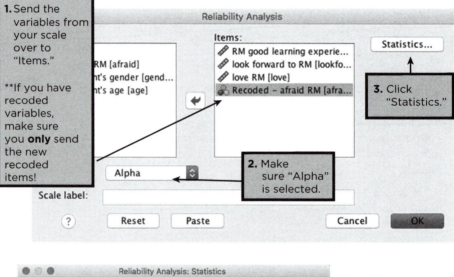

After you click OK, an output window will appear.

Reliability

Scale: ALL VARIABLES

Case Processing Summary

		N	%
Cases	Valid	10	100.0
	Excluded[a]	0	.0
	Total	10	100.0

a. Listwise deletion based on all variables in the procedure.

Reliability Statistics

Cronbach's Alpha	N of Items
.762	4

Cronbach's alpha is the measure of internal consistency and tells us how reliable the measurement scale is.

The higher the alpha, the better reliability. Ideally, the alpha should be .70 or above, although an alpha as low as .60 can be acceptable.

In this example, alpha = .76.

Item-Total Statistics

	Scale Mean if Item Deleted	Scale Variance if Item Deleted	Corrected Item-Total Correlation	Cronbach's Alpha if Item Deleted
RM good learning experience	7.9000	4.100	.605	.683
look forward to RM	8.5000	3.611	.763	.591
love RM	8.1000	4.989	.227	.882
Recoded-afraidRM	8.2000	3.733	.740	.607

This table allows you to examine each item. The last column tells you what your alpha would be if an item were deleted (or omitted).

Here we see that omitting the "love RM" question would raise our alpha to .88.

Scale Statistics

Mean	Variance	Std. Deviation	N of Items
10.9000	6.767	2.60128	4

Making Decisions Based on Reliability Analysis

- If the alpha is below .70, check first that your data were correctly coded and recoded and you selected the correct variables (e.g., the not recoded items plus the recoded items). If so, check to see if omitting an item will raise the alpha. If you cannot obtain an acceptable alpha, this means that the items are not consistent with each other and should be analyzed separately.

- If the alpha is above .70, your measure has good internal consistency. You can still check individual items to see if omitting an item will raise the alpha.

- The decision to omit an item should be based on how much it will help to improve the alpha *and* a review of the item itself. You may decide to keep an item if you believe it is important to your overall construct.

- In the example output, we have a pretty decent alpha with all four items (.76). However, if we omit the "love RM" question, the alpha will increase to .88, and this is a big increase. Plus, this question doesn't seem to fit as well with the other items because it assesses a general feeling of love. Consequently, we chose to omit it from further analyses.

- To omit an item, you don't actually delete it from your dataset. You simply leave it out when you compute a scale score in the next step.

3. Compute a scale score. This new variable will represent the total or average of all the individual items on a measurement scale. You will use this scale score for future analyses.

On the Menu bar, Click **Transform → Compute**

The "Compute Variable" box will open:

1. Name the measurement scale.

Target Variable:
RMattitudeTotal

Type & Label...

ID [ID]
RM good learning ...
afraid of RM [afraid]
look forward to RM...
love RM [love]
participant's gend...
participant's age [...
Recoded – afraid ...

Numeric Expression:
learnexp + lookforward + afraidR

+ < > 7 8 9
- <= >= 4 5 6
* = ~= 1 2 3
/ & | 0 .
** ~ () Delete

If... (optional case selection condition)

? Reset Paste

Cancel OK

2. To compute a total score, create a numeric expression that adds the individual items (*Don't forget to use any **recoded** variables, not the originals!*).

Send each variable over one at a time, followed by a + (as in this example), or type directly into the numeric box.

Alternatively, you can compute a mean score (this is a good option if you have missing data). Create a numeric expression:

mean (variable1, variable2, etc.)
In our example, we would have:
mean (learningexp, afraidR, lookforward)

3. Click "OK."

Practice Exercise 1

A researcher is interested in how much students value academic honesty. Here is the five-question scale she used to measure the value of academic honesty:

On a scale of 1 to 5, with 5 indicating *strongly agree*, how much do you agree that
Academic honesty is essential to a good education. _____
Talking about academic honesty is a waste of class time. _____
Cheating is sometimes necessary for academic success. _____
I would think less of a friend if I found out that he or she cheated on an assignment. _____
Honesty and integrity in my academic work are strong values for me. _____

She collected data from 10 people; here is a summary of the data:

ID	Age	Gender	Value of Academic Honesty: Question #s and Answers				
			#1	#2	#3	#4	#5
1	19	Male	5	2	1	4	4
2	21	Male	3	4	3	1	3
3	23	Female	3	2	1	3	4
4	18	Male	4	2	1	3	5
5	24	Female	4	1	2	4	3
6	50	Female	4	2	1	4	4
7	20	Female	3	3	4	3	1
8	19	Male	4	3	4	4	1
9	28	Male	3	2	2	3	3
10	26	Female	1	4	3	1	3

1. **Enter** the data using SPSS®. You can make up whatever variable names make sense to you. All variables should be numeric, so be sure to code gender as a number.

2. Look over the questionnaire. You will want a higher number to indicate stronger values for academic honesty. Right now there are some questions that need to be reverse coded. Using SPSS®, **recode** these into **different variables** so that a score of 1 = 5, 2 = 4, 3 = 3, 4 = 2, 5 = 1).

3. **Check the reliability of the scale** by calculating Cronbach's alpha. Remember to use the RECODED variables.

   a. What is the alpha (α)? _____

b. What decisions should you make based on these results?

_____

_____

4. **Compute** the total score on the value of academic honesty questionnaire. Remember to use the RECODED variables here, not the original ones.

5. Check your answers and make any corrections to the dataset, if necessary.

Practice Exercise 2

1. Go to https://edge.sagepub.com/adams2e

2. Click on Data Sets.

3. Open the file called Reminiscence Study, and view these files:

   a. Description of the Reminiscence datasets (reminiscence description.pdf)

   b. Reminiscence data set 1 (reminiscence1.sav)

4. Read over the description of the Reminiscence dataset, paying special attention to how variables are named and coded. It may be helpful to print this file.

5. Note that there are several measurement scales in the survey.

   a. There are two subscales from the Savouring Beliefs Inventory (Bryant, 2003):
      i. Savouring the Moment (8 items)
      ii. Anticipating the Future (8 items)

   b. Satisfaction with Life (5 items; Diener, Emmons, & Larson, 1985)

   c. Reminiscence Strategies (9 items created for this survey). Note that you can also create subscales for the strategies, such as cognitive (3 items) or behavioral strategies (6 items).

6. Download and open the dataset.

7. Choose one of the measurement scales (or subscales): _____

   a. Look at the individual items for the measurement scale or subscale you chose. Do you need to recode any of the items for the scale you chose? If so, recode the variables in the data set using SPSS®.

   b. Using SPSS®, calculate Cronbach's alpha for the scale you chose.

      α = _____

   c. Compute the scale score.

8. If you would like more practice, repeat with another of the measurement scales.

Basics of Research Design

DESCRIPTION, MEASUREMENT, AND SAMPLING

$$4$$

CHAPTER SUMMARY

A descriptive study examines the who, what, when, where, and how, but it does not examine relationships among them. In this chapter, we discuss when it is appropriate to use a descriptive study and how to evaluate the validity of descriptive research. The chapter also details methods such as surveys, observations, and archival research, which are common in various types of research studies. We also discuss the advantages and issues associated with each of these methods.

The second half of the chapter focuses on sampling. The chapter explains how to identify a population and follows with specific procedures for obtaining different types of probability or nonprobability samples from the population. Issues regarding sample size for probability and nonprobability samples are also discussed. The chapter ends with an introduction to other types of studies that will be detailed in later chapters.

REVIEW AND APPLICATION OF KEY CONCEPTS FROM CHAPTER 4

Exercise 4.1: Understand Prevalence and Trends (Review and Application)

Fill in the blank with either the term *prevalence* or *trend*.

1. Descriptive research is used to examine _____, or how common a behavior, attitude, characteristic, or condition is.

2. Descriptive research can also be used to examine a _____, or a pattern over time.

LEARNING OUTCOMES

After reading and reviewing Chapter 4, you should understand

- When a descriptive study is appropriate

- How to evaluate the validity of descriptive research

- Common methods used in research, including surveys, observations, and archives

- How to define a population and obtain a sample using probability and nonprobability sampling techniques

3. In 2012, the _____ of Facebook use among American adults was 67%.

4. Use of Facebook did not change much from 2012 to 2015, indicating a stable _____.

5. Use of Pinterest rose from 15% in 2012 to 31% in 2015, indicating an upward _____.

6. A public health researcher who examines the current rate of smoking in teenagers is examining _____.

7. A public health researcher who examines how rates of smoking among teenagers has changed over time is examining the _____.

Exercise 4.2: When Is a Descriptive Study Appropriate? (Application)

The following questions are all about the television series *Game of Thrones*. You may be familiar with the series or the books upon which the series was based, but you do not need to know anything about it for this exercise. Circle all the questions that can be tested with a descriptive study.

1. How many people watched the first six seasons of *Game of Thrones*?

2. Was the first season more popular among younger or older viewers? What about the other seasons?

3. How has the popularity of the series changed over time?

4. Who is the most loved character?

5. Does killing off a beloved character cause anxiety among viewers?

6. What did viewers like and dislike about the first season?

7. When did most people watch the episodes, as they aired or later?

8. Where did most people watch the episodes, at home or outside the home?

9. What will people think about the show 200 years from now?

Exercise 4.3: Validity in Descriptive Studies (Review)

1. _____ validity refers to the overall accuracy of a study's conclusion.

2. _____ validity is how accurately a measure, test, or instrument used in a study measures what it intended to measure.

3. A _____ is a preliminary study with a small sample to test measures and procedures prior to conducting a larger study.

4. Creating a measure from scratch _____ (is/is not) a good way to help ensure good measurement validity, whereas using a published scale _____ (is/is not) helpful in ensuring measurement validity.

5. Measurement validity is _____ (as/more/less) important in a descriptive study compared to other types of studies.

6. The ability to generalize to other samples, settings, and methods, or _____ validity, is _____ (as/more/less) important in a descriptive study compared to other types of studies.

7. The ability to show causality, or _____ validity, is _____ (as/more/less) important in a descriptive study compared to other types of studies.

Exercise 4.4: Measurement Methods (Review)

1. Interviews and questionnaires are types of _____.

2. A _____ interview is more flexible than a _____ interview.

3. An observer completing a(n) _____ observation would let the participants know that they are being observed, whereas in a(n) _____ observation, the observer would not let the participants know they are being observed.

4. _____ observations occur in a natural environment and do not involve any interference, whereas the researcher sets up the environment for _____ observations.

5. A _____ is someone who pretends to be a participant or bystander but is actually working for the researcher.

6. In a _____ observation, the researcher or observer is actively involved in the situation, whereas the researcher or observer is not involved in a _____ observation.

7. A _____ is a detailed description of observed behaviors.

8. A _____ is a list of qualities or behaviors that the observer checks off, if observed.

9. A _____ is a numerical rating of a particular quality (e.g., how loud someone spoke).

10. _____ is how long it takes a participant to respond, _____ is how long it takes to complete a task, _____ is how long a behavior lasts, and _____ is the time between stopping one task and starting another.

11. _____ research involves the analysis of existing data or existing records.

12. _____ is existing data that were collected by one researcher or group.

13. Fill in the table below on identifying and reducing bias:

Description of Bias	Name of Bias	How to Reduce (list strategies)
Observers focus on behaviors or interpretations that support their expectations		
Interviewers provide verbal or nonverbal cues that impact the participants' responses		
Participants respond based on what they think is socially acceptable or how the want to be perceived		

Exercise 4.5: Measurement Methods (Application)

Imagine that you are interested in understanding how students at your college or university view the women's basketball team (or another sports team, if your college or university does not have a women's basketball team).

1. Survey

   a. What would be the advantages and disadvantages of conducting a survey (interview or questionnaire) on this topic?

   Advantages: _____

   Disadvantages: _____

   b. If you chose to do a survey, would you choose interviews or questionnaires? Explain the rationale for your choice.

   _____

   _____

   _____

2. Observation

   a. What types of observations might you make that could help you better understand how students view the team, and where would you make them?

      _____

      _____

      _____

   b. What would be the advantages and disadvantages of such observations?

      Advantages: _____

      Disadvantages: _____

3. Archival Research

   a. What type of archives might help you understand student views of the team?

      _____

   b. What would be the advantages and disadvantages of conducting archival research on this topic?

      Advantages: _____

      Disadvantages: _____

4. Validity of the Study

   Choose one method of study—interviews, questionnaires, observations, or archives—to examine this topic.

   a. How might you ensure good measurement validity?

      _____

      _____

      _____

   b. How might you ensure good study validity? (Remember to focus on external validity, which is important in a descriptive study.)

      _____

      _____

      _____

Exercise 4.6: Defining the Population and Obtaining a Sample (Application)

1. If you are interested in examining how students at your school view a specific sports team, the _____ for your study is all the students at your school.

2. In question 1, athletes at your school would be a _____ _____.

3. The students who participated in your study on views of the sports team are your _____.

4. If athletes are overrepresented in your sample of students, you have a _____.

5. In _____ sampling, all students at your school would have an equal chance of being selected for your sample because you used the process of _____ (with or without replacement).

Exercise 4.7: How Will You Obtain a Sample From Your Population? (Review)

Identify the specific type of probability or nonprobability sampling described.

Description	Probability Sampling	Nonprobability Sampling
Uses random selection? (yes or no)		
Most basic method		
Sample proportions of a key characteristic match population proportions		
Identify clusters instead of individuals within population		not applicable
Sample represents extremes within a population	not applicable	
Participants recruit others	not applicable	

Exercise 4.8: Probability Sampling (Application)

1. Imagine you wanted to interview the actors who were in the first season of the television series *Game of Thrones*. You know that it would not be possible to interview all the actors, so you decide to use probability sampling in order to obtain a representative sample.

You define the population as all the actors who played named characters during the first season (so you would exclude extras who did not play a character with a name).

You obtain a list of all the named characters from online sources.

a. What would be the next steps if you used simple random sampling?

_____

_____

_____

b. Suppose you wanted your sample to accurately represent the proportion of female actors and male actors in the first season. What type of probability sampling would you use and how would you obtain your sample?

_____

_____

_____

c. There were 129 named characters on the first season of *Game of Thrones*.

i. Use either the formula in Chapter 4 or the online calculator found at www.surveysystem.com/sscalc.htm to calculate the minimum sample size you would need to have a confidence interval of 5 (meaning that the margin of error will be about 5%) and a confidence level of 95% (meaning that there is a 95% likelihood that you will achieve your desired margin of error). _____

ii. If you increased your confidence interval to 12 and kept your confidence level at 95%, what is the minimum sample size you would need? _____

2. Imagine you want to observe home basketball games at your school but realize that you will not be able to observe the entire population of home basketball games. Instead, you decide to randomly select a sample of home games that will be played on Saturdays.

a. What type of sampling is this? _____

b. What would be your next steps?

_____

_____

_____

Exercise 4.9: Nonprobability Sampling (Application)

Imagine again that you want to interview actors on the first season of *Game of Thrones*, but now you decide to use nonprobability sampling.

1. What is the advantage of using nonprobability sampling in this example?

   _____

   _____

   _____

2. How would you obtain a sample using convenience sampling?

   _____

   _____

   _____

3. How would you obtain a sample using snowball sampling?

   _____

   _____

   _____

4. Suppose you wanted your sample to accurately represent the proportion of female actors and male actors in the first season. What type of nonprobability sampling would you use and how would you obtain your sample?

   _____

   _____

   _____

5. Suppose you wanted your sample to represent extremes in the population, such as level of fame, how much screen time the actor got, whether or not the character died, etc. What type of nonprobability sampling would you use and how would you obtain your sample?

   _____

   _____

   _____

Exercise 4.10: The Big Picture: Description and Beyond Description (Application)

Suppose that a researcher examined weekly exercise routines and mental health issues including symptoms of depression and anxiety.

1. In the research report, the researcher reported frequency and type of exercise, as well as frequency and severity of mental health issues within the sample. This represents a _____ design.

2. In the same research report, the researcher examined the correlation between frequency of exercise and severity of mental health issues. This represents a _____ design.

3. If the researcher also examined whether or not increased exercised resulted in a decrease in severity of mental health issues, this would represent a _____ design.

4. Is it reasonable to report results from multiple designs in a single research report? Explain.

_____

_____

_____

YOUR RESEARCH

Designing a Descriptive Study on Your Topic

1. Identify one question that you could examine with a descriptive study and that you believe is important to study (based on what you know about existing research in this area).

_____

_____

2. What descriptive method (or combination of methods) would you use to help answer this question? Consider a survey (interview and/or questionnaire), observation, or archival research. Explain your rationale.

_____

_____

3. Would it be better to use probability or nonprobability sampling? Explain.

_____

_____

_____

4. Choose a specific sampling procedure. Define the population and then outline how you will obtain a sample from your population.

_____

_____

_____

_____

_____

_____

IBM® SPSS® DATA ANALYSIS AND INTERPRETATION

IBM® SPSS® can help you create groups, select groups, and select a random sample of cases. These tools can be useful when sampling from a population, if you have a dataset with basic information about every member of the population. These tools can also be useful for statistical analyses that you will learn about in the following chapters.

Creating Groups

You might want to identify a subpopulation or group of women or athletes. This is easily accomplished because gender and athlete status are both nominal variables (they are already categories). But what if you have interval or ratio data? If you wanted to examine a subpopulation or group who were under 21, for example, you could convert that ratio data into categories by creating groups in SPSS.

How to Create Groups Based on a Cutoff Score

You may create groups based on a predetermined cutoff. For example, in the research literature older adults are often categorized as "young old" (55–64), "middle old" (66–74), and "old old" (75 and older).

On the Menu Bar, click **Transform → Recode → into Different Variables**

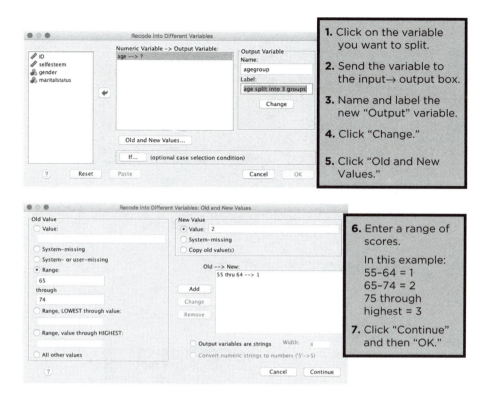

1. Click on the variable you want to split.

2. Send the variable to the input→ output box.

3. Name and label the new "Output" variable.

4. Click "Change."

5. Click "Old and New Values."

6. Enter a range of scores.

   In this example:
   55–64 = 1
   65–74 = 2
   75 through highest = 3

7. Click "Continue" and then "OK."

How to Create Groups Based on a Median Split

If you do not have a cutoff score that makes sense to use, or if you want approximately equal numbers in your groups, you can create groups using a median split. The median is the middle score in a sample distribution. There are two steps to a median split:

1. Find the median of the scale.

On the Menu Bar, click **Analyze → Descriptive Statistics → Frequencies**

1. Send the variable you want to split to the "Variable(s)" box.

2. Click "Statistics."

The "Statistics" box will open:

3. Click on "Median" and then "Continue."

You will return to the first Frequencies box, then click "OK."

After you click OK, the output window will open.

OUTPUT
Frequencies

Statistics

selfesteem		
N	Valid	25
	Missing	0
Median		14.0000

The output reports the median.

In this example, the median = 14.

selfesteem

		Frequency	Percent	Valid Percent	Cumulative Percent
Valid	6.00	1	4.0	4.0	4.0
	8.00	2	8.0	8.0	12.0
	9.00	1	4.0	4.0	16.0
	10.00	4	16.0	16.0	32.0
	12.00	4	16.0	16.0	48.0
	14.00	1	4.0	4.0	52.0
	15.00	4	16.0	16.0	68.0
	17.00	1	4.0	4.0	72.0
	18.00	1	4.0	4.0	76.0
	19.00	1	4.0	4.0	80.0
	20.00	5	20.0	20.0	100.0
	Total	25	100.0	100.0	

The frequency table tells you how scores are distributed.

In this example, 52% of the scores fall at or below the median of 14.

2. Recode the variable just as you would when using a cutoff score.

On the Menu Bar, click **Transform → Recode → into Different Variables**

1. Click on the variable you want to split. **2.** Send the variable to the input→ output box. **3.** Name and label the new "Output" variable. **4.** Click "Change." **5.** Click Old and New Values."

Recode into Different Variables: Old and New Values

Old Value
- ○ Value:
- ○ System-missing
- ○ System- or user-missing
- ○ Range:

  through

- ● Range, LOWEST through value:
  14
- ○ Range, value through HIGHEST:

- ○ All other values

New Value
- ● Value: 1
- ○ System-missing
- ○ Copy old value(s)

Old --> New:

  Add
  Change
  Remove

☐ Output variables are strings   Width: 8
☐ Convert numeric strings to numbers ('5'->5)

Cancel   Continue

Enter a range of scores. We can use the "Range, LOWEST through value" command to get the low category.

In this example, Lowest through 14 = 1.

Recode into Different Variables: Old and New Values

Old Value
- ○ Value:
- ○ System-missing
- ○ System- or user-missing
- ○ Range:

  through

- ○ Range, LOWEST through value:

- ● Range, value through HIGHEST:
  15
- ○ All other values

New Value
- ● Value: 2
- ○ System-missing
- ○ Copy old value(s)

Old --> New:
  Lowest thru 14 --> 1

  Add
  Change
  Remove

☐ Output variables are strings   Width: 8
☐ Convert numeric strings to numbers ('5'->5)

Cancel   Continue

To get the high category, use the "Range, value through HIGHEST" command.

In this example, 15 through highest = 2.

After you are finished adding values, click "Continue" and then "OK."

Split the Data File, Select Groups, or Select a Random Sample

Split File Command

Use this command if you want to run analyses separately for two or more groups (e.g., based on marital status). The Split File command will also organize your dataset according to the groups.

On the Menu Bar, click **Data → Split File**

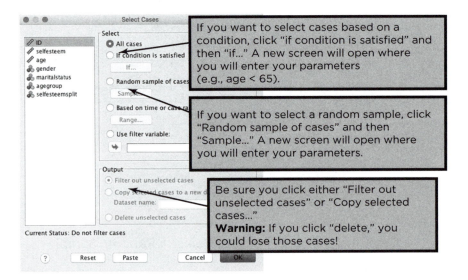

Select Cases Command

Use this command if you want to analyze data for only certain participants. For example, you may want to only examine those participants who are younger than 65. Or, you may want to select a random sample.

On SPSS Menu Bar, click **Data → Select Cases**

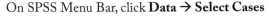

Remember: When you use the Split Data or Select Cases commands, *all* the subsequent analyses you do will follow this command until you return to the command screen and click "All cases."

Practice Exercises

1. Go to https://edge.sagepub.com/adams2e

2. Click on Datasets

   Open the file called "Game of Thrones." Here you will find two files:

   - Description of the Game of Thrones dataset (.pdf)

   - The dataset (.sav)

3. Read over the description of the Game of Thrones dataset, paying special attention to how variables are named and coded. Note that this is real data based on the first season of the television series.

   a. Use simple random sampling to select a sample of 44 of the 129 characters (which will give you a 12-point confidence interval with a 95% confidence level).

      Use the **Select Cases** command and click "Copy Selected Cases into a New Dataset." Click on "Sample" and select a random sample of 44 from the first 129 cases.

   b. Go back to the original dataset with all 129 cases. Suppose you want to have a random sample with about equal numbers of characters who appeared in a few seasons and who appeared in many seasons. To do this, you'll need to follow several steps.

      i. First, you'll need to convert the "totalseasons" variable, that is now ratio, into a nominal variable with two groups. Because you want about equal numbers, use a median split (see How to Create Groups Based on a Median Split for directions).

      ii. Use the **Frequency** command to calculate the median.

      iii. Use the **Recode into Different Variables** command to create a new variable, coded as 1 (scores at or below the median) and 2 (scores above the median). Name it whatever you like.

         Suppose you want a stratified random sample of 44 that represents the distribution in the population. Look at the frequency table. Notice that 75 scores in the population (58.1%) fall at or below the median. In a stratified random sample of 44, you will therefore want about 26 out of 44 (about 58%) to be from the low category and the remaining 18 of the 44 to be from the high category. Next, we will walk you through the steps to randomly select this sample.

   c. Use the **Split File** command to organize your dataset by your new variable. Cases coded as 1 (low number of seasons) should all be listed first in the dataset. Then use the **Select Cases** command to select a random sample of 26 from the first 75 cases. Click on "Copy Cases into a New Dataset." This new dataset will represent your sample from the low number of seasons.

d. Go back to the original dataset. Use the sort command (**Data → Sort Cases**) and sort cases by your new variable. Click "Descending" so that now those coded as 2 will appear first in your dataset. Use the **Select Cases** command to select a random sample of 18 from the first 54 cases. Click on "Copy Cases into a New Dataset." This new dataset will represent your sample from the high number of seasons.

Extra Practice

The following datasets are available for download. Choose one and practice some of the SPSS skills you have learned.

Dataverse Network: http://thedata.harvard.edu/dvn

This is a large repository of data created by the Institute for Quantitative Social Science at Harvard University (IQSS). Many datasets are available for immediate download, and others are available with permission.

General Social Survey (GSS): http://gss.norc.org

Data and codebook available for the General Social Survey that is used to assess demographics and attitudes of U.S. residents.

Health Information National Trends Survey (HINTS): http://hints .cancer.gov

Data and codebook available for the HINTS program, a study designed to monitor how adults use the Internet and other communication to learn about health issues.

Monitoring the Future: http://www.icpsr.umich.edu/icpsrweb/ ICPSR/studies/20022

Data and codebook available from Monitoring the Future, an ongoing study of the behaviors and attitudes of American youth.

Pew Research Center: http://www.pewresearch.org/data/

Data available from a variety of polls.

Describing Your Sample

CHAPTER SUMMARY

Describing a sample requires critical thinking about both ethical and practical issues in choosing the characteristics of the sample to describe. Quantitative (numerical) analyses are a popular way to summarize sample characteristics, and the majority of the chapter focuses on descriptive statistics. Specific descriptive statistics are organized by their overall purpose: to describe how often a score appears in the sample; to describe the central tendency; and to describe the variability. Definitions, formulas, and example calculations are included for each type of descriptive statistic. Note that statistical notations that are most common in published research are used throughout the book (e.g., M and SD).

In this chapter, an emphasis is placed on not only understanding different types of descriptive statistics and their purpose, but also choosing the appropriate descriptive statistics based on the scale of measurement and, for interval or ratio variables, the shape of the distribution of scores. The chapter ends with a reminder of the importance of thinking critically about the quality of your data and the meaning of your results.

REVIEW AND APPLICATION OF KEY CONCEPTS FROM CHAPTER 5

Exercise 5.1: Descriptive Statistics (Review)

1. If you wish to use descriptive statistics to describe qualitative responses, you must first categorize the data. This process is called
   _____.

LEARNING OUTCOMES

After reading and reviewing Chapter 5, you should understand

- The ethical and practical considerations of describing your sample

- How to describe your sample using descriptive statistics

- The appropriate statistics and graphs based on the type of data you have

- How to use z scores and percentiles to describe your sample

2. _____ statistics are quantitative analyses used to describe a sample.

3. The mean, median, and mode are all measures of _____.

4. The _____ is the most common score, the _____ is the average score, and the _____ is the middle score.

5. Range, observed minimum and maximum, variance, and standard deviation are all measures of _____.

6. The _____ and _____ both summarize how much scores deviate from the mean.

7. To describe how often a score appears in the sample, you may use the _____ or _____.

8. To describe how often a range of scores appears in the sample, you would use the _____.

9. A _____ is a standardized score.

10. A _____ is the percentage of a distribution that scored below a specific value.

Exercise 5.2: Describing Variables Measured on a Nominal Scale (Application)

A market researcher asked 20 participants whether they prefer to shop for clothes online, in a store, or using a paper catalog:

Participant #	Shopping preference	Participant #	Shopping preference
1	Store	11	Online
2	Catalog	12	Online
3	Store	13	Store
4	Store	14	Store
5	Store	15	Online
6	Online	16	Store
7	Store	17	Catalog
8	Online	18	Online
9	Online	19	Store
10	Store	20	Store

1. What is the frequency for online, store, or catalog preference?

   _____

2. What percentage chose shopping online as their preference?

   _____

3. The best measure of central tendency for nominal data such as this is the
   _____, which for these data equals _____.

4. Draw a bar graph to summarize these results. Be sure to label your axes.

Exercise 5.3: Describing Variables Measured on an Ordinal Scale (Application)

A highly selective university honors society only recruits incoming students who are in the top 10 of their class in high school. Following are the rankings of their 15 members, in order from lowest to highest ranking:

$$7, 7, 5, 5, 4, 3, 3, 3, 2, 1, 1, 1, 1, 1, 1$$

1. What percentage was ranked first in their high school class? _____

2. The best measure of central tendency for ordinal data such as this is the
   _____, which for these data equals _____.

3. What is the possible minimum score (lowest ranking)? _____

4. What is the observed minimum score (lowest ranking)? _____

5. What is the range? _____

Exercise 5.4: Describing Variables Measured on Interval and Ratio Scales (Review)

1. In a normal distribution, most scores cluster around the _____, and slightly less than 5% of the scores are above or below _____ standard deviations.

2. _____ is the degree of the peak of a distribution, with a very peaked curve called _____ and a flat curve called _____.

3. A _____ distribution has two peaks.

4. The frequency of the scores are all the same in a _____ distribution.

5. In a _____ distribution, scores cluster on one side.

6. If the distribution of an interval or ratio scale is normal, report the _____ as a measure of central tendency and the _____ as a measure of variability.

7. If the distribution of an interval or ratio scale is skewed, report the _____ as a measure of central tendency and either the _____ or _____ as a measure of variability.

8. If the distribution of an interval or ratio scale is uniform, report the _____ as a measure of central tendency and the _____ _____ as a measure of variability.

9. If the distribution of an interval or ratio scale is bimodal, ideally you should _____. If that is not possible, you should _____.

Exercise 5.5: Describing Variables Measured on Interval and Ratio Scales (Application)

1. A professor asks students how many hours they predict they will need to study for an upcoming exam, with the following results: 1, 2, 2, 2, 3, 3, 3, 3, 3, 4, 4, 5
   a. Complete the frequency table:

Hours (predicted)	f
1	
2	
3	
4	
5	

b. Graph a histogram of these results. Remember to label your axes.

c. Does the distribution appear to be normally distributed? _____

d. Calculate by hand and report the best measure of central tendency for this data. Show your work:

e. Calculate by hand and report the best measure of variability for this data. Show your work:

2. After the exam, the professor asks the students how many hours they actually spent studying, with the following results: 1, 1, 1, 2, 2, 2, 2, 3, 3, 3, 4, 8

   a. Complete the frequency table:

Hours (actual)	f
1	
2	
3	
4	
5	
6	
7	
8	

   b. Graph a histogram of these results. Remember to label your axes.

c. Based on the histogram, this appears to be a _____ distribution (be specific).

d. What statistic should you calculate to confirm your assessment of the shape of the distribution? _____

e. Assuming that you confirm your assessment of the shape of the distribution, what measure of central tendency and variability should you report for this data? _____

f. Calculate by hand and report the central tendency:

_____

g. Calculate by hand and report the variability:

_____

Exercise 5.6: Comparing Interval/Ratio Scores With *z* Scores and Percentiles (Application)

1. What is a *z* score and how might *z* scores be useful?

_____

_____

2. Professor K converts all his students' test scores to *z* scores. Julie has a *z* score of 0.5 and Alice has a *z* score of -2.7. How would you help Julie and Alice interpret their scores?

_____

_____

_____

3. What is the difference between earning 95% on an exam and being in the 95th percentile on an exam?

_____

_____

_____

4. If you scored in the 50th percentile on an exam, how would you interpret your performance? What is your *z* score?

_____

Exercise 5.7: The Big Picture: Know Your Data and Your Sample

1. List five things that might negatively impact your ability to accurately interpret your descriptive statistics.

   _____

   _____

   _____

   _____

2. How does the sampling technique impact how you interpret descriptive statistics?

   _____

   _____

   _____

   _____

YOUR RESEARCH

Find a primary research article on your topic. Look through the Method and Results sections.

1. Did the author(s) use frequencies to describe a characteristic of the sample? If so, explain.

   _____

   _____

   _____

   _____

2. Did the author(s) use percentages to describe a characteristic of the sample? If so, explain.

   _____

   _____

_____

_____

_____

_____

3. Did the author(s) report the central tendency and variability to describe any of the variables? If so, explain what variables and what measures of central tendency and variability the author(s) reported.

_____

_____

_____

_____

_____

4. Did the authors use z scores or percentiles? If so, explain.

_____

_____

_____

_____

_____

IBM® SPSS® DATA ANALYSIS AND INTERPRETATION

Calculating Frequencies for Nominal Variables

Calculate the frequency to describe nominal data such as gender, marital status, religious affiliation, etc.

On the Menu Bar, click **Analyze → Descriptive Statistics → Frequencies**

The Frequencies Box will open:

1. Click on the variable(s) you want to analyze in the variable list and send to "Variable(s)."

2. Be sure that "Display frequency tables" is checked.

3. Click "OK."

Then you will see the output window:

Frequencies

Statistics

participant's gender		
N	Valid	10
	Missing	0

participant's gender

Valid	Frequency	Percent	Valid Percent	Cumulative Percent
male	5	50.0	50.0	50.0
female	5	50.0	50.0	100.0
Total	10	100.0	100.0	

This output tells us

- How many total participants there are ($N = 10$)
- How many of these participants were male ($n = 5$) and female ($n = 5$)
- The percentage of the sample in each group or category (50% of the sample was male and 50% female)

Calculating the central tendency, variability, and skewness of interval or ratio variables (option 1: use the Frequency command)

On the Menu Bar, click **Analyze → Descriptive Statistics → Frequencies**

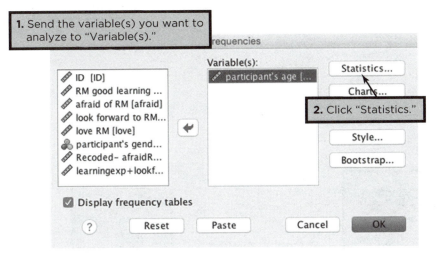

1. Send the variable(s) you want to analyze to "Variable(s)."

2. Click "Statistics."

The "Statistics" box will open:

3. Click on the Statistics you want to run.

- Select more options than you will report, including the Mean, Median, *SD*, Min, Max, and skewness.

- Use the skewness statistic to decide which measure of central tendency and variability to report.

Click "Continue" when you are done.

You can also request a chart of the distribution:

4. Click "Charts."

The Charts Box will open:

5. Click "Histograms" and "Show normal curve..." Then click "Continue."

6. Click "OK" when you are finished selecting your statistics and charts.

OUTPUT

Frequencies

Statistics

participant's age	
N Valid Missing	10 0
Mean	29.6000
Median	28.5000
Std. Deviation	10.89546
Skewness	2.224
Std. Error of Skewness	.687
Minimum	19.00
Maximum	58.00

In the output, you will first see the statistics you requested.

Notice here the skewness statistic (G_1) is 2.22. Recall from the textbook that there are two ways to determine skewness:

1. G_1 is greater than +/−2.

2. The absolute value of G_1 is greater than twice the standard error of the skew.

By both these criteria, age is skewed in this sample. Therefore, you should *not* report the mean and standard deviation. Instead report the median and the range (or the min and max).

participant's age

Valid	Frequency	Percent	Valid Percent	Cumulative Percent
19.00	1	10.0	10.0	10.0
21.00	1	10.0	10.0	20.0
23.00	1	10.0	10.0	30.0
25.00	1	10.0	10.0	40.0
28.00	1	10.0	10.0	50.0
29.00	1	10.0	10.0	60.0
30.00	1	10.0	10.0	70.0
31.00	1	10.0	10.0	80.0
32.00	1	10.0	10.0	90.0
58.00	1	10.0	10.0	100.0
Total	10	100.0	100.0	

The frequency table outlines the frequency for every age reported.

Looking at the cumulative percent can be useful with skewed data:

"The data were positively skewed due to one participant who was 58. The remaining ninety percent of the sample were between the ages of 19 and 32."

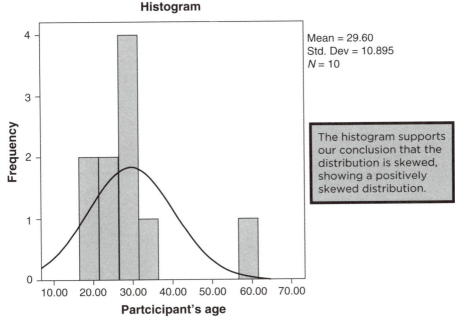

Histogram

Mean = 29.60
Std. Dev = 10.895
N = 10

The histogram supports our conclusion that the distribution is skewed, showing a positively skewed distribution.

Note that the histogram can give you an idea of what the data look like, and it might suggest a positive or negative skew. It can also alert you to a bimodal or uniform distribution that will not be detected by the skewness statistic (G_1).

If the histogram appears skewed, base the final decision about whether or not the distribution is skewed on the skewness statistic (G_1), not the graph.

REMEMBER, there are two ways to assess skewness:

1. If the skewness statistic (G_1) is between -2 and 2, the distribution meets the criteria for a normal distribution. If G_1 is greater than +/-2, the distribution is skewed.

OR

2. If the absolute value of the skewness statistic (G_1) is more than twice the standard error of the skew (SES), the distribution is skewed.

If you have a skewed distribution, the sign of G_1 (+ or -) will tell you the direction of the skew (positive or negative).

Calculating the central tendency, variability, and skewness for interval or ratio variables (option 2: use the Descriptives command)

On the Menu Bar, click **Analyze → Descriptive Statistics → Descriptives**

The "Descriptives" box will open:

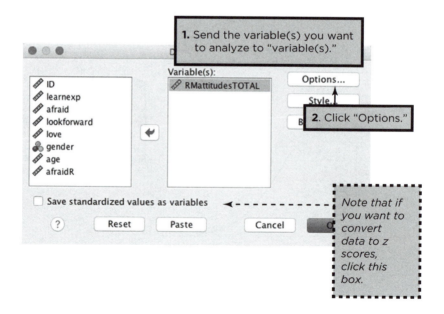

The Options Box will open:

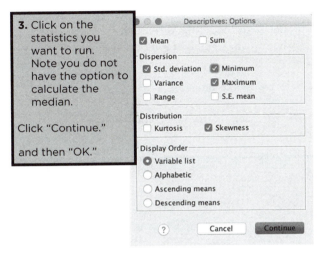

3. Click on the statistics you want to run. Note you do not have the option to calculate the median.

Click "Continue."

and then "OK."

OUTPUT

Descriptive Statistics

	N Statistic	Minimum Statistic	Maximum Statistic	Mean Statistic	Std. Deviation Statistic	Skewness Statistic	Std. Error
Total RM attitudes	10	4.00	11.00	8.1000	2.23358	–.754	.687
Valid N (listwise)	10						

Notice that many of the same types of statistics are obtained from the "Descriptives" command as from the "Frequencies" command.

A key benefit of using the "Descriptives" command is that you can easily convert data to standardized *z* scores.

A downside is that it does not provide the median, frequency table, or charts that are particularly useful if you have skewed data.

Selecting Cases to Describe

Suppose you want to analyze data for only certain participants. For example, recall that in the example about attitudes toward research methods, age was skewed because of one participant who was 58. You might want to see what happens when you exclude that participant.

1. Use the **Select Cases** command.

On Menu Bar, Click **Data → Select Cases**

---

1. Select "if condition is satisfied"

2. Click "If"

3. A new screen will open – type in the condition (age < 58 in this example) and click "continue"

4. Click "OK"

(See the Study Guide Chapter 4 for additional information about "Select Cases.")

2. Run descriptive statistics for the variable of interest (attitudes toward research methods, in this example).

(See directions earlier in this Study Guide chapter for additional information.)

The analyses will exclude anyone who did not meet the criteria. In this example, we have descriptive statistics for the nine participants who were under 58:

OUTPUT

Descriptive Statistics

	N Statistic	Minimum Statistic	Maximum Statistic	Mean Statistic	Std. Deviation Statistic	Skewness Statistic	Std. Error
Total RM attitudes	9	4.00	11.00	8.2222	2.33333	–.951	.717
Valid *N* (listwise)	9						

3. If you want to examine the entire sample again, you must turn off the "Select Cases" command:

Click **Data** → **Select Cases**, select "All cases" and then "OK."

Descriptive Statistics Comparing Groups

Suppose you want to compare the scores of two or more groups in your sample. For example, you might want to compare the mean attitudes toward research methods scores for males and females.

1. The first step is to use the **Split File** command.

On the SPSS Menu Bar, Click **Data**→**Split File**

1. Select "Compare Groups"
2. Select the grouping variable from the variable list (gender, in this example) and send it to the "Groups based on" box
3. Click "OK"

(See Study Guide Chapter 4 for additional information about "Split File.")

2. Run descriptive statistics for the variable of interest (attitudes toward research methods, in this example).

(See directions earlier in this Study Guide chapter for additional information.)

Because you are in "Split File" mode, the output will organize the descriptive information by groups. In this example, the data are split by gender.

OUTPUT

Descriptive Statistics

| participant's gender | | N Statistic | Minimum Statistic | Maximum Statistic | Mean Statistic | Std. Deviation Statistic | Skewness | |
							Statistic	Std. Error
male	Total RM attitudes	5	4.00	11.00	8.4000	2.70185	-1.339	.913
	Valid *N* (listwise)	5						
female	Total RM attitudes	5	5.00	10.00	7.8000	1.92354	-.590	.913
	Valid *N* (listwise)	5						

3. If you want to examine the entire sample again, you must turn off the "Split File" command:

Click **Data → Split File**, select "Analyze all cases" and then "OK."

Writing up Results

General Guidelines

- The goal in a Results section is to summarize the statistics that you believe are most important and useful in understanding your study. You should be selective in the results you report and how you report them. Do not just provide a laundry list of data that overwhelms the reader!

- Good writing skills are just as important in a Results section as in any other writing assignment. For example, you should use correct grammar and sentence structure, vary your sentence length and structure, avoid passive voice when possible, avoid awkward statements, be concise, and so on.

- In a Results section, you will be using statistical notation that is likely new to you. Use the examples in this workbook as models, but modify the wording according to your study and data. Think about what your data and results mean and then consider the best way to explain your results to your reader.

- When reporting numbers,
  - Use words for numbers that start a sentence (e.g., Seventy participants took surveys) or are less than 10 (e.g., There were three groups).
  - Use digits when the number doesn't start the sentence, when stating the number of participants, when reporting numbers 10 and over, or when reporting numbers in a series in which at least one number is 10 or above. For example, "There were 47 children who ranged in age from 7 to 15 ($M = 10.60$, $SD = 2.56$)."

- If you find that the text is getting too wordy or complicated, consider creating a table or graph in Word to help report your results. You can explain what the results mean in the text of your report, and then refer to the table for the specific statistics. (Note that you should never cut and paste SPSS output into a research report!)

Writing up Descriptive Statistics

Reporting Frequency Results for Nominal Data

Here are several options:

1. Option 1: A total of 10 (5 male, 5 female) participants completed surveys.

2. Option 2: A total of 10 participants completed surveys. Fifty percent were male and 50% were female.

3. Option 3: Five males and five females completed questionnaires.

4. Option 4: Our sample was evenly split between males ($n = 5$) and females ($n = 5$).

Reporting Descriptive Statistics for Normally Distributed Data

Here are a few examples:

The Research Methods Attitude Scale has a possible range of scores of 3–12. Observed scores ranged from 4–11 and were normally distributed ($M = 8.10, SD = 2.23$).

OR

The Research Methods Attitude Scale has a possible range of scores of 3–12. In this sample, the mean was 8.10 ($SD = 2.23$).

Reporting Descriptive Statistics for Skewed Data

Below is an example:

Ages ranged from 19–58, with a median of 28.50. Data were skewed due to one participant who was 58. Ninety percent of the sample was between the ages of 19 and 32.

Putting it All Together for the Method, Results, and Discussion

We have been using the example of the attitudes toward research methods study up to this point. Let's put it all together in sections of a research report.
Some important notes about this example:

- The numbers reported in this example are pulled from this chapter and previous chapters. Some details were added here for demonstration purposes.

- This example is not designed to be a template into which you can simply insert your results. Instead, it is designed to give you one example of how to integrate analyses and make sense of them.

- At this point, we have not covered statistical significance testing. You will be introduced to this important concept in Chapter 6 of the textbook.

- In a full research report, you would have an Introduction that builds a rationale for your study based on past research. In the Discussion section, you would also explain how your results fit or don't fit with past research. This example does not include those components.

Method

Participants

Ten students (five male and five female) enrolled in a psychology research methods course agreed to participate in the study. The students ranged in age from 19 to 58, with a median of 28.50. The inclusion of the 58-year-old student (who was female) skewed the age of the sample. All the other students were between the ages of 19 and 32.

Procedures

On the first day of class during the fall 2016 semester, students enrolled in the psychology research methods course ($N = 22$) were asked to volunteer to take a brief online survey about their attitudes toward the course. Students were asked to complete the survey right after class and to wait to do so until the instructor left the room. The students were informed that their answers would be anonymous and confidential and that they could withdraw from the study at any time without penalty. Because the survey was associated with a course they were taking, students were told that their participation or lack of participation would not impact their course grade and that the professor would not know which students opted to participate and which students opted out. The students had to acknowledge that they read and understood this before taking the survey.

Materials

The survey consisted of four items assessing the students' attitudes toward research methods (Research Methods is a good learning experience, I am afraid of Research Methods [recoded], I look forward to Research Methods, and I love Research Methods). The course instructor created the items based on feedback and comments from previous classes. Each item was rated on a 4-point Likert scale with 1 = *strongly disagree* and 4 = *strongly agree*. Cronbach's alpha was calculated on the four items and results indicated good internal consistency ($\alpha = .76$). However, the reliability analysis indicated that omitting the last question (I love Research Methods) would raise the alpha to .88. Because this was a substantial increase, and because the item was relatively vague, it was omitted from analyses. A total scale score was calculated by summing the three remaining items.

Results

The total of three attitude questions made up the Research Methods Attitude Scale and scores could range from 3 to 12. A score of 7.50 designates the middle and would indicate a neutral attitude. A score over 7.50 indicates a positive attitude. In this sample, scores ranged from 4 to 11, with a mean of 8.10 ($SD = 2.23$).

Because the age in our sample was positively skewed due to one woman who was 58, we ran analyses excluding this participant. The mean score increased just slightly with this exclusion ($M = 8.44$, $SD = 2.51$).

Analyses were conducted to compare male and female students. Because excluding the 58-year-old female did not seem to have a large impact on the data, we ran these analyses with all 10 participants. Males in our sample reported more positive attitudes toward Research Methods ($M = 8.80$, $SD = 2.95$) than females in our sample ($M = 7.80$, $SD = 1.92$).

Discussion

Results of this study suggest that the students who took the survey had slightly more positive than negative views toward the course at the beginning of the semester. This increased slightly when the 58-year-old participant was excluded from analyses. Male students scored in the positive range, whereas female students had less positive and closer to a neutral attitude toward the course.

It is important to note that statistical significance tests were not run, so these results can only be used to describe the sample of 10 students. Moreover, although males in the sample tended to have more positive attitudes than females, we cannot say that this is a statistically significant difference.

Less than half of the class opted to take the survey, and it is unclear what motivated some to participate and others not to and, more important, whether those who participated were very different from those who did not. Future studies should be done to attempt to obtain a larger and representative sample of Research Methods students. It would also be interesting to know how attitudes toward the course change throughout the semester and beyond, and whether attitudes predict student performance in the class.

Practice Exercise 1

Review and integration of research methods and statistics:

1. What evidence is presented that supports the reliability of the Research Methods Attitude Scale?

_____

_____

_____

2. What evidence is presented that supports the construct validity of the Research Methods Attitudes Scale?

_____

_____

_____

3. Rewrite one of the paragraphs in the Results section, in your own words.

_____

_____

_____

_____

_____

_____

Practice Exercise 2

Calculating frequencies is also a good way to check for data entry errors.

1. Go to https://edge.sagepub.com/adams2e

2. Click on "Datasets," open the file called "Reminiscence Study," and then open the "reminiscence with errors.sav" data file. This is real data from a study conducted as part of a class project. However, this file has errors added to the demographic data for the purpose of this practice exercise.

   a. Using SPSS, calculate frequencies for the variables named *age, gender,* and *collegestudent.*

3. Look at the frequency tables in the output to identify the two errors.

   a. What is one of the errors, and how do you know it is an error?

   _____

   b. What is the other error, and how do you know it is an error?

   _____

4. Now, you might be wondering what to do about errors such as these. If you have access to the raw data, you could identify the cases (by ID number) and examine the original data to identify the correct values. It would be a good idea to also do some spot checks to be sure there were no other data entry errors.

   a. In this example, you do not have access to the raw data. All you can do in such a situation is delete the erroneous value. First sort the data (click on *data* → *sort cases* and sort by the variable with the error), then scan the variable column to find the error, and then delete the error.

   b. Delete the two errors you identified and then calculate the appropriate statistics to describe age, and re-run the frequency of the variable *collegestudent.*

   c. Write a brief description of the age, gender, and college student distribution in the sample as you would in a Participants section of a research report. Be sure you only report the correct information (without errors) and use APA format.

   _____

   _____

   _____

_____

_____

_____

Practice Exercise 3

1. Go to https://edge.sagepub.com/adams2e

2. Click on "Datasets" and open the file called "Academic Honesty Study." This is real data from a study conducted as part of a class project.

   a. Review the file called "academic honesty survey codesheet.pdf" to learn about the variables and codes.

   b. Open the data file called "academic honesty.sav."

3. Using SPSS, calculate the appropriate descriptive statistics to answer these questions:

   a. Do most of the participants believe that those who plagiarize should have the opportunity to redo the assignment? (Hint: Calculate descriptive statistics using the variable called "responseC.")

   _____

   _____

   b. Do those who report they have never plagiarized believe that those who do should have the opportunity to redo the assignment? (Hint: Use the "Select if" command to select only those who reported that they have never plagiarized, and then run the same descriptive statistics you did for question 3a.)

   _____

   _____

   c. Do those who identified as undergraduates differ from those who were not currently undergraduates in their belief that those who plagiarize should have the opportunity to redo the assignment? (Hint: Turn off the "Select if" command, then split the file to compare those who are currently in college to those who are not, and then run the same descriptive statistics as you did above.)

   _____

   _____

d. Write up the results of your analyses as you would in a Results section of a research report. Remember not to refer to SPSS variable names (such as "responseC") and use APA format.

_____

_____

_____

_____

_____

_____

For additional practice, run additional descriptive statistics on the practice data set. Consider what questions you can ask based on the survey questions, and determine what analyses to run in SPSS to help answer those questions.

You might also practice with one of the data sets available for download, listed at the end of this study guide's Chapter 4.

Beyond Descriptives

MAKING INFERENCES BASED ON YOUR SAMPLE

6

CHAPTER SUMMARY

The chapter is focused on inferential statistics that allow us to make inferences about a population from findings with a sample. Sampling distributions are a distribution of some statistic and provide the basis for deciding whether our sample is representative (or not) of the population—or when a difference makes a difference. The decision-making process is called *hypothesis testing* and involves multiple steps: stating null and alternative hypotheses, defining the sampling distribution, setting the criterion level (.05 or .01), computing a statistic, and deciding whether to reject or retain the null hypothesis. The alternative hypothesis determines the region of rejection in the sampling distribution and can be one-tailed (directional) or two-tailed (nondirectional). If the results of our analysis fall in the region of rejection, we reject the null hypothesis and support the alternative hypothesis, but if the statistic falls in the region of acceptance, we retain the null hypothesis.

We design studies to try to reject a false null hypothesis (called *power),* but because hypothesis testing is based on probability, the decision to reject or retain the hypothesis is associated with a probability of error. Type I error occurs when we reject a true null hypothesis, and Type II error occurs when we retain a false null hypothesis. Ways to decrease the probability of either type of error are described as well as ways to increase power. Finally, effect sizes (magnitude of an effect), confidence intervals (margin of error), and practical significance (everyday implications) are described as tools to enhance our understanding of the results of a study.

LEARNING OUTCOMES

After reading and reviewing Chapter 6, you should understand

- The use of inferential statistics to determine whether the finding of a study is unusual

- The importance of the sampling distribution

- How to carry out the hypothesis testing process

- When to reject or retain a null hypothesis and the types of errors associated with each of these decisions

- The distinction between statistical significance, effect size, confidence intervals, and practical significance

REVIEW AND APPLICATION OF KEY CONCEPTS
FROM CHAPTER 6

Exercise 6.1: Inferential Statistics (Review)

1. _____ statistics are the statistical analysis of data from a sample used to draw a conclusion about a population from which the sample is drawn.

2. Statistics from a population are called _____.

3. _____ is the population mean.

4. _____ is the population standard deviation.

5. Fill in the table:

Descriptive	Inferential
sample	
	parameter
mean (M)	
	sigma (σ)

6. Inferential statistics are based on _____ theory, which examines random events, such as what card you will draw in poker.

7. _____ is the decision-making process of determining the probability of finding a particular result.

8. A _____ describes a distribution of statistics while a _____ describes a distribution of scores.

Exercise 6.2: Hypothesis Testing (Review)

1. The _____ hypothesis predicts what you expect to find in your study.

2. The _____ hypothesis predicts no difference between groups.

3. A study is always designed to _____ the null hypothesis.

4. The typical region of rejection is the extreme _____% of the sampling distribution, but sometimes we use the more strict extreme _____% to define the region of rejection.

5. If your results fall in the region of rejection, you should _____ (reject/retain) the null hypothesis and you _____ (have, have not) found statistical significance.

6. If your results fall in the region of acceptance, you should _____ (reject/retain) the null hypothesis and you _____ (have/have not) found statistical significance.

7. Statistical significance suggests that your results are not due to _____ and that the results _____ (do/do not) belong to the sampling distribution implied by the null hypothesis.

8. A one-tailed test makes it _____ (more/less) difficult to reject the null hypothesis because the region of rejection is located on one tail of the sampling distribution, while two-tailed tests divide the region of rejection between the two tails of the distribution.

9. A two-tailed test is a _____ (more/less) conservative test than a one-tailed test because _____.

10. Researchers typically compute a _____-tailed test because it is more conservative.

11. The value of a statistic that defines the region of rejection in a sampling distribution is called the _____ value.

12. The percentage of the distribution that the researcher selects for the region of rejection is called the _____ level and typically is less than _____%.

13. When you reject the null hypothesis, there is a probability of a _____ error and it is equal to the _____.

14. When you retain the null hypothesis, there is a probability of a _____ error.

15. Regardless of your decision to reject or retain the null hypothesis, there is always a chance of error because statistics are based on _____.

16. Why can't you have a probability of both a Type I and a Type II error in a study?

_____

_____

17. Correctly rejecting a false null hypothesis is called _____.

18. You can reduce the probability of a Type II error by (increasing/decreasing)

a. _____ sample size

b. _____ error in your research design

c. _____ strength of the effect

Exercise 6.3: Hypothesis Testing (Application)

1. "There will be no difference in the number of crimes committed by those in urban areas and those in rural areas" is an example of a(n) _____ hypothesis.

2. "The number of crimes committed in urban areas will differ from the number committed in rural areas" is an example of a(n) _____ hypothesis and it is _____ (directional/nondirectional).

3. "The number of crimes committed in urban areas will be greater than the number committed in rural areas" is an example of a(n) _____ hypothesis and it is _____ (directional/nondirectional).

4. "Males are more likely than females to physically bully their classmates." This is a _____ (directional/nondirectional) alternative hypothesis.

5. Define a sampling distribution for the following hypothesis: There is no difference in the percentage of income spent on housing by elderly households and the percentage of income spent on housing by all households. Hint: First name the percentage spent by all households (estimate a reasonable percentage).

   _____

6. In the figures below, the numbers on the *x*-axis are standard deviation units away from the mean. For example, –2 = 2 *SD*'s below the *M*, while 1 = 1 *SD* above the *M*.

   Figure A: Draw the region of rejection and region of acceptance for a two-tailed test where $p < .05$.

   Figure B: Draw the region of rejection and region of acceptance for a one-tailed test where $p < .05$.

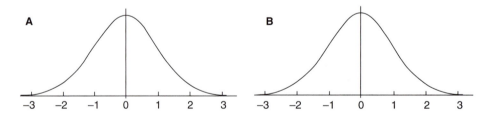

7. List the seven steps that you would follow to test the following hypothesis: "Males are more likely than females to physically bully their classmates." Make your steps relevant to this specific study (e.g., state the null and alternative hypotheses for this study).

   a. _____

   b. _____

c. _____

d. _____

e. _____

f. _____

g. _____

8. Which of the following p values would meet the criteria for statistical significance at $p < .05$? Circle them.

.001   .05   .006   .50   .047   .20   .02   .07   .70

9. If you find that, in your sample, girls verbally bully their classmates more often than boys ($p = .04$),

a. Are the results statistically significant?_____

b. Would you reject or retain the null hypothesis? _____

c. What is the probability of a Type I error? _____ Type II error? _____

d. Name two ways you could reduce your chance of a Type I error in the study.

    i. _____

    ii. _____

10. If you find, in your sample, that males physically bully their classmates more often than girls ($p = .07$),

a. Are the results statistically significant?_____

b. Would you reject or retain the null hypothesis? _____

c. Is there a probability of a Type I error? _____ Type II error? _____

11. Two studies were conducted on bullying at an elementary school. Study 1 selected a convenience sample of 10 boys and 10 girls from grades K–5. Study 2 selected a convenience sample of 25 boys and 25 girls from the fourth grade.

Which study is likely to have more power? _____ Why? (Hint: There are two reasons.)

a. _____

b. _____

Exercise 6.4: Effect size, Confidence Intervals, and Practical Significance (Review)

1. The magnitude of an effect in a study is the _____.

2. The margin of error in a study is defined by the _____.

3. The everyday usefulness of results is the _____.

4. The effect size used to examine mean differences and measured in standard deviation units is called _____.

5. Another way to measure the effect size is the _____.

6. Fill in the table, but remember that these numbers are guidelines and not designed to be strict cutoffs.

Interpretation of Effect Size	Effect Size: Cohen's d	Effect Size: Proportion of Variability Accounted for
Small/Weak		
Medium/Moderate		
Large/Strong		

Exercise 6.5: Effect size, Confidence Intervals, and Practical Significance (Application)

1. Interpret each of the following effect sizes as weak, moderate, or strong:

   a. 2% of the variability accounted for _____

   b. 50% of the variability accounted for _____

   c. $d = .48$ _____

   d. $d = 1.20$ _____

   e. $d = .12$ _____

   f. 10% of the variability accounted for _____

   g. $d = .25$ _____

2. A teacher reports that exam grades ranged from 64% to 98%, with a mean of 79.85 ($SD = 10.18$), 95% CI [75.09, 84.61]. The confidence interval tells you that you are _____ confident that the sample mean of _____ represents a population mean that falls between _____ and _____.

3. Another teacher reports exam scores based on academic year.

   First-year students: $M = 75.25$, $SD = 5.16$, 95% CI [71.70, 78.88]

   Second-year students: $M = 80.33$, $SD = 7.33$, 95% CI [74.11, 86.55]

   a. Do the confidence intervals for the population means overlap? _____

   b. A second-year student brags that their year outperformed first-year students. Based on the confidence intervals, how might you counter this student's claim?

   _____

   _____

   _____

   c. What would you say about the practical significance of these results?

   _____

   _____

   _____

Exercise 6.6: The Big Picture: Making Sense of Results (Application)

1. What are the benefits of reporting each of the following in describing the results of a study?

   a. Statistical significance _____

   _____

   b. Effect size _____

   _____

   _____

   c. Confidence interval _____

   _____

   _____

   d. Practical significance _____

   _____

   _____

2. Statistical significance, effect size, confidence intervals, and practical significance _____ (can/cannot) vary independently.

3. A study examined whether convenience affected recycling behavior. The researchers operationally defined recycling behavior based on the weight (in pounds) of material recycled by each household. They found that households who were supplied a large recycling bin and weekly pickup ($M = 25.00$, $SD = 5.00$, 95% CI [20.25, 29.75]) recycled significantly more material than the households who were sent flyers encouraging them to recycle ($M = 10.00$, $SD = 4.00$, 95% CI [6.50, 13.50], $p = .003$). Convenience accounted for 22% of the variance in recycling.

   a. Explain what the p value indicates and how you would interpret it.

   _____

   _____

   b. Interpret the effect size.

   _____

   _____

   c. Interpret the confidence intervals.

   _____

   _____

   d. Interpret the practical significance of the study.

   _____

   _____

4. The researchers replicated the study in a different city and found that those supplied with a recycling bin ($M = 25.00$, $SD = 7.00$, 95% CI [16.20, 33.80]), recycled more than those who were just given an informational flyer ($M = 10.00$, $SD = 5.50$, 95% CI [2.50, 17.50]). This time, they found that $p = .10$, Cohen's $d = .25$.

   a. Explain what the p value indicates and how you would interpret it.

   _____

   _____

   b. Interpret the effect size.

   _____

   _____

c. Interpret the confidence intervals.

_____

_____

d. Interpret the practical significance of the study.

_____

_____

5. Which of the two recycling studies

a. Found statistically significant results? Explain your answer.

_____

_____

b. Had a stronger effect size? Explain your answer.

_____

_____

_____

_____

c. Has more practical significance? Explain your answer.

_____

_____

_____

_____

_____

_____

YOUR RESEARCH

Find a primary research article on your topic. If possible, find an article that has a simple design. If the article describes multiple studies, pick one of the studies as the focus of this exercise. Before beginning to work on this section, look through the entire article.

You will see that in order to answer these questions, you will have to read the article very carefully and probably several times. This practice should give you some idea of the care that you should take in digesting research. Even though you need to take a lot of time to read articles, you may end up summarizing the article in your own literature review with a single sentence or by simply citing the article because of the measure you use from the study or for the procedure you adopt. But by attending to the details of published articles, you will learn a great deal about the format for reporting research, different methods for conducting research, various ways to analyze data, and appropriate interpretations of statistics. All of this will support you as you learn to design, carry out, analyze, and report your own studies.

1. Focus on the Introduction of the article.

   a. Identify one hypothesis that most interests you. (Remember that it is important to learn how to write about research in your own words. Be sure that you do not plagiarize in writing the hypothesis!)

   _____

   _____

   b. Is the hypothesis directional or nondirectional? How do you know?

   _____

   _____

2. Now examine the Method section.

   What do you learn about the sample and procedure of the study that may help the researchers to avoid Type II errors (e.g., sample size, error in the research design, strength of effect)? You may want to review the section "Reducing the Chance of a Type II Error" in Chapter 6 before answering this question.

   Sample:

   _____

   _____

   _____

   Research design:

   _____

   _____

   _____

   Strength of effect:

   _____

   _____

   _____

3. Review the Results section of the article. Even though there may be statistics you do not understand, focus on the statistics that you are familiar with: M, SD, range, possible and observed scores, p, percentage of variability accounted for (could be noted as r^2, r_{pb}^2, η^2), Cohen's d, confidence intervals. Consider the hypothesis you selected in question 1 and answer the following questions regarding the analyses used to test this hypothesis.

   a. Did the author(s) report any descriptive statistics (e.g., M, SD) related to the hypothesis you selected? _____ If yes, explain what the descriptive statistics tell you about the variable(s) under examination.

   _____

   _____

   _____

   b. Did the researchers find statistically significant results for the hypothesis you noted in question 1? Explain.

   _____

   _____

   c. Is there a probability of a Type I error? _____ If yes, what is the exact probability? _____ Is there a probability of a Type II error? _____

   d. Did the authors report an effect size? _____ If yes, list it here and interpret its meaning.

   _____

   _____

   e. Did the authors include a confidence interval for their findings? _____. If yes, list the confidence interval(s) and interpret the meaning.

   _____

   _____

   _____

   _____

4. Reread the Discussion section.

   a. Did the authors indicate that they found support for the hypothesis you selected?

   _____

b. How do they interpret the meaning of the support or nonsupport for their hypothesis?

_____

_____

_____

c. What do the researchers state or imply about the practical significance of their study? They may not use the term *practical significance;* instead, they may discuss the implications or usefulness of their results.

_____

_____

_____

_____

_____

d. Researchers also discuss limitations of their study in the Discussion. Do you see any limitations they mention that you can relate to the possibility of Type I or Type II errors? How do the authors suggest that future researchers should address or overcome these limitations?

_____

_____

_____

_____

_____

_____

_____

As you read other primary research articles on your topic, we recommend you use some or all of these questions to help you evaluate the research.

Calculating a Confidence Interval for a Mean Score

You can use IBM® SPSS® to calculate confidence intervals for means by running an analysis called a one-sample *t* test. You will learn more about the one-sample *t* test in Chapter 7. For our purposes here, we are only using it to calculate a confidence interval.

Data Entry

You need a variable measured on an interval or ratio scale to calculate the confidence interval for the mean of that variable. In the example below, we have 20 students and their final exam scores (out of 100), which is a ratio variable.

You can then calculate descriptive statistics and verify that the distribution meets the criteria for a normal curve, using either the Frequency or Descriptives command (see Chapter 5 of this study guide). The following analysis will repeat some of that information.

	studentID	finalexam
1	1.00	98.00
2	2.00	85.00
3	3.00	78.00
4	4.00	64.00
5	5.00	70.00
6	6.00	88.00
7	7.00	72.00
8	8.00	88.00
9	9.00	70.00
10	10.00	70.00
11	11.00	77.00
12	12.00	85.00
13	13.00	70.00
14	14.00	95.00
15	15.00	85.00
16	16.00	77.00
17	17.00	85.00
18	18.00	65.00
19	19.00	80.00
20	20.00	95.00

Calculating the Confidence Interval for the Mean

On the Menu Bar, click **Analyze → Compare Means → One-sample *t* test**

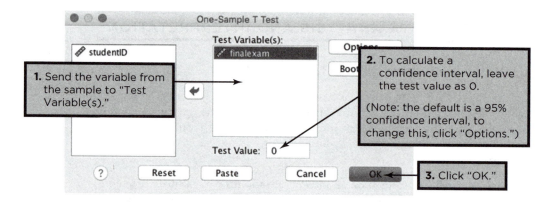

OUTPUT

One-Sample Statistics

	N	Mean	Std. Deviation	Std. Error Mean
finalexam	20	79.8500	10.17880	2.27605

The first table provides descriptive statistics for the sample.

One-Sample Test

	Test Value = 0					
					95% Confidence Interval of the Difference	
	t	df	Sig. (2-tailed)	Mean Difference	Lower	Upper
finalexam	35.083	19	.000	79.85000	75.0862	84.6138

When you are interested in the confidence interval for the mean, focus on the last two columns of the second table and ignore the rest.

Writing Up Results

When reporting a confidence interval for a mean, include the following:

- The mean and standard deviation (*M, SD*)

- What confidence level you are using (e.g., 95%, 99%)

- The confidence interval, typically but not always, is formatted as CI [lower, upper]

You may also opt to include other descriptive information, such as the sample size or minimum and maximum scores or other information you gained from conducting descriptive statistics (see Chapter 5 of this study guide).

Examples:

Twenty students completed a final exam. The mean score was 79.85 (SD = 10.18), 95% CI [75.09, 84.61].

OR

Student scores on the final exam ranged from 64 to 98 out of 100 possible (M = 79.85, SD = 10.18), 95% CI [75.09, 84.61].

OR

Final exam scores for 20 students indicated an average score of C+/B- (M = 79.85, SD = 10.18). At a 95% confidence level, we estimate that the population mean falls between 75.09 and 84.61.

Review and Practice Exercise

One evening, two waiters record what percentage of the bill their first 10 customers left as tips:

Waiter 1	Waiter 2
.15	.18
.16	.12
.15	.25
.12	.30
.18	.15
.22	.10
.15	.20
.25	.18
.20	.22
.14	.15

1. Review: Enter the data into SPSS.

2. Review: Using SPSS, calculate the appropriate descriptive statistics to describe the tip percentage for the entire sample. Write the statistics below.

_____

3. Review: Using SPSS, calculate the appropriate descriptive statistics to compare the two waiters' tip percentages. Write the statistics below.

_____

_____

4. Practice with confidence intervals: Using SPSS, calculate the confidence interval for the entire sample mean and for each waiter separately. Write the intervals below.

_____

_____

_____

5. Write up your results using correct APA format. Include a brief interpretation of the results based on the confidence interval.

_____

_____

_____

_____

_____

_____

_____

_____

_____

6. What is the practical significance of the results? What other information would be useful in understanding the practical significance?

_____

_____

_____

Comparing Your Sample to a Known or Expected Score

CHAPTER SUMMARY

The chapter's focus is on the statistics used to compare a sample score to a known or expected score. The appropriate statistical test depends upon the scale of measurement. The chi-square goodness of fit is the appropriate test for nominal data, and the one-sample t test is the appropriate test for interval or ratio data. This chapter focuses on the one-sample t test. Using an example comparing a sample of first-year students' scores on a citation format knowledge quiz to the national average for the quiz, the steps of the hypothesis testing process were described. For the statistical analysis, you learned how to compute a one-sample t test, which is used when you have interval or ratio data. Then two options for the effect size (eta squared and Cohen's d) were covered. Finally, you learned how to compute a 95% confidence interval for the difference between the sample mean and the known mean in a study. This section concluded with instruction about how to write up Results and Discussion sections for a one-sample study when you have computed these statistics.

LEARNING OUTCOMES

After reading and reviewing Chapter 7, you should understand

- How to compare a sample to a known population value when you have interval or ratio data using the one-sample t test
- How to compute the effect size when comparing a sample to a known population
- How to compute the confidence interval when comparing a sample to a known population value

REVIEW AND APPLICATION OF KEY CONCEPTS FROM CHAPTER 7

Exercise 7.1: Choosing the Appropriate Test (Review)

1. The _____ is an inferential statistic used to compare a sample mean to a known population mean or to an expected mean.

2. The _____ is an inferential statistic used to compare observed frequencies to known or expected frequencies.

3. The chi-square goodness of fit is appropriate for variables measured on a
_____ scale of measurement.

4. The one-sample *t* test is appropriate for variables measured on either a
_____ or _____ scale of
measurement.

Exercise 7.2: One-Sample *t* Tests (Review)

1. The _____ hypothesis for a one-sample *t* test is that the sample mean
equals the population mean.

2. The _____ hypothesis for a one-
sample *t* test is that the sample mean is different from the population mean.

3. The _____ hypothesis for a
one-sample *t* test is that the sample mean is either greater or less than the
population mean.

4. The assumptions of a one-sample *t* test include the following:

a. _____

b. _____

c. _____

5. Complete the following table.

A Results section should include
1.
2. Type of statistical test(s)
3.
A Discussion section should include
1.
2. Interpretation of findings, including how they fit with previous research
3.
4. Possible limitations of the study
5.

Exercise 7.3: One-Sample *t* Tests (Application)

1. Do fathers who have completed a parenting class spend more time each day
talking to their toddlers than the average number of minutes reported in a
national survey of fathers?

a. The researcher should compute a _____
(type of statistical test).

b. Should your alternative hypothesis for this study be directional or nondirectional? _____ Explain why.

_____

_____

c. State an appropriate alternative hypothesis for this study:

_____

_____

2. A professor finds that the age of students in her class is skewed, and she wants to compare the median age in her class to that of the university. Why should the professor *not* use a one-sample t test to analyze this data?

_____

3. A political scientist asks voters leaving the polling center for whom they voted in the city council election; she plans to compare her data to the actual voting outcome. Why should the researcher *not* use a one-sample t test to analyze this data?

_____

Exercise 7.4: Formulas and Calculations: One-Sample t Test (Review)

1. The standard deviation for a sampling distribution of means is called the

_____.

2. Because we do not have the standard deviation of a sampling distribution, we use the _____ to compute the one-sample t test. This term is symbolized as _____.

3. In order to calculate a one-sample t test, we must have four statistics. Name them and note their symbol.

Statistic	Symbol

4. The number of scores free to vary in a sample is called the _____ _____ and is symbolized by _____.

5. The _____ t value is the value that defines the region of rejection for the sampling distribution if the null hypothesis is true.

6. To be statistically significant, the calculated or computed t value must be _____ (greater than/less than) the critical t value.

Exercise 7.5: Formulas and Calculations: One-Sample *t* Test (Application)

1. If a sample from question 1 in Exercise 7.3 consists of 25 fathers, then $df = $ _____.

2. If for a study we find $p = .02$, this means _____

   _____

   _____

3. Suppose you found the result of $t(14) = 3.12$.

   a. The critical *t* value for this finding for a two-tailed test at the .05 level is _____. (Hint: Use Table C.4 in Appendix C.)

   b. Would your result be significant for $p < .05$ for a two-tailed test? _____

   c. How do you know?

   _____

   d. The number of participants in this study is _____.

   e. How do you interpret these results?

   _____

   _____

   _____

4. Suppose you found for a study that $t(29) = 2.50$.

   a. Would this result be significant for $p < .01$ for a two-tailed test? _____

   b. How do you know?

   _____

   c. Would this result be significant for $p < .01$ for a one-tailed test? _____

   d. How do you know?

   _____

   e. Why is there a difference in your conclusions for the one- and two-tailed tests?

   _____

   _____

5. After surveying drivers at multiple sites throughout the country, the National Transportation Board reports that drivers report using their cell phones during 60% of their trips in their car. You think that better-educated people will use their cell phones less frequently while driving. You ask 25 of your classmates during what percentage of trips in their car (of any duration) do they use their cell phones. Your classmates report a mean of 52%, with a standard deviation of 10%. Do your classmates use their cell phones significantly less than the general population when driving?

a. State your null hypothesis.

H_0: _____

_____

b. State a directional *and* a nondirectional alternative hypothesis.

Directional H_a: _____

_____

Nondirectional H_a: _____

_____

c. Which alternative hypothesis is more appropriate for the problem above? Explain.

_____

_____

d. Calculate the appropriate statistical test.

e. Can you reject the null hypothesis? _____ Why or why not?

_____

_____

f. What is the probability of a Type I error? _____ Type II error? _____

g. Compute the effect size using Cohen's *d*.

h. Write a Results section for your findings. Use APA format and include the descriptive statistics, type of statistical test and results of the test, and effect size.

_____

_____

_____

_____

_____

_____

i. Write a Discussion section for your findings. Include the findings, interpretation/explanation/implication of the findings, limitations of the study, and possible next studies.

_____

_____

_____

_____

_____

_____

Exercise 7.6: Calculating an Effect Size (Review and Application)

1. APA requires that researchers report the _____ as well as the statistical significance.

2. The two statistics that can be used to assess the effect size for a one-sample _t_ test are

    a. _____

    b. _____

3. A researcher compares the number of calories consumed daily by a sample of obese 5-year-olds to the recommended calories for this age group. As part of her analysis, she finds $\eta^2 = .15$.

    a. The name of this test is _____.

    b. She should interpret this finding to mean _____

        _____ which suggests a _____
        (weak/moderate/strong) effect.

4. Another researcher compares the amount of time a sample of high school juniors spent on their phones during a school day to the average time found in a national survey of high school students. He finds $d = .35$.

    a. The name of this test is _____.

    b. He should interpret this result to mean _____
        _____ which suggests a
        _____ (weak/moderate/strong) effect.

Exercise 7.7: Calculating a Confidence Interval (Review and Application)

1. We are confident that the difference between the population mean and our sample mean falls within an interval of mean differences called the

   _____.

2. Researchers typically use the _____% confidence interval.

3. The researcher who assessed the time high school juniors spent on their phones (measured in minutes) during a school day finds $(M - \mu) = 4.50$, 95% CI [3.30, 5.70]. How would you interpret this finding?

   _____

   _____

Exercise 7.8: Using Data Analysis Programs: One-Sample *t* Test (Application)

The Pew Research Center sampled a large national group on basic science facts using a 12-item quiz. The average correct score on the quiz was 7.9. You decide to see whether a sample of 16 students in a study group at a local bookstore is more knowledgeable than the general adult public. The output from a one-sample *t* test comparing the students to the national average is below.

One-Sample Statistics

	N	Mean	Std. Deviation	Std. Error Mean
Science Facts	16	8.8125	1.55858	.38964

One-Sample Test

	Test Value = 7.9					
					95% Confidence Interval of the Difference	
	t	df	Sig. (2-tailed)	Mean Difference	Lower	Upper
Science Facts	2.342	15	.033	.91250	.0820	1.7430

$\eta^2 = .27, d = .58$

1. Write a Results section following APA format.

   _____

   _____

   _____

   _____

_____

_____

2. Write a Discussion section following APA format.

_____

_____

_____

_____

_____

_____

Exercise 7.9: The Big Picture: Examining One Variable at a Time (Application)

Identify the appropriate inferential statistic to examine each of the following variables:

1. rating of child's language skills _____

2. whether or not child can walk without assistance
   _____

3. child's age (in months) _____

4. child's height (in inches) _____

5. mother's marital status _____

6. presence or absence of father in child's life _____

7. family income _____

IBM® SPSS® DATA ANALYSIS AND INTERPRETATION

Conducting a One-Sample *t* Test

On the Menu Bar, click **Analyze → Compare Means → One-sample *t* test**

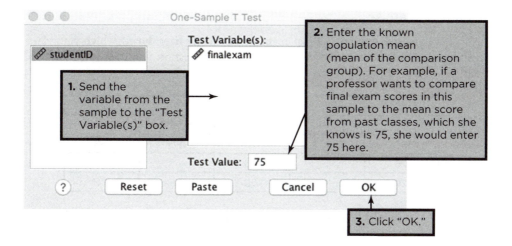

1. Send the variable from the sample to the "Test Variable(s)" box.

2. Enter the known population mean (mean of the comparison group). For example, if a professor wants to compare final exam scores in this sample to the mean score from past classes, which she knows is 75, she would enter 75 here.

3. Click "OK."

OUTPUT
T Test

One-Sample Statistics

	N	Mean	Std. Deviation	Std. Error Mean
finalexam	20	79.8500	10.17880	2.27605

The first table provides descriptive statistics for the sample.

One-Sample Test

	Test Value = 75					
					95% Confidence Interval of the Difference	
	t	df	Sig. (2-tailed)	Mean Difference	Lower	Upper
finalexam	2.131	19	.046	4.85000	.0862	9.6138

The second table provides your *t* statistic, *df*, and *p* value.

In this example, our *t* is statistically significant at *p* < .05 and we would report:
t(19) = 2.13, *p* = .046.

Practice Exercise

You now have the individual percentage of driving trips during which your classmates reported that they used their cell phone (see question 5 in Exercise 7.5). Their data are below.

.25	.10	.60	.75	.29
.33	.50	.85	.33	.30
.50	.20	.20	.80	.65
.25	.45	.50	.65	.40
.20	.10	.60	.75	.50

1. Enter the data and compute the appropriate test to respond to your belief that your classmates will use their cell phones significantly less than the national average reported by the National Transportation Board.

2. Can you support your hypothesis? Why or why not?

   _____

   _____

3. What is the probability of a Type I error? _____ Type II error? _____

4. Compute the effect size.

5. Discuss the practical significance of your findings.

   _____

   _____

   _____

   _____

6. Write a Results section, including all information and in the format required by APA.

_____

_____

_____

_____

_____

_____

7. Write a Discussion section, including all elements required by APA format.

_____

_____

_____

_____

_____

_____

Examining Relationships Among Your Variables

CORRELATIONAL DESIGN

8

CHAPTER SUMMARY

The chapter begins with a discussion of correlation research, which investigates the relationship between variables. Correlation designs are employed for many reasons, such as when the manipulation of variables is impossible or unethical, in a pilot study to check whether a relationship exists before testing for causation in an experiment, to test validity or reliability of measures, or to increase external validity. The major drawback of correlation designs is that they do not meet the requirements for causation. The ethical interpretation of correlation research and analysis is reviewed throughout the chapter in terms of focusing on relationships and not implying causation, even when a relationship is strong.

The chapter describes types of correlation statistics that are used to analyze the relationship between two variables. These statistics may be the primary or secondary analysis in a study, and thus, correlation statistics are used in experimental as well as correlational designs. The type of correlation statistic that is appropriate is dependent on the scale of measurement of the two variables being analyzed. The most commonly used correlation is Pearson's r, which examines the relationship between two interval or ratio variables. Other correlation statistics include the point-biserial correlation (r_{pb}) between a dichotomous and interval/ratio variable (described in this chapter), the chi-square test for independence (χ^2) between two nominal variables, and the Spearman rho (r_s) between two ordinal variables (both described in Chapter 13).

When there is a statistically significant Pearson's correlation, a researcher may choose to compute a regression equation or the equation for the line of best fit for the data ($Y' = bX + a$). This equation can then be used to predict one of the variables in the relationship from the other. In addition, multiple regression, an analysis that predicts a variable based on its relationship to two or more other variables, is briefly described.

LEARNING OUTCOMES

After reading and reviewing Chapter 8, you should understand

- The advantages and limits of correlational designs

- How to distinguish between correlational design and correlation as a statistic

- How to compute and interpret the statistics assessing correlations between variables of different measurement scales

- How to predict scores of one variable based on another

Exercise 8.1: Correlation Design (Review)

1. A research design that examines the hypothesis that there is a relationship between variables is called a _____ design.

2. _____ is the term used to describe a pattern or relationship between two variables.

3. Fill in the chart below.

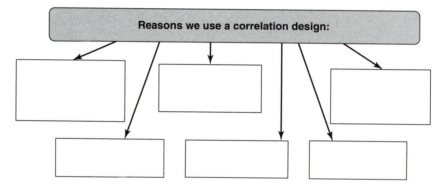

4. The major disadvantage of correlation designs is

_____

5. A valid correlation depends on obtaining a variation in the scores for each measure.

   a. When the obtained scores all fall at the upper end of the possible scores, the measure may have a _____ effect.

   b. When the obtained scores all fall at the lower end of the possible scores, the measure may reflect a _____ effect.

Exercise 8.2: Correlation Design (Application)

1. If we wanted to study whether depriving children of adequate nutrition during their first year of life is related to their language abilities at 3 years of age, we might use a _____ design because it would be _____ to manipulate the nutritional intake of infants.

2. A correlation design is more appropriate than an experiment if we want to study whether visits to a mental health clinic increase after a town

experiences a severe hurricane because _____
_____.

3. A student researcher wants to examine risk-taking behaviors among emerging adults in comparison to their health status. She wants to use a correlation design, but her classmate argues for an experimental design. Which design would you recommend and why?

_____

_____

4. A student researcher finds that attractiveness and confidence are positively correlated. He tells a classmate that his study shows that "high levels of attractiveness cause people to have greater confidence." How would you respond to his claim?

_____

_____

5. A researcher is exploring the relationship between intelligence and work performance, with both variables rated by the supervisor on a 10-point scale. Does this study meet the criteria for a powerful correlational design? _____ Explain.

_____

_____

6. Suppose you find for the work performance ratings in the example above that the ratings of all the employees range from 1–3, although it is possible to score from 1 to 10 on the measure. Would you be able to find a valid correlation with this measure? Explain.

_____

_____

7. Suppose the intelligence ratings for employees vary from 7–10 when the possible range is 1–10. The scores may reflect a _____ effect, which could _____ (increase/decrease) the power of the correlation design.

Exercise 8.3: Relationship Between Two Interval or Ratio Variables (Review)

1. _____ is the statistic used to test correlation when you have two variables on an interval or ratio scale.

2. Pearson's r provides information about the _____ and _____ of the relationship between two variables.

3. When the scores of two variables either increase together or decrease together, this is called a _____ correlation.

4. When the scores of one variable increase as the scores of another variable decrease, this is called a _____ correlation.

5. The value of Pearson's r can vary between _____ and _____.

6. The strength of Pearson's r is determined by how close the value is to

_____.

7. A _____ is a graph that depicts the participant scores on two measures.

8. What do we say about a relationship between two variables when the value of Pearson's r is close to zero (0)? _____

9. If two variables were perfectly positively correlated, the points on a graph would depict a _____ and the value of Pearson's r would equal _____.

Exercise 8.4: Relationship Between Two Interval or Ratio Variables (Application)

1. The more alcohol consumed, the poorer a person's scores on a driving skills simulation. This is an example of a _____ (positive/negative) correlation.

2. As the number of likes for a news story on Facebook increases, the time spent viewing the story also increases. This is an example of a _____ (positive/negative) correlation.

3. Suppose you find that the correlation between hours of study and scores on a statistics exam is .34, while the correlation between math anxiety and the statistics exam is −.63.

   Which relationship is stronger? _____ Explain your answer.

   _____

   _____

   _____

4. The correlation between hours of study and scores on a statistics exam ($r = .34$) would be interpreted as a _____ (weak, moderate, strong) correlation, while the correlation between math anxiety and statistics exam ($r = −.63$) would be interpreted as a _____ (weak/moderate/strong) correlation.

5. Examine the graph below.

    a. How would you interpret the graph?

    _____

    b. What statistic(s) would you compute to check that your interpretation of
       the contents of the graph was correct? _____

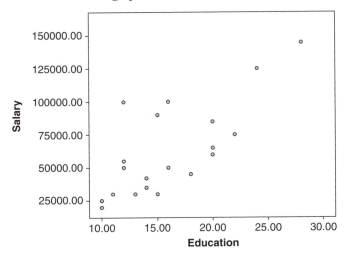

6. The graph below seems to depict a _____ (strong/
   moderate/weak) relationship between life satisfaction and total reminiscing
   (anticipating the future and savoring the moment) because the data points
   on the graph _____
   _____.

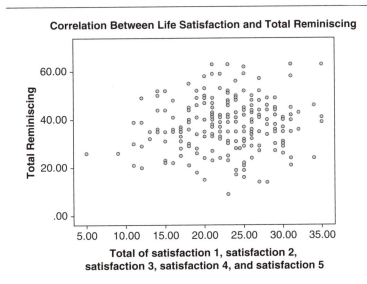

Exercise 8.5: Formulas and Calculations: Pearson's *r* (Application)

1. A researcher finds for a group of 30 residents in an assisted living facility that general health status (assessed on a 20-point scale) and minutes spent exercising per week are correlated, $r = .32$.

   a. State a null hypothesis for the study.

   _____

   b. State a directional alternative hypothesis for the study.

   _____

   c. What is the *df* for the study? (Hint: for a Pearson's *r*, $df = N - 2$.) _____

   d. Is the relationship statistically significant for a two-tailed test at $p < .05$? (Hint: see Table C.6 in Appendix C.) _____ Explain your answer.

   _____

   _____

2. A developmental psychologist observes seven children with their parents, rating levels of family support and child behavior problems. The data appear below (Note that this is a very small sample size for demonstration purposes. If you were conducting an actual study, you would want a larger sample size.)

Child ID number	Ratings of Family Support	Ratings of Child Behavior Problems
1	8	4
2	5	4
3	2	7
4	9	3
5	7	4
6	5	7
7	3	5

   a. State a null hypothesis for the study.

   _____

   b. State a directional alternative hypothesis for the study.

   _____

   _____

c. Using the formula in Chapter 8 of the textbook, calculate Pearson's r

_____

d. Calculate the df _____

e. Using Table C.6 in Appendix C, what is the critical r for this study for a two-tailed test at $p < .05$? _____

f. Is the relationship statistically significant? In other words, is the r you calculated at or stronger than the critical r? _____

Exercise 8.6: Formulas and Calculations: Point-Biserial r (Application)

1. The relationship between living status (live alone or lives with others) and life satisfaction (rating scale) can be analyzed using the _____ _____. The statistical notation for this correlation statistic is _____ .

2. A researcher is interested in the relationship between owning a home (yes/no) and educational attainment (years of education completed). After surveying 100 individuals at a local farmer's market, he finds $r_{pb} = .23$.

   a. What is the df for this study? _____

   b. Is the relationship significant at $p < .05$ for a two-tailed test? _____ Explain.

   _____

   _____

   _____

   c. Is the relationship significant at the $p < .01$ for a two-tailed test? _____ Explain your answer.

   _____

   _____

Exercise 8.7: Using Data Analysis Programs: Pearson's r and Point-biserial r (Application)

The data presented below are for demonstration purposes only, and some are based on very small sample sizes. For these examples, it is likely that a larger N would be needed so that we would have sufficient power.

1. Examine the output below from a survey that students completed regarding the use of different types of humor in the classroom:

Correlations

		Related Humor	Disparaging Humor
Related Humor	Pearson Correlation	1	.154*
	Sig. (2-tailed)		.021
	N	232	227
Disparaging Humor	Pearson Correlation	.154*	1
	Sig. (2-tailed)	.021	
	N	227	233

*. Correlation is significant at the 0.05 level (2-tailed).

a. What correlation statistic was computed?

_____

_____

_____

b. Name the two variables being correlated.

i. _____

ii. _____

c. Is the relationship statistically significant? _____ How do you know?

_____

d. Calculate the proportion of variance accounted for: $r^2 =$ _____.
You interpret this as meaning _____
and the effect size is _____ (strong/moderate/weak).

e. Describe these findings as you might in a Results section.

_____

_____

_____

f. Interpret the meaning of the findings.

_____

_____

_____

2. Examine the output below:

Correlations

		Gender Stereotypes	Openness to New Experiences
Gender Stereotypes	Pearson Correlation	1	–.789**
	Sig. (2-tailed)		.000
	N	21	21
Openness to New Experiences	Pearson Correlation	–.789**	1
	Sig. (2-tailed)	.000	
	N	21	21

**. Correlation is significant at the 0.01 level (2-tailed).

a. How many participants were in this study? _____

b. Is the relationship statistically significant? _____ How do you know?

_____

_____

c. Calculate the proportion of variance accounted for: _____. You interpret this as meaning _____ _____ and the effect size is _____ (strong/moderate/ weak).

d. The probability of a Type I error = _____ and a Type II error = _____.

e. Describe these findings as you might in a Results section.

_____

_____

_____

_____

_____

3. A gerontologist computes the correlation between pet ownership (yes or no) and happiness among a group of elderly participants (80 years or older) who live in their own homes. The output is shown below when Owning a pet = 1 and Not owning a pet = 2:

Correlations

		Pet Owner	Happiness
Pet Owner	Pearson Correlation	1	−.416*
	Sig. (2-tailed)		.022
	N	30	30
Happiness	Pearson Correlation	−.416*	1
	Sig. (2-tailed)	.022	
	N	30	30

*. Correlation is significant at the 0.05 level (2-tailed).

a. Even though the output above says this is a Pearson's *r*, what correlation statistic was computed? _____

b. Is the relationship statistically significant? _____ How do you know?

_____

c. The probability of a Type I error = _____ and a Type II error = _____.

d. Describe these findings as you might in a Results section.

_____

_____

_____

_____

_____

e. What recommendation would you make to those working with the elderly, based on these results?

_____

_____

f. What variable(s) (other than the two in this study) could be responsible for the relationship?

_____

4. Below is an example output with the interval variables *frustration tolerance* and *self-control*, the ratio variable *income*, and the nominal variable *health status* (healthy or unhealthy). Notice also that each of the correlations is listed twice, so you need to pay attention only to the top or bottom half of the matrix.

Correlations

		Frustration Tolerance	Self-Control	Annual Income	Health Status
Frustration Tolerance	Pearson Correlation	1	.704*	.673*	−.436
	Sig. (2-tailed)		.023	.033	.208
	N	10	10	10	10
Self-Control	Pearson Correlation	.704*	1	.842**	−.748*
	Sig. (2-tailed)	.023		.002	.013
	N	10	10	10	10
Annual Income	Pearson Correlation	.673*	.842**	1	−.529
	Sig. (2-tailed)	.033	.002		.116
	N	10	10	10	10
Health Status	Pearson Correlation	−.436	−.748*	−.529	1
	Sig. (2-tailed)	.208	.013	.116	
	N	10	10	10	20

a. Fill in the blanks. Round to two decimal places, except where rounding would result in a $p = .00$:

The correlation between frustration tolerance and self-control:

$r =$ _____, $p =$ _____

The correlation between frustration tolerance and income: $r =$ _____,

$p =$ _____

The correlation between frustration tolerance and health status:

$r_{pb} =$ _____, $p =$ _____

The correlation between self-control and income: $r =$ _____,

$p =$ _____

The correlation between self-control and health status: $r_{pb} =$ _____,

$p =$ _____

The correlation between income and health status: $r_{pb} =$ _____,

$p =$ _____

b. Which of the correlations are statistically significant? Circle them.

c. Indicate the strength of the relationship (weak/moderate/strong) next to each.

Exercise 8.8: Regression (Review)

1. Simple linear regression is appropriate when you have _____ variables measured on a _____ or _____ scale.

2. You would only use the regression equation to predict one variable based on another if _____.

3. The _____ variable is the predicted variable in a regression.

4. The _____ is the value used to predict another variable.

5. Sometimes we are interested in using a relationship between three or more variables to predict a variable and, in this case, we compute a _____ _____, which is symbolized as _____.

Exercise 8.9: Formulas and Calculations: Simple Linear Regression (Review)

1. The value that results when you enter a particular X value in a regression equation is called _____ and is symbolized by

   _____.

2. Each X value and its predicted Y value falls on the _____.

3. The regression equation is always in the format of $Y' = bX + a$, with $b =$ _____ and $a =$ _____.

4. The value where the line of best fit crosses the Y axis is called the _____ and is symbolized by _____ in the regression equation.

5. The slope of the regression equation represents _____ and is symbolized by _____.

6. The direction of the slope (positive or negative) is determined by the _____

   _____.

7. The average difference between predicted Y values (Y') and the actual Y values in the data is called the _____ _____ and is symbolized by _____.

8. A small standard error of estimate suggests that _____

   _____.

9. _____ is the proportion of variability accounted for by knowing the relationship between two variables and is symbolized by

   _____.

10. The larger r^2, the _____ (more/less) accurately we can predict Y from X.

Exercise 8.10: Using Data Analysis Programs: Simple Linear Regression (Application)

A researcher asked 35 participants to rate the importance of environmental issues and how much time they spend outside. The output is shown below:

Model Summary

Model	R	R Square	Adjusted R Square	Std. Error of the Estimate
1	.379[a]	.144	.118	4.15513

a. Predictors: (Constant), I think the environment is the most important political issue today.

ANOVA[a]

Model		Sum of Squares	df	Mean Square	F	Sig.
1	Regression	95.794	1	95.794	5.548	.025[b]
	Residual	569.749	33	17.265		
	Total	665.543	34			

a. Dependent Variable: On average, how many hours do you spend outside each week?

b. Predictors: (Constant), I think the environment is the most important political issue today.

Coefficients[a]

Model		Unstandardized Coefficients		Standardized Coefficients	t	Sig.
		B	Std. Error	Beta		
1	(Constant)	−1.597	2.934		−.544	.590
	I think the environment is the most important political issue today	2.079	.882	.379	2.356	.025

a. Dependent Variable: On average, how many hours do you spend outside each week?

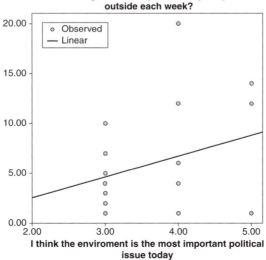

On average, how many hours do you spend outside each week?

1. Is the relationship statistically significant? _____ How do you know?

   _____

2. The effect size is _____ (name the exact value). You interpret this as meaning _____
   _____. The effect size is _____ (strong/moderate/weak).

3. The probability of a Type I error = _____ and a Type II error = _____.

4. _____ is the predictor variable and _____ is the criterion variable.

5. Write the regression equation for the relationship. _____
   _____

6. a. What is the average deviation between actual hours spent outside and the hours predicted by the regression equation? _____

   b. If a person rates as 4 (mostly agree) that the environment is the most important political issue, how many hours do you predict he or she spends outside, according to the regression equation? _____
   _____

7. Describe these findings as you might in a Results section, using APA format.

   _____

   _____

   _____

   _____

   _____

   _____

8. Interpret the findings as you would in a Discussion section.

   _____

   _____

   _____

   _____

   _____

Exercise 8.11: The Big Picture: Correlational Design vs. Correlational Analysis

1. Complete the following chart:

Scale of Measurement	Correlational Analysis	Appropriate for What Design(s)?
Two interval/ratio variables		
	Point-biserial correlation coefficient (r_{pb})	
Two nominal variables with two or more categories		Correlational or experimental design
	Spearman rho (r_s)	Correlational design

2. Name the most appropriate inferential statistic and its statistical symbol for the following questions:

Is a measure of hardiness (scores can range from 20 to 100) reliable? High school students complete a scale assessing the trait of hardiness and then complete the same scale again one week later. _____
_____

Are visits to a mental health clinic (yes/no) related to family stress as assessed by a scale ranging from 0–20? _____
_____

A school counselor and teacher rank students in the class in terms of frequency of misbehavior. Are the counselor and teacher rankings correlated?
_____

Is SES (high/middle/low) related to political views (conservative/moderate/liberal)? _____

Is suicide ideation (scores range from 0–84) related to work-related traumatic stress (scores range from 0–10) among police officers? _____
_____

If compulsivity and attention to detail are strongly correlated, what is the score for attention to detail if compulsivity = 25? _____
_____

Is participation in after-school activities in high school (yes/no) related to self-reported acts of delinquency (yes/no)? _____
_____

What is the line of best fit for the relationship between years on a job and salary? _____

YOUR RESEARCH

Find and Evaluate a Nonexperimental Study on Your Topic

1. Use your library database to find a primary research article that describes a nonexperimental study on your topic (or related to your topic).

2. After you have found an appropriate nonexperimental study, read the entire article carefully and answer the following questions.

3. Look through the entire Results section to identify any inferential statistics with which you are familiar (from Chapters 7 and 8). List them and explain how the authors used the statistic.

_____

_____

_____

_____

_____

_____

_____

_____

IBM® SPSS® DATA ANALYSIS AND INTERPRETATION

Calculating a Pearson's Correlation Coefficient (*r*)

Data Entry		frustration	selfcontrol
Here are data that have been entered for 10 participants. Note that each participant has a pair of data entered—one value for each variable in the relationship *(in this example, the variables are frustration tolerance and self control, both measured on an interval scale).*	1	8.00	42.00
	2	9.00	48.00
	3	5.00	25.00
	4	6.00	40.00
	5	8.00	38.00
	6	7.00	42.00
	7	5.00	29.00
	8	8.00	28.00
	9	4.00	26.00
	10	7.00	32.00

It is a good idea to first create a scatterplot to determine whether there are outliers in your data and to determine whether the relationship appears linear.

To create a **scatterplot,** on the menu bar, click

Graphs → Legacy Dialogs → Scatter/Dot → Simple Scatter → Define

Send your Y variable to the "Y axis" (the vertical axis) box and your X variable to the "X axis" (the horizontal axis) box.
X is the predictor variable (in this example, self-control) and Y is the predicted variable (in this example, frustration tolerance). When you do not have a clear predictor and outcome, it doesn't matter how you identify X and Y.
Click "OK."

A scatterplot will appear in the output.

In the example to the left, we see that there is a positive and mostly linear relationship between self-control (X) and frustration tolerance (Y). Notice that there are some data points that don't fit with the overall pattern, but they are not extreme enough to be considered outliers.

To calculate Pearson's r, on the Menu Bar, click

Analyze → Correlate → Bivariate

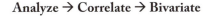

1. Send your X and Y variables to the "Variables" box.

2. Click "OK."

Notes: _Pearson's r_ is used when you have two interval or ratio variables.

If one of your variables is nominal with two groups, you would use the same commands to calculate a _point-biserial correlation_.

If both your variables are ordinal, click "Spearman" to calculate _Spearman's rho_.

OUTPUT

Correlations

		Frustration Tolerance	Self-control
Frustration Tolerance	Pearson Correlation	1	.704*
	Sig. (2-tailed)		.023
	N	10	10
Self-control	Pearson Correlation	.704*	1
	Sig. (2-tailed)	.023	
	N	10	10

$r = .704$

$p = .023$ (and is statistically significant at the $p < .05$ criteria)

Notice that this information is repeated at the top and bottom of the correlation table.

*. Correlation is significant at the 0.05 level (2-tailed).

To find the **proportion of variance accounted for**, simply square r. In this example, $r^2 = .50$, indicating that 50% of the variance in one variable is accounted for by the other.

SPSS does not provide the **confidence interval** when you run a Pearson correlation. If you would like to find out how to calculate a confidence interval for r by hand, go to http://onlinestatbook.com/chapter8/correlation_ci.html

Calculating a Point-Biserial Correlation (r_{pb})

A point-biserial correlation is used to examine the relationship between a nominal variable with two groups (dichotomous) and a variable measured on an interval or ratio scale. When entering your data, be sure to code the dichotomous variable as a number (0 and 1, 1 and 2, etc.). Then follow the same commands as for a Pearson's r.

OUTPUT

Correlations

		Self-control	Health status
Self-control	Pearson Correlation	1	-.748*
	Sig. (2-tailed)		.013
	N	10	10
Health status	Pearson Correlation	-.748*	1
	Sig. (2-tailed)	.013	
	N	10	10

In this example, self-control is an interval variable and health status is a dichotomous variable.

The output in SPSS will look the same as for Pearson's r, but will be interpreted as $r_{pb} = -.75$, $p = .013$.

Pay attention to how you coded the dichotomous variable. In this case, healthy = 1, unhealthy = 2, indicating that healthy is related to higher self-control.

*. Correlation is significant at the 0.05 level (2-tailed).

To find the **proportion of variance accounted for**, simply square r_{pb}. In this example, $r_{pb}^2 = .56$.

Conducting Multiple Pearson's *r* and Point Biserial Correlations (r_{pb})

Because r and r_{pb} are conducted with the same commands in SPSS, you can run multiple correlations by entering multiple interval, ratio, and dichotomous variables in the "Variables" box. Below is an example output with the interval variables *frustration tolerance* and *self-control*, the ratio variable *income*, and the nominal variable *health status* (healthy or unhealthy).

Correlations

		Frustration Tolerance	Self-control	Annual income	Health status
Frustration Tolerance	Pearson Correlation	1	.704*	.673*	–.436
	Sig. (2-tailed)		.023	.033	.208
	N	10	10	10	10
Self-control	Pearson Correlation	.704*	1	.842**	–.748*
	Sig. (2-tailed)	.023		.002	.013
	N	10	10	10	10
Annual income	Pearson Correlation	.673*	.842**	1	–.529
	Sig. (2-tailed)	.033	.002		.116
	N	10	10	10	10
Health status	Pearson Correlation	–.436	–.748*	–.529	1
	Sig. (2-tailed)	.208	.013	.116	
	N	10	10	10	20

*. Correlation is significant at the 0.05 level (2-tailed).
**. Correlation is significant at the 0.01 level (2-tailed).

The output is a matrix that correlates each variable with all the other variables. Notice also that each of the correlations is listed twice so you need to pay attention only to the top or bottom half of the matrix.

For this example, *self-control* is significantly positively correlated with *frustration tolerance* ($r = .70$, $p = .02$) and *annual income* ($r = .84$, $p = .002$) and significantly negatively correlated with *health status* ($r_{pb} = -.75$, $p = .01$). *Frustration tolerance* and *annual income* are also significantly positively correlated ($r = .67$, $p = .033$).

Writing Up Results

When you write up results from a Pearson's *r*, you will include the following information:

- The statistical analysis used (e.g., Pearson's correlation)

- The variables examined (*never* use SPSS codes such as Q1, etc.)

- The *r*, rounded to two decimal places

- The direction of the relationship (positive or negative)

- The strength of the relationship (weak, moderate, strong, etc.)

- The results of statistical significance testing (the *p* value)

- Optional: r^2 or the proportion of variance accounted for

Use this same format for a point-biserial correlation or Spearman's rho, but use the appropriate statistical notation (r_{pb} and r_s, respectively).

Examples:

Option 1: Report all the results in text.

Results

We calculated a series of Pearson's *r* correlations to examine the relationship between self-control, frustration tolerance, and income. Self-control had strong, positive, and statistically significant correlations with frustration tolerance ($r = .70$, $p = .02$) and annual income ($r = .84$, $p = .002$). The correlation between frustration tolerance and annual income was strong, positive, and statistically significant ($r = .67, p = .033$).

Option 2: To avoid the redundancy of listing all the correlation coefficients, you might consider using a table to summarize the results. You would highlight the major findings in the Results section and refer to the table.

Results

Pearson's *r* correlations indicated that the relationship between self-control, frustration tolerance, and income were strong and positive. All correlations were also statistically significant at the $p < .05$ criteria (see Table 1).

(In an APA-style research report, Tables appear after the Reference section.)

Table 1

Correlations Among Study Variables

	Self-Control	Frustration Tolerance
Self-Control	—	
Frustration Tolerance	.70*	—
Income	.84**	.67*

*$p < .05$, **$p < .01$

Conducting a Linear Regression

Linear regression is used when you want to examine a linear relationship between two or more variables. Simple linear regression is used when you have two interval/ratio variables and you wish to predict the value of one based on the other. Multiple regression is used when you have more than two variables.

To calculate a linear regression, click

Analyze → Regression → Linear

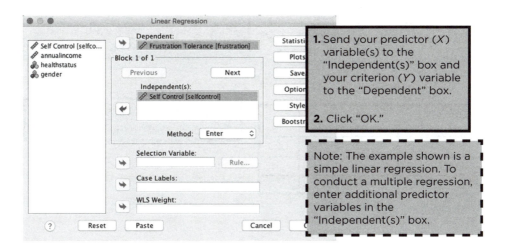

You can also request a graph of the regression line (line of best fit) for a simple linear regression:

Click **Analyze → Regression → Curve Estimation**

1. Send your variables to the Independent (X) and Dependent(s) (Y) variable boxes.

2. Make sure "Linear" is checked.

3. Click "OK."

OUTPUT (abbreviated)

Regression

Model Summary

Model	R	R Square	Adjusted R Square	Std. Error of the Estimate
1	.704a	.496	.433	1.23186

a. Predictors: (Constant), Self-control

When you only have 2 variables, $R = r$ and R Square $= r^2$.

Std. Error of the estimate is the average error of Y' in predicting Y.

ANOVAa

Model		Sum of Squares	df	Mean Square	F	Sig.
1	Regression	11.960	1	11.960	7.881	.023b
	Residual	12.140	8	1.517		
	Total	24.100	9			

a. Dependent Variable: Frustration Tolerance
b. Predictors: (Constant), Self-control

The ANOVA table tells you if the r is statistically significant.

Coefficients[a]

Model		Unstandardized Coefficients		Standardized Coefficients	*t*	Sig.
		B	Std. Error	Beta		
1	(Constant)	1.657	1.838		.901	.394
	Self-control	.144	.051	.704	2.807	.023

a. Dependent Variable: Frustration Tolerance

If your *r* is statistically significant, you can calculate the regression equation ($Y' = bX + a$). You find the a and b for your regression equation in the B column.

The value labeled "Constant" (1.657) is **a** (the y intercept) and the value labeled as the x variable (.144) is **b** (the slope). These values are used to create the regression equation. In this case,

$Y' = .14X + 1.66$

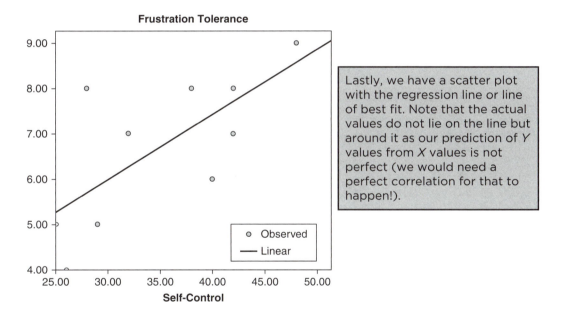

Frustration Tolerance

Lastly, we have a scatter plot with the regression line or line of best fit. Note that the actual values do not lie on the line but around it as our prediction of *Y* values from *X* values is not perfect (we would need a perfect correlation for that to happen!).

Now that you have the regression equation, $Y' = .14X + 1.66$, you can use it to predict frustration tolerance (*Y*) based on specific self-control (*X*) values.

If self-control = 40, then we predict frustration tolerance will be

$$Y' = .14(40) + 1.66 = 5.60 + 1.66 = 7.26$$

The *Y'* of 7.26 will lie on the line of best fit, while the actual value for frustration tolerance = 6.00 when self-control = 40. See the scatter plot above. This difference contributes to the standard error of the estimate (average difference between actual and predicted Y values), which we can see in the above output is 1.23.

Practice Exercises

A marketing consultant for an online dating site wonders whether time spent on the Internet during leisure hours is related to whether a person believes he or she can find a romantic partner online. She surveys 20 young adults who are not in a committed relationship about their recent time online (in minutes) and their belief about the likelihood of finding a romantic partner online (as assessed with a 5-point scale where 1 = *very unlikely* and 5 = *very likely*). The data are below:

Time online	Find partner?	Time online	Find partner?
60	4	10	1
5	1	300	4
14	2	45	2
30	3	15	1
30	4	60	4
60	2	240	5
120	2	60	3
60	3	15	1
120	5	45	3
120	4	150	4

1. Using SPSS, enter the data and calculate the statistics below. Alternatively, or additionally, calculate these statistics by hand by following the directions in Chapter 8 of the textbook.

   a. Compute the appropriate descriptive statistics for the two variables. Describe them.

   _____

   _____

   b. What is the appropriate correlational statistic to compute for these data?

   _____

   c. Compute a scatterplot for the data. What type of relationship does it suggest?

   _____

   _____

d. State a null and directional alternative hypothesis for the relationship.

_____

_____

e. Compute the correlation coefficient.

f. Is the relationship between time on the Internet and belief in finding a partner on the Internet significant? _____ How do you know?

_____

_____

g. What proportion of variability is accounted for by the relationship?

_____

h. Is it appropriate to predict belief in finding a partner on the Internet from the time spent online? _____ Explain your answer.

_____

_____

i. Compute the regression for the relationship in question g and write the regression equation. _____

_____

j. Comment on the standard error of estimate (small/moderate/large). How do you know how to interpret this value?

_____

_____

k. If a person spends 90 minutes on the Internet, what is the predicted score on the likelihood to believe he or she will find a romantic partner on the Internet? _____

l. Describe your findings as you would in a Results section, using APA format.

_____

_____

_____

_____

_____

_____

m. Write a Discussion section for your results. Include all the information that belongs in this section.

_____

_____

_____

_____

_____

_____

2. For additional practice with the different correlation statistics and regression, pull up the datasets that are available for this course or datasets your instructor has made available.

a. Identify variables you would like to correlate and their scale of measurement, then decide on the appropriate correlation to compute.

b. Compute the statistic(s) and interpret your results.

c. Check your work with classmates, a TA (if available), or your instructor. (This practice would be a good group activity with classmates.)

Examining Causality

CHAPTER SUMMARY

How do you determine that one variable caused a change in another variable? Chapter 9 begins by outlining the requirements for causality, including sequence, correlation, and the ability to rule out alternative explanations. *Internal validity* is the extent to which a research design ruled out alternative explanations, and the key threats to internal validity are discussed in detail in this chapter. These threats are inherent in the nonexperiment designs, such as a pre/posttest or quasi-experimental design.

An experiment is the only type of design that can demonstrate causality, although simply conducting a study is not enough to show causality. This chapter discusses basic issues in designing an experiment and increasing internal validity. Additionally, the chapter discusses practical and ethical issues in recruiting participants, randomly assigning them to groups, maintaining experimental control, manipulating the independent variable, and measuring the dependent variable.

This chapter also introduces other issues with experimental design, including demand characteristics, experimenter expectancy effects, diffusion of treatment, and balancing internal and external validity. The chapter ends with a discussion of the limitations of experimental design.

REVIEW AND APPLICATION OF KEY CONCEPTS FROM CHAPTER 9

Exercise 9.1: Testing Cause and Effect (Review)

1. What are some terms that researchers use to suggest that one variable caused a change in another variable?

   _____

   _____

LEARNING OUTCOMES

After reading and reviewing Chapter 9, you should understand

- The key components necessary to test cause and effect

- How to design an experiment

- How to manipulate an independent variable (IV)

- How to measure the dependent variable (DV)

- How to balance internal and external validity in an experiment

- Limitations to experimental design

2. Students sometimes confuse the words "effect" and "affect." Remember that when discussing causality, effect is a noun and affect is a verb. Practice by filling in the blanks below with the word "effect" or "affect"

   a. Researchers have examined the _____ of smell on memory.

   b. The color of a car might _____ the likelihood of getting into an accident.

   c. We hypothesize that spending time in nature will _____ mood.

   d. Do you think that taking practice quizzes will have an _____ on your exam score?

3. List the three requirements for causality: _____

   _____

   _____

4. _____ validity is the degree to which one can say that one variable caused a change in another.

5. A _____ is an alternative explanation for causality.

6. What conditions for causality are lacking in a correlational design?

   _____

   _____

Exercise 9.2: Threats to Internal Validity (Review)

Fill in the blanks with names of potential threats to internal validity.

1. _____ is a statistical phenomenon in which extreme scores become less extreme.

2. _____ occurs when participants withdraw from the study.

3. _____ indicates that preexisting differences in the sample caused the observed change in the dependent (or outcome) variable.

4. _____ indicates inconsistency in measures, administration, or scoring.

5. _____ is any event that might impact the outcome of a study.

6. _____ occurs when a pretest changes the outcome of a study.

7. _____ occurs naturally over time.

Exercise 9.3: Why the One-Group Pretest-Posttest Design Does not Demonstrate Causality (Application)

A political candidate's approval rating was very low, a mere 20%, prior to unveiling his economic plan. After the plan was shared, the candidate's approval rating rose to 28%.

1. Based on the information above, fill in the model for a one-group pretest-posttest design. We started this for you:

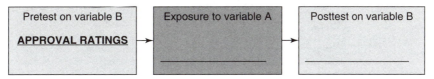

2. Identify the threats to internal validity that help explain why this design cannot demonstrate that the economic plan is the reason for the increased approval ratings:

_____

_____

_____

_____

_____

_____

Exercise 9.4: Group Designs (Application)

A marketing executive wants to know whether a new website might improve sales. She plans to compare the new website to the original one.

1. The marketing executive is considering a two-group pretest-posttest design. Fill in the blanks. We started this for you:

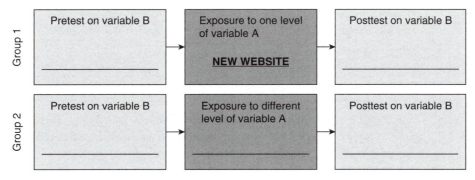

2. Alternatively, she might conduct a two-group posttest-only design. Fill in the blanks:

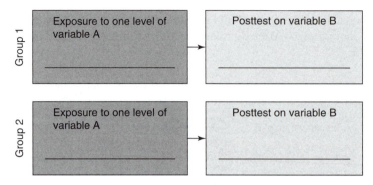

3. In which of these designs (from question 1 or 2) might testing be a threat to internal validity? How could the marketing executive avoid this threat?

_____

_____

4. Why would it be a problem if the marketing executive gave one group up to 30 minutes to explore the new website, but gave the other group only 10 minutes to explore the old website? Identify the specific threat to internal validity.

_____

_____

5. Why would it be a problem if the marketing executive had one group look at the new website in pairs and the other group look at the old website individually? Identify the specific threat to internal validity.

_____

_____

6. Why would it be a problem if the marketing executive had all the people who were under 30 explore the new website and had all those who were 30 and older explore the old website? Identify the specific threat to internal validity.

_____

_____

7. Why would it be a problem if the marketing executive asked those in one group to report the items they would like to purchase and looked at the

online shopping carts of those in the other group? Identify the specific threat to internal validity.

_____

_____

8. When would attrition be a threat to internal validity of the marketing executive's study?

_____

_____

Exercise 9.5: How an Experiment Can Demonstrate Causality (Review)

1. An experiment requires the following: _____

_____

_____

2. A quasi-experiment is missing the requirement of

_____.

3. The _____ variable is predicted to affect the _____ _____ variable.

4. The _____ group receives a certain amount or level of the IV, and a _____ group receives a zero level of the IV.

5. It is not always necessary or possible for an experiment to have a _____ group.

6. _____ helps ensure that the IV groups are as similar as possible prior to the manipulation.

7. A _____ helps verify that the participants attended to the manipulation.

8. A _____ is someone who pretends to be a participant or bystander but is actually working with the researcher.

Exercise 9.6: Application of Experimental Design

1. In an experiment testing the effect of listening to the news on anxiety, listening to news is the _____ variable and anxiety is the _____ variable.

2. In an experiment testing whether hunger increases after exposure to the color red, hunger is the _____ variable and color is the _____ variable.

3. A police department wants to know whether citizens will better comprehend verbal police instructions if an officer repeats the information twice or if an officer adds listenability features, such as an introduction ("I am going to tell you three things") and lists (first . . . second . . . third).

Help them design a simple experiment:

Recruit participants

Prescreen for: _____

Inform potential participants: _____

_____

Randomly assign participants to independent variable (IV) conditions

What type of random assignment? _____

How will you carry out this random assignment? _____

_____

| **IV condition (or level) 1:** | **IV condition (or level) 2:** |
| _____ | _____ |

Keep everything else constant (the same) across the two conditions

What will be constant across your IV conditions? _____

_____

Measure Dependent Variable (DV)

What is the DV? _____ How might you operationally

define (measure) the DV? _____

Exercise 9.7: Other Threats to Internal Validity (Review)

1. The _____ occurs when participants change their behavior simply because they are part of a study.

2. You should reduce _____ of a study to decrease the likelihood that participants will guess at your hypothesis and purposely try to support or contradict your hypothesis.

3. Even if you do not intentionally try to bias your experiment, it is possible that you might treat the groups differently and therefore impact your results. This is called _____.

4. If participants interact with each other before the end of the experiment, it is possible that _____ will occur.

5. A _____ receives an intervention or treatment only after the completion of the study.

6. In a _____ experiment, participants do not know to which group they have been assigned. In a _____ _____ experiment, neither the participants nor the researchers interacting with the participants know to which group the participants have been assigned.

Exercise 9.8: Other Threats to Internal Validity (Application)

1. What might you do to reduce demand characteristics of the study from Exercise 9.6?

    _____

    _____

    _____

2. What might you do to reduce experimenter expectancy effects of the study from Exercise 9.6?

    _____

    _____

    _____

3. Comment on the ecological validity of the experiment from Exercise 9.6.

    _____

    _____

    _____

YOUR RESEARCH

Find and Evaluate an Experiment on Your Topic

Use your library database to find a primary research article that describes an experiment on your topic (or related to your topic). Limit your search to experiments published in the last 10 years. See Chapter 2 for search strategies.

1. How do you know it is an experiment? _____

_____

2. How did the researchers recruit participants (or obtain animal subjects)?

_____

_____

3. What type of random assignment did they use? _____

4. Identify the IV(s). How did the researchers manipulate the IV(s)?

_____

_____

5. Was there a manipulation check? If so, describe.

_____

6. Identify at least one way, other than random assignment, that the researchers controlled threats to internal validity.

_____

7. Identify the DV(s). How did the researchers operationally define the DV(s)?

_____

_____

8. How might you build on this study?

_____

_____

Independent-Groups Designs

10

CHAPTER SUMMARY

In this chapter, you learned about independent-groups designs in which the participants in different groups are unrelated. These designs can be correlational, quasi-experimental, or experimental studies. Although the statistical tests used to analyze the three types of independent-groups designs is the same, the interpretation of the results differs. Both correlational and quasi-experimental results are described as a correlational relationship between the predictor (IV) and outcome (DV), while experiments are described as a causal relationship between the IV and DV. The chapter reviewed the controls and considerations you learned about in previous chapters regarding designing powerful independent-groups studies.

The simplest independent-groups design involves two groups, and you learned how to analyze the data from such studies using an independent-samples t test. This statistical test assumes that you have two unrelated groups, an IV (predictor) and DV (outcome), interval/ratio data, normally distributed DV, and similar variability of scores in the two groups (homogeneity of variance). The independent-samples t test compares the means of the two groups in relation to an estimate of the standard deviation of the sampling distribution (standard error of the difference between the means). You also compute an effect size (r_{pb}^2 or Cohen's d) and confidence intervals, either by hand or using a statistical package (e.g., SPSS, Excel).

You then learned about multiple-groups designs when you have one IV (predictor) with three or more independent groups. The advantages of multiple-groups designs (in comparison to two-group designs) were described. The findings of these designs are analyzed using a one-way analysis of

LEARNING OUTCOMES

After reading and reviewing Chapter 10, you should understand

- Different types of independent-groups designs with two levels

- How to analyze a two-group design with an independent-samples t test

- How to calculate and interpret the effect size and the confidence interval for an independent-samples t test

- The characteristics and advantages of multiple-groups designs

- How to calculate and interpret data for multiple-groups designs using a one-way ANOVA

- The purpose and interpretation of post hoc tests

variance (ANOVA), which compares the variability between groups (treatment variance) to the variability within groups (error variance). The assumptions are similar to those for the independent-samples t test. If you find a significant F (the end statistic for the ANOVA), you compute a post hoc test, which examines differences between all possible pairs of the groups in the study. Eta squared (η^2) is the effect size appropriate for the ANOVA, and it is interpreted the same way as r_{pb}^2. In reporting your results for a t test or one-way ANOVA, you should make clear the type of relationship you have examined (correlational or causal) and discuss the practical and statistical interpretation of your findings.

REVIEW AND APPLICATION OF KEY CONCEPTS FROM CHAPTER 10

Exercise 10.1: Designs With Independent Groups (Review)

1. The three designs with independent groups are _____, _____, and _____.

2. The independent-groups designs discussed in the chapter compare groups analyzed on _____ or _____ scale of measurement.

3. Differences between correlational designs and experimental designs include that correlational designs do *not* _____ _____, _____, or _____ _____.

4. In a correlational design, we examine the _____ variable, which predicts a value of the _____.

5. When interpreting the findings of a correlational design, we _____ (do/do not) imply causation.

6. Quasi-experimental designs are like correlational designs in that they _____ _____ and _____ _____.

7. Quasi-experimental designs differ from correlational designs in that they _____.

8. Quasi-experimental designs differ from experiments in that they _____ _____.

9. When interpreting the findings of a quasi-experimental design, we _____ (do/do not) imply causation.

Exercise 10.2: Designs With Independent Groups (Application)

1. A study finds that children who read at home every day are more likely to enjoy school than children who never read at home. This is a/an _____ (type of design) independent-groups design; reading at home is the _____ variable and enjoying school is the _____ variable.

2. A researcher interested in environmental issues completes a study on recycling. She arranges to have one neighborhood's recycling picked up each week and a second neighborhood's recycling picked up each month. The amount of recycling (in pounds of material) for each resident in the two neighborhoods is measured over 6 months.

   What type of study is this? _____

   What type of variable does timing of recycling represent? _____

   What type of variable does amount of recycled material represent? _____

   _____

   Can we make assumptions about causality regarding this study? Explain.

   _____

   _____

3. How would you make the recycling study an experiment?

   _____

   _____

Exercise 10.3: Designing a Simple Experiment (Application)

Suppose children who are encouraged to gesture while generating creative ways to use objects generate significantly more novel uses for the objects than those who are not encouraged to gesture.

1. If the children are randomly assigned to one of the instruction types, what type of design is this? _____

2. The IV for the gesturing study is _____; the DV is _____.

3. Would this design allow you to conclude that encouraging gesturing causes an increase in the generation of novel uses for objects? _____ Explain your answer.

   _____

   _____

4. List three ways a researcher could maximize the power of the gesturing study.

   a. _____

   b. _____

   c. _____

5. Name two steps you could take to ensure the reliability and validity of the DV in this study.

   _____

   _____

6. Name two potential confounds that you would want to eliminate from this study.

   _____

   _____

7. What ethical concerns might arise from the study and how might you address them?

   _____

   _____

Exercise 10.4: Independent-Samples *t* Tests (Review)

1. The inferential statistic used to analyze two independent-samples designs is

   _____ .

2. Circle which of the following assumptions should be met in order to appropriately compute an independent-samples *t* test.

Nominal/ordinal data	Homogeneity of variance
Interval/ratio data	Study is an experiment
Three or more groups	Normally distributed measurement variable
Random assignment to groups	Pilot study

3. An independent-samples *t* test is used to determine whether the means of two groups differ more than we would expect by _____ .

4. In an independent-samples *t* test, the difference between the means of two groups is compared to a sampling distribution composed of differences between the means of two groups, when _____ .

Exercise 10.5: Formulas and Calculations: Independent-Samples *t* Test (Review and Application)

1. In the formula for an independent-samples *t* test, the difference between the means is divided by _____ which is symbolized by _____.

2. The standard error of the difference between means is _____ (larger or smaller) than the standard deviation of each group in a study because _____ _____.

   _____

3. The _____ represents the variability of the entire sample and is computed by squaring the _____ of each group; this value also weights the sample variability according to the _____ in each group.

4. The computed or obtained *t* value represents the deviation units our mean difference is from the zero difference predicted by the _____ _____.

5. If there is no difference between the means for our samples, we would expect *t* = _____.

6. The _____ (larger/smaller) the difference between our means, the _____ (more/less) likely we will find statistical significance.

7. In order to determine whether a t_{obt} is significant, we must compare this value with the _____ in a *t* table.

8. To find the t_{crit} for a study, we need the following: _____, _____, and _____.

9. Suppose for one of our groups *SD* = 1.5 and for the other group *SD* =15. What assumption of a *t* test might we be worried about? _____

   _____

10. If a study has 16 participants in each of two groups, the *df* = _____. If we have a two-tailed test and *p* < .05, t_{crit} = _____ for this study. (See Table C.4 in Appendix C.)

11. A study investigates the effect of different methods of taking notes in class (entering notes on a laptop or writing notes in longhand on paper) on student retention of material. Students (*N* = 27) are randomly assigned to one of the two conditions. They hear the same 30-minute lecture and 30 minutes later take a short-answer test on the material.

a. What type of independent-groups design is this study? _____ _____ Explain what characteristics define the design you selected.

_____

_____

b. State a directional alternative hypothesis for this study.

_____

_____

c. For this study: IV is _____; levels of the IV are _____ and _____.
DV = _____
df = _____ for a two-tailed test at $p < .05$, t_{crit} = _____

d. Suppose $t(25) = 5.32$. Are these results statistically significant for a two-tailed test at $p < .05$? Explain.

_____

_____

e. A second study examines the effect of the two types of note taking on a multiple-choice test. The results show $t(38) = 1.98$. Are these results statistically significant for a two-tailed test at $p < .05$? Explain.

_____

_____

12. A developmental psychologist observed seven children with their parents. She recorded whether or not the parents used any harsh language (yes or no) and rated the level of child behavior problems exhibited. The data appear below.

Child ID number	Use of Harsh Language	Ratings of Child Behavior Problems
1	No	4
2	No	4
3	Yes	7
4	No	3
5	No	4
6	Yes	7
7	Yes	5

a. Using the formula in Chapter 10 of the textbook, calculate t _____

b. Calculate the *df* _____

c. Using Table C.4 in Appendix C, are the results statistically significant for a two-tailed test at $p < .05$? _____ For $p < .01$? _____

Exercise 10.6: Confidence Intervals (Review and Application)

1. The _____ _____ tells us the range of values within which we can be confident our mean difference would fall 95% (or 99%) of the time.

2. Suppose you find 95% CI [1.65, 4.80] for an independent-groups study. Write a sentence describing the meaning of this result.

   _____

   _____

3. In a second study exploring the same variables, you find 95% CI [1.65, 9.32]. Which of these confidence intervals are you more satisfied with? _____. Explain your choice.

   _____

   _____

Exercise 10.7: Effect Size (Review and Application)

1. Measures of the effect size for an independent-samples t test are _____ and _____.

2. The effect size that describes the percentage of variability in a DV accounted for by the IV is _____ and is symbolized by _____.

3. The effect size that describes the standard deviation units between the means is _____ and is symbolized by _____.

4. A researcher finds that $d = .50$. Interpret the meaning of this finding.

   _____

   _____

5. Another researcher finds that $r_{pb}^2 = .50$. Interpret the meaning of this finding.

   _____

   _____

Exercise 10.8: Practical Significance (Review)

1. What is practical significance?

   _____

   _____

2. How do we evaluate the practical significance of findings from an independent-groups design?

   _____

   _____

Exercise 10.9: Using Data Analysis Programs: Independent-Samples *t* Test (Application)

1. A student is interested in whether faculty who use humor in the classroom are liked more than faculty who do not use humor. She arranges for a graduate student to be the "guest teacher" in two sections of the same class. The content of the class is the same but the graduate student uses humor in one section and omits humor in the other class. At the end of each class, the students complete a survey about the guest teacher, including how much they liked the class.

   a. What type of independent-groups design is this study? _____ _____ Explain what characteristics define the design you selected.

      _____

      _____

      _____

   b. State a directional alternative hypothesis for this study.

      _____

   c. For this study: IV is _____; levels of the IV are _____ _____ and _____.

      DV = _____

   Use the output in the following tables to answer questions 1(d)–1(j).

Group Statistics

	Teach Group	N	Mean	Std. Deviation	Std. Error Mean
Likability	Humor	12	8.0833	2.90637	.83900
	No humor	12	6.1667	1.19342	.34451

Independent Samples Test

Likability	Levene's Test for Equality of Variances		t-test for Equality of Means					95% Confidence Interval of the Difference	
	F	Sig.	t	df	Sig. (2-tailed)	Mean Difference	Std. Error Difference	Lower	Upper
Equal variances assumed	8.637	.008	2.113	22	.046	1.91667	.90697	.03572	3.79761
Equal variances not assumed			2.113	14.607	.052	1.91667	.90697	-.02104	3.85438

Correlations

		Teach Group	Likability
Teach Group	Pearson Correlation	1	−.437*
	Sig. (2-tailed)		.033
	N	24	24
Likability	Pearson Correlation	−.437*	1
	Sig. (2-tailed)	.033	
	N	24	24

*Correlation is significant at the 0.05 level (2-tailed).

d. Which of the assumptions for an independent-samples t test was not met? _____ How do you know?

_____

_____

e. How does this change your interpretation of and conclusions about the output?

_____

_____

_____

f. Compute r_{pb}^2 as an effect size for the study: _____

g. Compute d as an effect size for the study: _____

h. Write a few sentences summarizing the findings as you would in a Results section.

_____

_____

_____

_____

i. What conclusions can you make about the findings?

_____

_____

_____

j. Name a possible flaw in the study and at least one suggestion for future studies.

_____

_____

_____

2. Are male presidents of community colleges paid a higher salary than female presidents at these institutions? A researcher documents the salaries of 20 presidents who were hired within the last 2 years.

a. What type of independent-groups design is this study? _____ _____ Explain what characteristics define the design you selected.

_____

_____

_____

b. State a directional alternative hypothesis for this study.

_____

c. For this study, the predictor = _____; the outcome = _____.

Use the output in the following tables to answer questions 2(d)–2(g). Values/dollars are expressed in thousands.

Group Statistics

	Gender	N	Mean	Std. Deviation	Std. Error Mean
Salary (in thousands)	female	10	170.5000	20.06240	6.34429
	male	12	198.3333	33.46187	9.65961

	Levene's Test for Equality of Variances		t test for Equality of Means							
									95% Confidence Interval of the Difference	
Salary (in thousands)	F	Sig.	t	df	Sig. (2-tailed)	Mean Difference	Std. Error Difference	Lower	Upper
Equal variances assumed	1.907	.183	-2.303	20	.032	-27.83333	12.08756	-53.04753	-2.61913
Equal variances not assumed			-2.408	18.361	.027	-27.83333	11.55673	-52.07895	-3.58772

d. Compute Cohen's *d* as an effect size: _____

e. Are the salaries of male and female community college presidents significantly different? _____ How do you know?_____

f. Write a Results section, describing the results of this study.

_____

_____

_____

_____

_____

g. Based on these findings, what conclusions can you make about gender and community college presidents' salaries?

_____

_____

Exercise 10.10: Designs With More Than Two Independent Groups (Review)

1. Designs with more than two independent groups are called _____
   _____.

2. A study that examines the relationship between year in college (first year, sophomore, etc.) and cumulative GPA is called a _____
   _____ design.

3. The three types of multiple independent-groups design are _____,
   _____, and _____.

4. Circle all of the advantages of multiple independent-groups designs relative to multiple independent-groups designs.

Decreased probability of Type I error	Can use multiple control groups
Increased external validity	Increased probability of Type II error
Increased internal validity	More efficient
Decreased number of participants	Allows examination of functional relationships
Easier to analyze	

5. A multiple independent-groups design allows us to examine most or many of the levels of a particular variable and so is _____ (more/less) reflective of reality than a two independent-groups design.

6. Why is it a bad idea to compute multiple t tests comparing each of the groups with every other group?

   _____

Exercise 10.11: One-Way Analysis of Variance (Review)

1. The statistical test used to analyze data from multiple-groups designs is called a _____.

2. A one-way ANOVA has _____ independent variable(s) with _____ levels.

3. A one-way ANOVA compares the _____ variance to the _____ variance.

4. Another name for between-group variance is _____ variance.

5. Another name for error variance is _____ variance.

6. Researchers try to increase the _____ variance and minimize the _____ variance.

7. Because we can never eliminate individual differences or uniqueness of individuals, the between-group variance consists of both _____ variance and _____ variance.

8. The statistic representing the result of a one-way ANOVA is _____.

9. $F =$ _____ variance/_____ variance

10. If our null hypothesis is true (our treatment has no effect), we would expect $F =$ _____.

11. The _____ (larger/smaller) the F, the more likely it is to be statistically significant.

12. Assumptions for computing a one-way ANOVA include _____ groups (#), independent groups, DV = _____ scale of measurement, DV is normally distributed, and _____.

Exercise 10.12: Formulas and Calculations: One-Way ANOVA (Review and Application)

1. The values computed for an ANOVA are presented in a _____ table.

2. The first step in computing an ANOVA is to subtract the mean from each of its scores and then square the deviation scores and sum them. This value is called the _____.

3. We also subtract the total mean from each group mean, square the deviation scores and sum them. This value is called the _____ _____.

4. We have two dfs in a one-way ANOVA, one for _____ groups and one for _____ groups.

5. We lose one from the number of groups/levels to compute the df _____ _____.

6. We subtract the number of groups from the total N to compute the df ___ _____.

7. The df_{tot} is computed by subtracting _____ from N and is also equal to _____ + _____.

8. When the F value is significant in a one-way ANOVA, we must then compute a _____ to learn about _____ _____.

9. Using the formulas in Chapter 10 of the textbook, complete the following Summary Table for an experiment comparing four independent groups:

	Sum of Squares	df	Mean Square	F
Between Groups	43.844	??	??	??
Within Groups	??	28	??	
Total	65.219	31		

10. a. Calculate the effect size (η^2) using the formula in Chapter 10 of the textbook: _____

   b. What does this effect size tell you?

   _____

11. Based on the summary table:

   a. How many total participants are in the study? _____

   b. If the n is equal in each condition, how many participants are in each condition? _____

   c. Is the result statistically significant at $p < .05$? _____ How can you tell?

   _____

   d. What test should you compute next and why should you do this?

   _____

   e. How many paired comparisons are there for this study? _____

Exercise 10.13: Using Data Analysis Programs: One-Way ANOVA

1. A social psychologist is interested in the impact of men's clothing on views of their attractiveness. College students are randomly assigned to a condition in the study. The output for the study is below.

ANOVA

Attractiveness					
	Sum of Squares	df	Mean Square	F	Sig.
Between Groups (Dress Style)	43.844	3	14.615	19.155	.000
Within Groups	21.375	28	.763		
Total	65.219	31			

Report

Attractiveness			
Dress Styles	Mean	N	Std. Deviation
Jeans & polo	7.0000	8	.75593
Jeans & t-shirt	6.0000	8	.75593
Business suit	4.6250	8	1.06066
Khakis & vest	7.7500	8	.88641
Total	6.3438	32	1.45046

Test of Homogeneity of Variances

Attractiveness			
Levene Statistic	df1	df2	Sig.
1.167	3	28	.340

Measures of Association

	Eta	Eta Squared
Attractiveness * Dress Styles	.820	.672

Multiple Comparisons

Dependent Variable: Attractiveness						
LSD						
		Mean Difference (I-J)	Std. Error	Sig.	95% Confidence Interval	
(I) Dress Styles	(J) Dress Styles				Lower Bound	Upper Bound
Jeans & polo	Jeans & t-shirt	1.00000*	.43686	.030	.1051	1.8949
	Business suit	2.37500*	.43686	.000	1.4801	3.2699
	Khakis & vest	−.75000	.43686	.097	−1.6449	.1449
Jeans & t-shirt	Jeans & polo	−1.00000*	.43686	.030	−1.8949	−.1051
	Business suit	1.37500*	.43686	.004	.4801	2.2699
	Khakis & vest	−1.75000*	.43686	.000	−2.6449	−.8551
Business suit	Jeans & polo	−2.37500*	.43686	.000	−3.2699	−1.4801
	Jeans & t-shirt	−1.37500*	.43686	.004	−2.2699	−.4801
	Khakis & vest	−3.12500*	.43686	.000	−4.0199	−2.2301
Khakis & vest	Jeans & polo	.75000	.43686	.097	−.1449	1.6449
	Jeans & t-shirt	1.75000*	.43686	.000	.8551	2.6449
	Business suit	3.12500*	.43686	.000	2.2301	4.0199

a. What is the IV and how many groups/levels does it have? _____

b. What is the DV? _____

c. What is the probability of a Type I error? _____ Type II error? _____

d. Which clothing style was rated as least attractive? _____

e. As most attractive? _____

f. Was the homogeneity of variance assumption violated in this study? ___ Explain how you know.

_____

g. What is the effect size for the study and its strength? _____

h. List the comparisons that met the criteria for statistical significance at the $p < .05$. Indicate the exact p value for each of these comparisons, except report $p < .001$ when SPSS reports a p of .000.

_____

_____

i. Report your findings as if you were writing a Results section. Be sure to identify the IV and DV, descriptive statistics, and all of the required statistical analyses and their findings. Use APA format.

_____

_____

_____

_____

_____

_____

j. Interpret the results as you would in a Discussion section. Include one limitation and one way to address the limitation.

_____

_____

_____

2. Iam Phuny is investigating the effect of facial expression on ratings of females' job success. Participants are randomly assigned to view a picture showing only the head and shoulders of a woman (similar to one that would appear in a newspaper announcement on a business page). They then rate the female on several characteristics using a 10-point scale (1= *not at all* to 10 = *extremely*). Iam is only interested in ratings of job success. The results of the analysis are below.

Means

Report			
Job Success			
Facial Express	Mean	N	Std. Deviation
neutral	7.4667	15	1.95911
frown	5.7333	15	2.31352
smile	5.6000	15	2.26148
Total	6.2667	45	2.30020

Measures of Association

	Eta	Eta Squared
Job Success * Facial Express	.374	.140

Test of Homogeneity of Variances

Job Success			
Levene Statistic	df1	df2	Sig.
.332	2	42	.720

ANOVA

Job Success					
	Sum of Squares	df	Mean Square	F	Sig.
Between Groups	32.533	2	16.267	3.411	.042
Within Groups	200.267	42	4.768		
Total	232.800	44			

Multiple Comparisons

Dependent Variable: Job Success						
LSD						
(I) Facial Express	(J) Facial Express	Mean Difference (I-J)	Std. Error	Sig.	95% Confidence Interval	
					Lower Bound	Upper Bound
neutral	frown	1.73333*	.79735	.035	.1242	3.3425
	smile	1.86667*	.79735	.024	.2575	3.4758
frown	neutral	−1.73333*	.79735	.035	−3.3425	−.1242
	smile	.13333	.79735	.868	−1.4758	1.7425
smile	neutral	−1.86667*	.79735	.024	−3.4758	−.2575
	frown	−.13333	.79735	.868	−1.7425	1.4758

*. The mean difference is significant at the 0.05 level.

a. Name the IV and levels of the IV: _____

b. Name the DV: _____

c. What type of design is the study? _____

d. What scale of measurement does the IV represent? _____

e. What scale of measurement does the DV represent? _____

f. State the null and directional alternative hypotheses for the experiment.

H_0: _____

_____

H_a: _____

_____

g. Describe two potential threats to internal validity and what the researcher can do to avoid/minimize each threat.

i. _____

_____

ii. _____

_____

h. What is the total number of participants in the study? _____

i. What is the probability of a Type I error? _____ Type II error? _____

j. Graph the results (the group means).

k. Describe the results in APA format.

_____

_____

_____

_____

_____

_____

l. Comment on the external validity of the study.

_____

_____

m. What would you recommend to employed females?

_____

_____

n. Discuss the statistical significance, effect size, and practical significance for this study.

_____

_____

_____

_____

_____

_____

Exercise 10.14: The Big Picture: Selecting Analyses and Interpreting Results for Independent-Groups Designs

1. Identify the flaw in each item below **and** correct it.

a. Caroline is interested in whether there are more male or more female professors at her university. She counts the number of male and female faculty in each department and computes a t test comparing these numbers. The t test is significant and Caroline concludes that significantly more females than males teach at her school.

_____

_____

_____

b. Jack is conducting a study on math anxiety. He has participants take the same 10-item math test, but the groups differ in how long they have to complete the test (10 minutes, 20 minutes, 30 minutes). He assigns the first 25 participants to the 30-minute group, the next 25 participants to the 20-minute group, and the last 25 participants to the 10-minute group. He finds that the 30-minute group members score significantly better on the exam and report lower anxiety, and he concludes that math teachers should allow more time for all tests because it can cause a decrease in math anxiety.

_____

_____

_____

_____

c. Sharon has just completed a study on the effect of different fonts on reading comprehension. Her analysis shows $F(2, 47) = 1.04, p = .45$. She reports that she had a 45% chance of a Type I error and no chance of a Type II error.

_____

_____

_____

_____

2. For the following studies, name the type of design and what characteristics define the design, the appropriate statistical analyses, and the appropriate interpretation. We have completed some of this for you.

Study	Design	Characteristics	Inferential Statistic and Effect Size	Interpretation
Does choice impact enjoyment? Fifth graders in one class were assigned a book by their teacher while students in a second class chose from 10 books. After two weeks, students rated how much they enjoyed reading their book on 10-point scale.	two independent groups, quasi-experiment	two groups, IV manipulated, DV is interval, no random assignment	independent-samples t test, with either r_{pb}^2 or Cohen's d as the effect size	correlation

Do people who belong to different political parties (Democrat, Independent, Republican) differ in their suspicions of politicians, as rated by four items that sum to a maximum of 20 points?	**multiple independent groups, correlational**			
Do Latinos/as and African Americans receive harsher sentences than Caucasians for the same crime? Judges read the same case but are randomly assigned one of three ethnicities for the convicted man and recommend a prison sentence (in years).		**three groups, random assignment, IV manipulated, DV is ratio**		**causation**
Are people more traumatized by hurricanes or tornados? Trauma is measured with a 50-point questionnaire, with higher scores representing more trauma.		**two preexisting groups, no manipulation, outcome is interval**		
Do adults who are obese show more attention to visual food cues than to attractive nonfood cues? The participants who had just eaten were randomly assigned to view a series of either food or nonfood cues and gaze (in seconds) was recorded.	**two independent groups, experiment**			
What techniques can undocumented immigrants learn to reduce their anxiety? Groups of immigrants who had been in the United States for less than a year were taught yoga, meditation, stress reduction techniques, or nothing. Anxiety was measured after a month of sessions.			**one-way between-groups ANOVA, with η^2 as effect size, post hoc tests if F is statistically significant**	

YOUR RESEARCH

1. State a hypothesis for a simple experiment on your topic (one IV, with two levels, and one DV). This should be based on past research on your topic.

   _____

   _____

2. What inferential statistic would you use to test your hypothesis? Explain.

   _____

   _____

3. Turn your simple experiment into a multiple-groups design by adding at least one more level to your DV. This should be based on past research on your topic.

   _____

   _____

4. What inferential statistic would you use to test your hypothesis? Explain.

   _____

   _____

5. Which of these two designs is more appropriate, given the state of the research on this topic? Explain.

   _____

   _____

   _____

   _____

IBM® SPSS® DATA ANALYSIS AND INTERPRETATION

Conducting an Independent-Samples *t* Test

You need at least two variables to run an independent-samples *t* test. One variable is the IV (if you have an experiment) or grouping variable (predictor, if you have a correlational design); the other is the test variable (DV for experiment or outcome for correlation).

Assumptions of the Independent-Samples *t* Test

1. Groups are independent.

2. IV (or grouping variable) is nominal and dichotomous.

3. DV (or outcome variable) is interval or ratio.

4. DV is normally distributed (although you can still run a *t* test if this assumption is violated).

5. The variability (or *SD*) in both groups are about equal. (A test called the Levene's test will tell you if this assumption is violated, and if it is, you simply need to report a different *t*, *df*, and *p*.)

A Simple Experiment Example

For a simple experiment, we will use a study mentioned above (a version of a study by Kirk & Lewis, 2016) in which gesturing was or was not encouraged as children named novel uses for objects. In this case, we have a variable called "gesturing" that is coded as 0 = *no* and 1 = *yes*. We also have the dependent variable called "creativity" that is the number of novel, feasible uses for an object generated by each participant.

- The independent variable: Gesturing (no vs. yes)

- The dependent variable: Creativity (number of novel, feasible uses for object)

- Null hypothesis: Gesturing will not affect the number of novel, feasible uses generated (creativity) by children.

- Alternative directional hypothesis: The children who are encouraged to gesture will generate more novel, feasible uses of objects than those not encouraged to gesture

Data Entry

The variable view would look like this:

	Name	Type	Width	Decimals	Label	Values	Missing	Columns	Align	Measure	Role
1	gesturing	Numeric	8	2	experimental condition	{.00, no gesturing}...	None	10	Right	Nominal	Input
2	creativity	Numeric	8	2	number of uses for object	None	None	11	Right	Scale	Input

The data view would look like this:

	gesturing	creativity
1	.00	7.00
2	.00	4.00
3	.00	8.00
4	.00	6.00
5	.00	7.00
6	.00	9.00
7	.00	7.00
8	.00	7.00
9	.00	4.00
10	.00	5.00
11	.00	5.00
12	.00	6.00
13	1.00	7.00
14	1.00	4.00
15	1.00	8.00
16	1.00	6.00
17	1.00	11.00
18	1.00	9.00
19	1.00	9.00
20	1.00	7.00
21	1.00	8.00
22	1.00	10.00
23	1.00	8.00
24	1.00	10.00

Conducting an Independent-Samples *t* Test

On the Menu Bar, click

Analyze → Compare Means → Independent Samples *t* test

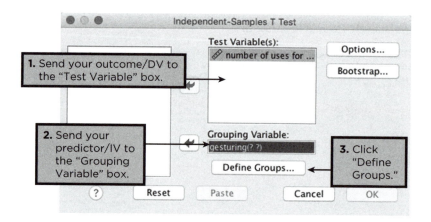

The "Define Groups" box will open:

<table>
<tr>
<td>

4. Tell SPSS how you coded your predictor or IV.

In this example:

Group 1 (no gesturing) = 0

Group 2 (gesturing) = 1

(Enter the codes that match YOUR data.)

</td>
<td>

Define Groups

◉ Use specified values

Group 1: 0

Group 2: 1

◯ Cut point:

(?) Cancel **Continue**

</td>
</tr>
</table>

5. Click "Continue" and then click "OK" to run your *t* test.

OUTPUT
T **Test**

Group Statistics

	experimental condition	*N*	Mean	Std. Deviation	Std. Error Mean
Creativity	no Gesturing	12	6.2500	1.54479	.44594
	Gesturing	12	8.0833	1.92865	.55675

The first table provides descriptive information for each of your groups.

The *t* test results are in the second table.

Interpreting the independent-samples *t* test is a two-step process.

Step 1: Look at Levene's test to tell you what row to use. The *p* value of the Levene's test compares the variance in each group; it tests the assumption of equal variances, *not* the hypothesis.

Step 2: Look at the *t* test results in the appropriate row. The *p* value of the *t* test tells you whether or not there is a statistically significant difference between the means of the two groups. In other words, the *t* test is what tests your hypothesis.

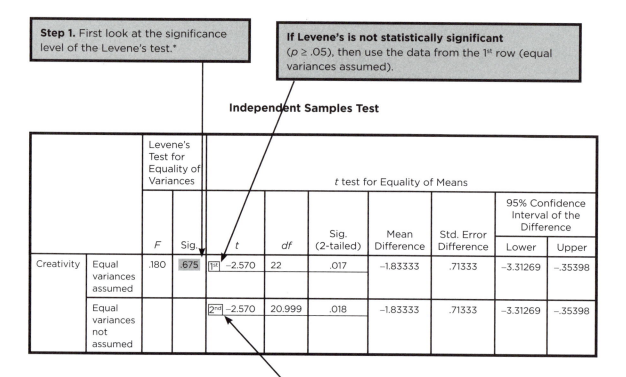

Step 1. First look at the significance level of the Levene's test.*

If Levene's is not statistically significant ($p \geq .05$), then use the data from the 1st row (equal variances assumed).

Independent Samples Test

		Levene's Test for Equality of Variances		t test for Equality of Means						
									95% Confidence Interval of the Difference	
		F	Sig.	*t*	*df*	Sig. (2-tailed)	Mean Difference	Std. Error Difference	Lower	Upper
Creativity	Equal variances assumed	.180	.675	1st −2.570	22	.017	−1.83333	.71333	−3.31269	−.35398
	Equal variances not assumed			2nd −2.570	20.999	.018	−1.83333	.71333	−3.31269	−.35398

If Levene's is statistically significant ($p < .05$), then use the data from the second row (equal variances not assumed).

In this example, Levene's is not statistically significant because p = .68 is greater than .05. Consequently, we can assume equal variances and will use the t test data from the 1st row.

*What is Levene's test?

Levene's tests the assumption that the groups have equal variances. In other words, that one group doesn't have a much higher variance (or *SD*) than the other. You want Levene's to be > .05 because it allows you to use a more powerful test. If Levene's is significant, you have to use a less powerful test with less *df*, which may impact your ability to find a statistically significant difference between the two groups.

Step 2. Once you have figured out which row to examine, determine if the *t* value meets the criteria for statistical significance.

Independent Samples Test

		Levene's Test for Equality of Variances		*t*-test for Equality of Means					95% Confidence Interval of the Difference	
		F	Sig.	*t*	*df*	Sig. (2-tailed)	Mean Difference	Std. Error Difference	Lower	Upper
Creativity	Equal variances assumed	.180	.675	–2.570	22	.017	–1.83333	.71333	–3.31269	–.35398
	Equal variances not assumed			–2.570	20.999	.018	–1.83333	.71333	–3.31269	–.35398

In this example, we will look at the first row's data in order to determine if there is a statistically significant difference in creativity between the gesturing and no gesturing conditions.

We see that *p* = .02 (rounded from .017), and this meets the criteria for statistical significance at the *p* < .05 level.

We would report: *t*(22) = –2.57, *p* = .02.

Computing the Effect Size for a Two Independent-Groups Design

You can report either the proportion of variance accounted for, which is r_{pb}^2 for a two independent-groups design, or Cohen's *d*.

Proportion of variance accounted for. Use the following equation to convert your t statistic to a squared point-biserial correlation (r_{pb}^2):

$$r_{pb}^2 = \frac{t^2}{t^2 + (N-2)} \quad \text{Using our example:} \quad r_{pb}^2 = \frac{-2.57^2}{-2.57^2 + (24-2)} = .23$$

Alternatively, you can run a bivariate correlation in SPSS just as you would run a Pearson's r.

Correlations

		gesturing	creativity
gesturing	Pearson Correlation	1	.481*
	Sig. (2-tailed)		.017
	N	24	24
creativity	Pearson Correlation	.481*	1
	Sig. (2-tailed)	.017	
	N	24	24

> Square the correlation coefficient to calculate the proportion of variance accounted for.
>
> In this example, r_{pb} = .48 and r_{pb}^2 = .23, indicating that 23% of the variance in creativity is accounted for by the gesturing condition.

Cohen's d. Use the online calculator at http://www.uccs.edu/~faculty/lbecker/ or compute Cohen's d using the following formula:

$$d = M_{Group1} - M_{Group2} \Big/ \sqrt{\left[\left(SD_{Group1}^2{}^2 - SD_{Group2}^2{}^2 \right) \Big/ 2 \right]}$$

The sign (+ or –) of Cohen's d depends on how you labeled your variables. We recommend you ignore the sign and just report the absolute value of d. Cohen's d is the size of the difference between the two group means in standard deviation units. In this example, $d = 1.05$, indicating that the two means differ by just over one standard deviation.

In your write-up, describe the effect size (either r_{pb}^2 or Cohen's d) as weak, moderate, or strong. The chart below provides guidelines rather than absolute cutoffs for this description. For example, you may use "moderate to strong" to describe an effect size.

Overview of Effect Size Interpretations (Cohen, 1988)

Effect Size		Interpretation
Proportion of Variance Accounted for	Cohen's d	
≈ 1%	≈ .20	Small/Weak
≈ 9%	≈ .50	Medium/Moderate
≈ 25%	≈ .80	Large/Strong

A Nonexperimental Example

Do children who speak more than one language (multilingual) come up with more or less ways to use an object than those who speak one language (unilingual)?

OUTPUT

Group Statistics

	language	N	Mean	Std. Deviation	Std. Error Mean
number of uses for object	multilingual	28	6.5714	4.46740	.84426
	unilingual	29	6.4483	1.76445	.32765

Independent Samples Test

		Levene's Test for Equality of Variances		*t*-test for Equality of Means							
										95% Confidence Interval of the Difference	
		F	Sig.	t	df	Sig. (2-tailed)	Mean Difference	Std. Error Difference	Lower	Upper
number of uses for object	Equal variances assumed	5.272	.026	.138	55	.891	.12315	.89387	–1.66821	1.91451
	Equal variances not assumed			.136	34.981	.893	.12315	.90561	–1.71537	1.96167

Step 1. In this example, Levene's is statistically significant ($p = .03$). Consequently, we cannot assume equal variances and will use the *t* test results from the 2nd row.

Step 2. Looking at the 2nd row, we find that the difference between means is not statistically significant ($p = .89$).

Because we violated the assumption of equal variances, we had to use a less powerful test with fewer degrees of freedom (in this case, $df = 34.98$). We would report: $t(34.98) = 0.14$, $p = .89$.

Effect Size

Using SPSS to calculate r_{pb} and then squaring the coefficient, $r_{pb}^2 = .0004$

Using the online calculator to find Cohen's *d* (http://www.uccs.edu/lbecker/index.html), $d = .04$

Writing up Results

Include the following:

- The type of analysis you conducted and the variables examined.

- A comparison of the mean and *SD* for each group
  - Here are a couple examples from the gesturing experiment:
    - The gesture-encouraged group (*M* = 8.08, *SD* = 1.93) generated more novel uses than the no encouragement group (*M* = 6.25, *SD* = 1.54).
    - The children who were encouraged to gesture generated an average of 8.08 novel uses (*SD* = 1.93), whereas the children in the control group generated an average of 6.25 (*SD* = 1.54).

- The *t* value, *df*, *p* value, and effect size.
  - Examples:
    - $t(22)= -2.57$, $p = .02$. Twenty-three percent of the variance in novel uses was accounted for by the gesture condition.
    - $t(22)= -2.57$, $p = .02$, $r_{pb}^2 = .23$
    - $t(22)= -2.57$, $p = .02$, $d = 1.05$

- A statement about whether or not the difference between the two groups was statistically significant. You can simply add a word or two to one of the above statements.
  - Examples:
    - The gesture-encouraged group (*M* = 8.08, *SD* = 1.93) generated statistically significantly more novel uses than the no encouragement group (*M* = 6.25, *SD* = 1.54).
    - The difference between the groups was statistically significant, $t(22)= -2.57$, $p = .02$, $d = 1.05$.

- If Levene's test was not significant, you don't need to mention it at all. If Levene's was significant, explain that you had to use a more stringent test because Levene's was significant (or because the assumption of equal variances was violated). In the latter case, be sure to cite the statistics on the second line of the *t* test output.

Example Results for the Nonexperimental Study

Results

We conducted an independent-samples *t* test to compare children's ability to generate different uses for an object between those who are multilingual ($M = 6.57$, $SD = 4.47$) and those who are unilingual ($M = 6.45$, $SD = 1.76$). Results were very weak and not statistically significant, $t(34.98) = 0.14$, $p = .89$, $d = 0.04$. The results violated the assumption of equal variance in that the variability within the multilingual group was much higher than within the unilingual group.

Conducting a One-Way Between-Subjects ANOVA

A one-way between-subjects analysis of variance (ANOVA) is used to compare three or more independent groups when the outcome or DV is measured on an interval or ratio scale. You can use the one-way ANOVA for experimental and nonexperimental data.

Assumptions of the One-Way Between-Subjects ANOVA

1. Groups are independent

2. IV or grouping variable is nominal (with two or more groups)*

3. DV or test variable is interval or ratio

4. DV or test variable is normally distributed

5. Variability is approximately equal across groups

*You can calculate the analysis with just two groups, but the independent-samples *t* test is the preferred method to compare the means of two independent groups.

Overview of the Analyses for a One-Way Between-Subjects ANOVA

- The ANOVA analysis will give you an *F* (instead of a *t*), although like the *t*,

    F = Between-group differences ÷ Within-group differences (error)

- When you report an *F* statistic, you need to report two types of degrees of freedom:

between-groups (treatment) df = number of groups (k) – 1

within-groups (error) df = number of participants (N) – number of groups (k)

- You also need to report the effect size. Eta (η) is a correlation coefficient used to describe the magnitude of a relationship containing two or more levels.

Eta squared (η^2) tells you the proportion of variance in the DV or outcome accounted for by the IV or predictor.

- If you find a statistically significant F, you will need to run post hoc tests.

A Multiple-Group Experiment Example

A researcher hypothesizes that aerobic exercise will reduce anxiety. She randomly assigns 30 college students to three groups: 10 minutes of aerobics (low), 20 minutes of aerobics (medium), 30 minutes of aerobics (high). After the students are done with the aerobic exercise, she has each of them fill out a questionnaire rating their level of anxiety.

Data Entry

To run a one-way ANOVA, you need at least two variables. One variable is the grouping predictor or IV, the other is the outcome or DV.

Data entry for the one-way ANOVA is very similar to the independent-samples t test, except that your IV will have three or more levels.

In the multiple-group experiment example, we would have a variable called "group" that is coded as $1 = $ low, $2 = $ medium, $3 = $ high. We would also have a variable called "anxiety" that is scored on an interval scale.

Conducting a One-Way ANOVA

First, you want to find out whether there is a significant difference between your groups and the magnitude of this difference.
On the Menu Bar, click

Analyze → Compare Means → Means

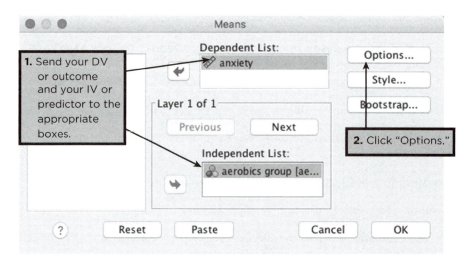

The options box will appear:

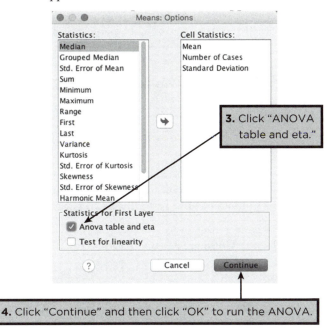

3. Click "ANOVA table and eta."

4. Click "Continue" and then click "OK" to run the ANOVA.

OUTPUT

Report

Anxiety

Aerobics group	Mean	N	Std. Deviation
low	5.7000	5	.97468
medium	7.8000	5	1.09545
high	5.0000	5	1.58114
Total	6.1667	15	1.68678

Descriptive information is presented under "Report."

ANOVA Table

			Sum of Squares	df	Mean Square	F	Sig.
Anxiety * Aerobics group	Between Groups	(Combined)	21.233	2	10.617	6.849	.010
	Within Groups		18.600	12	1.550		
	Total		39.833	14			

The ANOVA Table tells you the between groups df, within groups df, F, and p value. Here, we have $F(2, 12) = 6.85$, $p = .01$.

Measures of Association

	Eta	Eta Squared
Anxiety * Aerobics group	.730	.533

$\eta^2 = .53$, which means that 53% of the variance in anxiety is accounted for by aerobic exercise.

If the *F* is statistically significant, this only tells you that differences exist among the groups. It doesn't tell you which groups differ.

To find this out, you need to do post hoc comparisons.

Post Hoc Comparisons

You only do these if you have a statistically significant *F* from your ANOVA analysis. The post hoc tests compare one level of the IV to all the other levels (pairwise comparisons). There is a ton of post hoc tests; here we use LSD (least significant difference). On the Menu Bar, click

Analyze → Compare Means → One-Way ANOVA

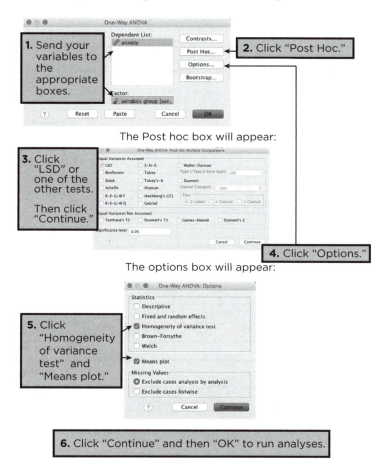

1. Send your variables to the appropriate boxes.

2. Click "Post Hoc."

The Post hoc box will appear:

3. Click "LSD" or one of the other tests.

Then click "Continue."

4. Click "Options."

The options box will appear:

5. Click "Homogeneity of variance test" and "Means plot."

6. Click "Continue" and then "OK" to run analyses.

OUTPUT

Test of Homogeneity of Variances

Anxiety			
Levene Statistic	df1	df2	Sig.
.719	2	12	.507

The first table depicts the results of the Levene's test. A significant Levene's serves as a warning. If significant, you should make sure your data are normally distributed and look for outliers. Here, Levene's is *ns* (non significant), $p = .51$.

ANOVA

Anxiety					
	Sum of Squares	df	Mean Square	F	Sig.
Between Groups	21.233	2	10.617	6.849	.010
Within Groups	18.600	12	1.550		
Total	39.833	14			

You get the same ANOVA tables as when you computed the means analysis.

Multiple Comparisons

Dependent Variable: Anxiety						
LSD						
(I) Aerobics group	(J) Aerobics group	Mean Difference (I-J)	Std. Error	Sig.	95% Confidence Interval	
					Lower Bound	Upper Bound
low	medium	−2.10000*	.78740	.021	−3.8156	−.3844
	high	.70000	.78740	.391	−1.0156	2.4156
medium	low	2.10000*	.78740	.021	.3844	3.8156
	high	2.80000*	.78740	.004	1.0844	4.5156
high	low	−.70000	.78740	.391	−2.4156	1.0156
	medium	−2.80000*	.78740	.004	−4.5156	−1.0844

* The mean difference is significant at the 0.05 level.

The LSD post hoc test compares each level of the IV to every other level. Here we have low vs. medium ($p = .02$), low vs. high ($p = .39$), and medium vs. high ($p = .004$).

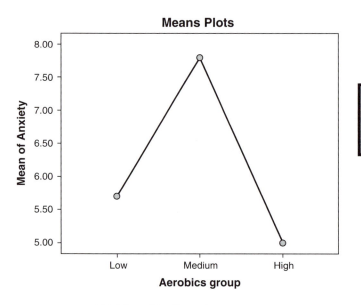

Means Plots

The Means Plot allows you to see how different levels of the IV impact the DV.

Writing Up Results

Include the following:

- The type of analysis(es) conducted and the variable examined.
  - One-way between-subjects ANOVA
  - If you did post hoc tests, report which one you used (e.g., Least Significant Differences).
- The mean and standard deviation for each group.
- The F value, dfs, p value, and effect size (in this example, $F(2,12) = 6.85$, $p = .01$, $\eta^2 = .53$).

Note: An η^2 around .01 is weak, around .06 is moderate, and around .16 is strong (Cohen, 1988).

- A statement about whether or not the difference between the groups was statistically significant.
- If the F was statistically significant, report the results of the post hoc tests. Indicate which groups were significantly different from each other with p value and the direction of the difference.

Example

Results

Participants who completed 20 minutes of aerobics ($M = 7.80$, $SD = 1.10$) had

higher levels of anxiety than those who completed 10 minutes ($M = 5.70$, $SD = 0.97$)

or 30 minutes (M = 5.00, SD = 1.58). A one-way between-subjects ANOVA revealed a strong and statistically significant effect, $F(2,12)$ = 6.85, p = .01, η^2 = .53. Post hoc least significant difference (LSD) tests further indicated statistically significant differences between 20 minutes and 10 minutes of aerobics, p = .02, and between 20 and 30 minutes, p = .004, but no statistically significantly difference between 10 and 30 minutes, p = .39.

Practice Exercise 1

A researcher is investigating the effect of continuing education on supervisors' effectiveness. He has supervisors take either a month-long online course that focuses on mindfulness as an approach to leadership or one that focuses on general skills of leaders. The supervisors' effectiveness is rated by a researcher blind to the conditions of the study, one month after the continuing education courses are completed. The following data result:

Mindfulness	General Leadership
7.00	4.00
6.00	4.00
7.00	7.00
6.00	5.00
5.00	7.00
5.00	7.00
7.00	5.00
4.00	4.00
6.00	6.00
7.00	4.00
8.00	5.00
7.00	7.00
5.00	3.00
7.00	5.00
5.00	2.00

1. What is the design of this study (be specific)? _____

2. What is the IV? _____ DV? _____

3. State a directional alternative hypothesis for the study.

   _____

   _____

4. Compute (by hand or using SPSS) all the appropriate statistics to test your hypothesis.

5. Are the findings significant? _____ How do you know? _____

6. State and interpret the effect size. _____

7. Describe the results using APA format.

_____

_____

_____

_____

_____

_____

8. Interpret the results as you would in a Discussion section. Include one limitation and one way to address the limitation.

_____

_____

_____

_____

_____

_____

Practice Exercise 2

A math professor decides to investigate whether stereotype threat is operating in her class for students of color. She randomly assigns students in her classes to one of two instructions for a practice test. In one condition, students are told that they are taking a practice test and to do their best. In the other condition, students are told that they are taking a standardized test that was designed by several professors at MIT, but to do their best. The test scores for her students of color are shown below.

Regular Instructions	Stereotype Threat
90.00	95.00
85.00	65.00
70.00	35.00
75.00	65.00
80.00	70.00
75.00	60.00

75.00	80.00
80.00	50.00
85.00	85.00
85.00	75.00

1. State a directional alternative hypothesis for the study.

   _____

2. Compute the statistics needed to test your hypothesis.

3. Are your findings significant? _____ Explain your answer. _____

   _____

4. What is the probability of a Type I error? _____ Type II error?

   _____

5. What potential problem(s) do you identify based on the findings?

   _____

   _____

6. Write a few sentences describing the findings as you would in a Results section.

   _____

   _____

   _____

   _____

   _____

7. Interpret the findings as you would in a Discussion section (what are the implications?).

   _____

   _____

   _____

8. What do you suggest for future researchers to improve upon the study?

   _____

   _____

   _____

Practice Exercise 3

A consultant who specializes in political campaigns tests the success of three ads in convincing registered voters to support a candidate. The ads run for 30 seconds and feature issues of the campaign. One ad presents the candidate's rationale for supporting issues, a second ad berates the opponent of the candidate and encourages people to vote for the candidate, and the third ad contrasts the two candidates' positions on issues. Registered voters are randomly assigned to view one of the three ads and then rate on their likelihood (0%–100%) of voting for the candidate. The responses are below:

Rationale	Berate opponent	Contrast positions
70	25	95
65	30	55
90	55	70
85	60	80
65	35	60
55	40	75
35	65	100
70	15	90
40	75	40
60	30	55
30	35	85
25	45	80

1. What is the design of this study (be specific)?

   _____

2. What is the IV? _____ DV? _____

3. Compute (by hand or using SPSS) all the appropriate statistics to test your hypothesis.

4. Are the findings significant? _____ How do you know?

   _____

5. State and interpret the effect size. _____

   _____

6. Describe the results using APA format.

   _____

   _____

   _____

_____

_____

_____

7. Interpret the results as you would in a Discussion section. Include one limitation and one way to address the limitation.

_____

_____

_____

_____

_____

_____

Practice Exercise 4

Studies suggest that time outside increases one's sense of well-being, but does more time increase one's well-being or is there only an initial gain and then a leveling of well-being? A researcher has students spend no time (control), 10 minutes, 30 minutes, or 90 minutes outside and then has them complete a well-being scale (higher scores reflect a greater sense of well-being). The following data result:

Control	10 minutes	30 minutes	90 minutes
18.00	16.00	20.00	21.00
22.00	20.00	25.00	23.00
25.00	23.00	28.00	28.00
15.00	16.00	29.00	18.00
22.00	19.00	30.00	19.00
16.00	25.00	25.00	17.00
22.00	27.00	22.00	19.00
17.00	19.00	16.00	24.00
21.00	16.00	28.00	22.00
15.00	19.00	18.00	15.00

1. What type of design is this? _____

2. State a directional alternative hypothesis. _____

3. Compute (by hand or using SPSS) all the statistical analyses needed to test your hypothesis.

4. Describe your findings.

_____

_____

_____

_____

_____

_____

5. Interpret these findings.

_____

_____

_____

_____

_____

_____

Additional Practice

If you want additional practice with independent-samples *t* tests and one-way ANOVAs, open one of the databases found in the Web Resources. Identify variables that can serve as IV (predictor) and DV (outcome) for correlational, quasi-experimental, or experimental studies. Check your answers by comparing them with a classmate or study group members, or check with your instructor.

Dependent-Groups Designs

11

CHAPTER SUMMARY

In this chapter, you learned about two types of dependent designs: matching and repeated measures. Their major advantage is the increased power they provide by decreasing variability caused by the unique characteristics of participants. By decreasing error variability, you should be able to better see the effect of your IV (in experiments) or predictor variable (in correlational studies). The two types of dependent designs reduce participant variability in different ways. In a matched design, you identify a variable that is highly correlated to the dependent (or outcome) variable and match participants on this variable. You then ensure that one of the matched partners is in each of the study conditions. In a repeated-measures design, each participant experiences each condition in the study. Dependent designs may involve two groups or multiple groups, but the rationale and implementation are the same.

As with all designs, the dependent designs have potential disadvantages. Both dependent designs require extra steps that can complicate the implementation of the study. In a matched design, you must be able to identify an appropriate matching design that doesn't sensitize the participants to your hypothesis or the purpose of the study. Repeated-measures designs are vulnerable to sensitization, fatigue, practice, and carryover effects and require counterbalancing of the order of treatments. In addition, you can't use a repeated-measures design when your IV creates a permanent change.

In addition to learning about the types of dependent designs, you learned about the statistics used to analyze the data generated from them. The dependent-samples (or paired samples or repeated measures) *t* test examines the differences between matched pairs, or the same participant under

LEARNING OUTCOMES

After reading and reviewing Chapter 11, you should understand

- The two types of dependent designs—matched and repeated measures

- How to identify the advantages and drawbacks of dependent designs

- How to compute and interpret dependent-groups *t* tests

- How to compute the confidence interval and effect size for dependent *t* tests

- How to compute and interpret dependent-groups one-way ANOVAs

- When and how to calculate post hoc tests for dependent one-way ANOVAs

different conditions, and compares this mean difference to the error within conditions. The dependent-samples (or within subjects or repeated measures) one-way ANOVA is used to analyze the data from a dependent multiple-groups study. This ANOVA separates error variability into the variability associated with a particular participant (in a repeated-measures study) or with the matched participants (in a matched design) and the variability that is error due to other sources (subject by condition interaction).

As a researcher, you should consider the advantages and disadvantages of different designs before deciding what type of design (independent or dependent and correlation, quasi-experiment, or experiment) will best test your hypothesis.

REVIEW AND APPLICATION OF KEY CONCEPTS FROM CHAPTER 11

Exercise 11.1: Dependent-Groups Designs (Review)

1. In independent-groups designs, we try to get equal groups (in terms of personal characteristics) through _____.

2. Dependent-groups designs are _____ (more/less) powerful that independent-groups designs because they _____ (decrease/increase) random error created by participant characteristics.

3. Dependent-groups designs are _____ (more/less) sensitive to the changes created in the DV by the IV or variability in the outcome associated with the predictor variable.

4. The two types of dependent-groups designs are _____ and _____.

Exercise 11.2: Matched-Pairs Design (Review)

1. In a matched-pairs design, participants are matched on _____ _____ _____.

2. In an experiment that uses a matched design, you _____ _____ after you match them.

3. In a correlational study or quasi-experiment, you match the participants _____.

4. Participants who are matched _____ (must/need not) score exactly the same on the matching variable.

5. In order to be effective and decrease error variance, the matching variable must be _____ with the DV or outcome variable.

6. Name three potential problems or disadvantages of matching designs.

a. _____

b. _____

c. _____

Exercise 11.3: Matched-Pairs Design (Application)

1. Suppose a researcher wants to examine the effect of different language instruction on the learning of English by immigrants. She decides to match the immigrants on age.

a. Comment on the effectiveness of this matching variable.

_____

_____

_____

b. What matching variable might you suggest for this study and why?

_____

_____

_____

2. Another researcher decides to replicate the language instruction study but matches participants on the variable you suggested and on their time since arrival in the United States. Explain why this might be a good or bad idea.

_____

_____

_____

3. A researcher is examining perceptions of violence in romantic relationships involving young adults. Participants in the study will read a scenario describing violence (a slap during an argument) where the perpetrator is either a male or a female. They rate several aspects of the relationship as well as the violence of the act. The researcher believes that one's view of women may influence attitudes toward violence against and by women, and she decides to match participants on the Attitudes toward Women scale (AWS) before assigning them to the perpetrator condition. Below are the scores for the participants on the AWS. Match them so that they can be randomly assigned to the two groups, and enter the matched pairs' participant numbers in the last column.

Participant	AWS Score	Participant	AWS Score	Matched Pairs
1	25	11	5	
2	18	12	13	
3	12	13	14	
4	14	14	17	
5	21	15	20	
6	15	16	23	
7	11	17	15	
8	16	18	25	
9	6	19	7	
10	5	20	6	

Exercise 11.4: Repeated-Measures Design (Review)

1. In a repeated-measures design, participants serve as their own
_____, which decreases _____ variance.

2. Another name for a repeated-measures design is _____
_____ design.

3. Explain the difference between a repeated-measures design and the use of multiple trials in a study.

_____

_____

_____

4. Having participants randomly assigned to the order of the conditions is called _____ and controls for _____ effects.

5. Complete counterbalancing controls for both _____
and _____.

6. Repeated-measures designs provide a check on the consistency of responses by _____ .

7. Repeated-measures designs require _____ (more/fewer) participants than independent-groups designs or matched-pairs designs.

8. Name three potential problems of repeated-measures designs and how these problems might occur.

a. _____

b. _____

c. _____

Exercise 11.5: Repeated-Measures Design (Application)

1. A gerontologist studying the effect of mental stimulation on the alertness of those 90 years or older has 8 participants available. They are randomly assigned to the order of two conditions: playing a word game for 10 minutes and watching a comedy segment for 10 minutes. Alertness is assessed after each session. In order not to overtax the energy of the participants, the researcher has the participants complete both of the 10-minute sessions back to back. What potential confound(s) can you identify in this study and how would you correct it/them?

_____

_____

_____

2. A high school basketball coach wants to try a different approach to teaching her players how to make free throws. She has a session one day when she gives her regular instruction, has players practice free throws for 15 minutes, and then has each team member attempt 10 free throws. The next day, she follows the same pattern but tries a new method of instruction before the free throw practice and attempts. She finds that the players make an average of 1.5 more free throws on the second day. Name a potential confound in this exercise and explain how to correct it.

_____

_____

_____

3. A teacher wants to examine which of two methods of teaching long division is more effective. Can the teacher use a repeated-measures design? Why or why not?

_____

_____

_____

4. Ima Ipad is a senior psychology major. For her senior thesis, she wants to study the effect of sleep deprivation on driving skills. After months of negotiating with the engineering department, she is granted access to the needed driving simulation equipment. She must now decide whether to use an independent or dependent design. What would you advise her and why?

Exercise 11.6: Analysis of Dependent Two-Group Designs (Review)

1. Dependent two-group designs (matched or repeated measures) are analyzed using a _____ test.

2. Alternative names for the dependent-samples t test are _____ _____.

3. The independent-samples t test focuses on individual scores while the dependent-samples t test focuses on differences _____ _____.

4. The major difference in the assumptions for the independent- and dependent-samples t test is that _____ _____.

Exercise 11.7: Formulas and Calculations: Dependent-Samples t Test (Review and Application)

1. The numerator for the dependent-samples (or within-subjects or paired-samples) t test is computed by adding up the differences between the matched scores or repeated measures and is called the _____ _____; it is symbolized by _____.

2. The denominator for the dependent-samples t test represents the standard deviation of the _____ for $\mu_D = 0$. It is called the _____ and is symbolized by _____.

3. The standard error of the mean difference is always _____ (larger/smaller) than the standard deviation for the sample because _____ _____.

4. The formula for df for a paired-samples t test is _____ where $N =$ _____, rather than individual scores.

5. Suppose we find in a study comparing student retention in an online ($M = 7.08$, $SD = 1.00$) vs. in-person ($M = 7.92$, $SD = 1.56$) lecture with 24 students paired on their GPA that $t_{obt} = 2.41$. Retention was measured with a 10-point multiple choice test.

   a. $df = $ _____

   b. t_{crit} for a two-tailed test, $p < .05 = $ _____

   c. Do the two lecture presentation modes result in a significant difference in student retention? _____ How do you know?

   _____

   d. If $SD_D = .34$, compute the 95% confidence interval using the following formula:

   $$(SD_D)(-t_{crit}) + (M_D) < \mu_D < (SD_D)(+t_{crit}) + (M_D)$$

   _____

   _____

   _____

   e. Compute Cohen's d as the effect size for the study and comment on its strength. (See the effect size formula for two dependent samples.)

   _____

   _____

   _____

   f. Comment on the practical significance of the study's findings.

   _____

   _____

   _____

Exercise 11.8: Using Data Analysis Programs: Dependent-Samples *t* Test (Application)

1. Suppose you are the gerontologist above who is examining the effect of two types of stimulation (30 minutes of word games or comedy on TV) on the alertness of those who are over 90 years of age. Each participant is randomly assigned to the order of the two stimulations, which are provided two days apart. Alertness is measured on a 25-point scale immediately following each stimulation session.

a. What type of dependent design is this? _____

b. What ethical concerns should the researcher be sure to address in this study?

_____

_____

_____

_____

_____

_____

_____

c. State the null and a directional alternative hypothesis for the study.

H_0: _____

H_a: _____

The output for the study is below:

Paired Samples Statistics

		Mean	N	Std. Deviation	Std. Error Mean
Pair 1	word game	14.5000	8	5.29150	1.87083
	comedy	13.0000	8	4.65986	1.64751

Paired Samples Correlations

		N	Correlation	Sig.
Pair 1	word game & comedy	8	.950	.000

Paired Samples Test

		Paired Differences							
					95% Confidence Interval of the Difference				
		Mean	Std. Deviation	Std. Error Mean	Lower	Upper	t	df	Sig. (2-tailed)
Pair 1	word game - comedy	1.50000	1.69031	.59761	.08687	2.91313	2.510	7	.040

d. $df =$ _____

e. How many participants were in the study? _____ How do you know?

_____

_____

f. Does mental alertness differ significantly for elderly people after playing word games vs. watching comedy? Explain your response.

_____

_____

g. Describe the findings in APA format, including all information that is expected in a Results section.

_____

_____

_____

_____

_____

_____

h. Interpret the results as you would in a Discussion section. Include one limitation and one way to address the limitation.

_____

_____

_____

_____

_____

2. Are people with harder-to-pronounce names considered more threatening than those with easier-to-pronounce names? A researcher matches participants (college students) on a scale measuring openness to new experiences. One of each matched pair of students is assigned to rate people with easy-to-pronounce names while the other rates people with hard-to-pronounce names with the same number of letters. All students view the same pictures of a diverse group of 10 adults who are rated on several characteristics. The findings for ratings of "threatening" are shown below. Threatening was rated on a 7-point scale, with higher scores reflecting more perceived threat.

Paired Samples Statistics

		Mean	N	Std. Deviation	Std. Error Mean
Pair 1	easy pronounce	3.7333	15	1.43759	.37118
	hard pronounce	4.6667	15	1.34519	.34733

Paired Samples Correlations

		N	Correlation	Sig.
Pair 1	easy pronounce & hard pronounce	15	.025	.931

Paired Samples Test

		Paired Differences						t	df	Sig. (2-tailed)
		Mean	Std. Deviation	Std. Error Mean	95% Confidence Interval of the Difference					
					Lower	Upper				
Pair 1	easy pronounce - hard pronounce	–.93333	1.94447	.50206	–2.01014	.14348	–1.859	14	.084

a. What type of dependent design is this? _____

b. State the null and a directional alternative hypothesis for the study.

   H_0: _____

   H_a: _____

c. $df =$ _____

d. How many participants were in the study? _____ How do you know?

   _____

e. Do perceptions of people with easy-to-pronounce names differ significantly from those with hard-to-pronounce names in terms of their threat to others? _____ Explain your answer.

   _____

f. Is there a probability of a Type I error? _____ Is there a probability of a Type II error? _____

g. Describe the results using APA format.

   _____

   _____

   _____

h. Interpret the meaning of the results in a few sentences.

_____

_____

_____

_____

Exercise 11.9: Designs With More Than Two Dependent Groups (Review)

1. The _____ (same/different) advantages occur for two-group and multiple-group dependent designs.

2. When participants are assigned in all possible sequences of the conditions of a study, it is called _____ counterbalancing.

3. The number of orders possible in a study is computed by the formula _____.

4. Complete counterbalancing includes every _____ and _____ of all the conditions.

5. _____ counterbalancing occurs when you randomly assign your participants to some of the possible sequences.

6. _____ counterbalancing occurs when you include a smaller number of conditions in which each condition occurs equally in each order.

7. When a researcher randomly assigns the order of conditions to each participant, this is called _____ counterbalancing.

8. Counterbalancing controls for _____ effects but not for _____ effects, so the researcher should ensure adequate time between conditions.

9. In comparison to two-group matched designs, matching with multiple-groups designs is _____ (more/less) complicated because _____

_____

_____.

10. With correlational or quasi-experimental designs, matching occurs _____

_____

_____

_____

_____.

Exercise 11.10: Designs With More Than Two Dependent Groups (Application)

1. Suppose a weight loss program was examining the effect of weighing every day (1), every other day (2), every third day (3), or once a week (4) on participants' confidence that they could lose weight. Participants were matched on their age and BMI. The possible number of sequences for this study is _____.

   a. If the experimenter randomly assigned participants to all possible sequences, this would be an example of _____ counterbalancing.

   b. The experimenter decided to randomly assign each group of participants to the following sequences: 1234, 2341, 3412, 4123.
   This is an example of _____ counterbalancing.

   c. Evaluate the matching variables. Can you think of a more effective matching variable?

   _____

   _____

   _____

   _____

   _____

2. A researcher explores the impact of time outside on third graders' completion of work in the classroom. Each day of one week each child spends 10, 15, 20, 25, or 30 minutes outside (every child spends each of the time periods outside over the course of one week). The completion of work immediately after the child returns to the classroom is measured.

   a. What type of design is this? _____

   b. What potential confound do you see in the study?

   _____

   c. What additional step would the researcher need to take in order to avoid this confound? Explain in detail what the researcher would need to do.

   _____

   _____

   _____

   _____

3. A researcher is investigating the impact of verbal reinforcement on 4-year-olds' scores on a vocabulary test. The test is individually administered and requires the examiner to read a question and then have the child choose a picture from several choices. He uses a sample of children who receive 10 questions followed by verbal reinforcement ("good") for correct answers only (C), 10 questions followed by verbal reinforcement for both correct and incorrect answers (B), and 10 questions followed by no reinforcement (N).

   a. How many different orders of the reinforcement conditions are possible?

   _____

   b. Show how would you use complete counterbalancing to decide the order of the conditions (C, B, N) that each child would receive. Remember that the number of orders should match the number you named in the previous question.

   _____

   c. How would the process of assigning children to conditions differ if you used Latin square counterbalancing? Name the specific orders you might use.

   _____

   _____

Exercise 11.11: Analysis of Dependent Multiple-Groups Designs (Review)

1. Dependent multiple-groups studies are analyzed using a _____-_____, also called a _____-_____ _____ or a _____-_____.

2. Assumptions for the dependent-groups ANOVA include which of the following (circle all that apply)?

Independent groups	A manipulated variable
Causation	Three or more conditions or groups
Ordinal or interval data	Interval or ratio data
Equal variances for the differences between pairs of groups	Measurement variable that is normally distributed
Dependent groups	

3. The term used to describe equal variances for the differences between groups in a one-way dependent-groups ANOVA is _____.

Exercise 11.12: Formulas and Calculations: Within-Subjects ANOVA (Review and Application)

1. Like the one-way independent-groups ANOVA, the resulting F_{obt} for a dependent-groups ANOVA is obtained by dividing _____ by _____.

2. The mean square between in a dependent-groups ANOVA represents ___ _____ and is symbolized by _____.

3. The SS_w (or error variability) in a dependent ANOVA is divided into two sources: the differences in scores associated with specific participants, called _____ and symbolized by _____, and the error associated with differences in scores between participants in the same condition, called _____ and symbolized by _____.

4. The more we can identify and extract the error associated with individual participants, the _____ (larger/smaller) F_{obt} will be because _____ _____.

5. In a dependent-groups ANOVA, the total sums of squares (SS_{tot}) is equal to which three sources of variability?

   _____

   _____

6. In a within-groups ANOVA, MS_w = _____ divided by _____ and F_{obt} = _____ divided by _____. (Use symbols for your answers.)

7. The effect size for a within-subjects ANOVA is called _____ and is symbolized by _____.

8. a. Complete the following summary table.

Source	SS	df	MS	F
Condition (A)	126.20	2	??	??
Subject	??	??		
Interaction (A x S)	22.47	??	??	
Total	224.47	29		

   b. Are the results of this study statistically significant? _____ How do you know? _____

   c. Compute the effect size using information from the Summary Table above. _____

d. Interpret the meaning of the effect size. _____

_____

_____

e. What next step (in terms of analysis) should you take? _____

_____

f. How many paired comparisons should you make in the post hoc tests?
_____

g. Suppose the following descriptive statistics are found for the groups in the study.

Descriptive Statistics

	Mean	Std. Deviation	N
Group 1	15.4000	3.62706	10
Group 2	15.5000	4.50309	10
Group 3	19.8000	3.19026	10

Compute LSD and complete the matrix below. Note with an asterisk which paired-comparisons meet the criteria for statistical significance at $p < .05$.

_____

_____

	1	2	3
Means	(15.400)	(15.500)	(19.800)
Group 1	—	??	??
Group 2	—	—	??
Group 3	—	—	—

$^*p < .05$

9. a. State a null and an alternative hypothesis for a study that examined the effect of weighing every day (1), every other day (2), every third day (3), or once a week (4) on participants' confidence that they could lose weight.

H_0: _____

H_a: _____

b. Complete the Summary Table below for the weigh-in study.

Source	SS	df	MS	F
Weighing (A)	24.60	??	??	??
Subject	72.72	36		
Interaction (A x S)	??	??	??	
Total	151.32	39		

c. What is F_{crit} for $p < .01$? _____ Are these results significant at $p < .01$? _____

d. Are these results significant at $p < .05$? _____ How do you know?

_____

e. Compute the effect size and interpret its meaning.

_____

_____

f. How many paired comparisons should you make in the post hoc tests? _____

g. The descriptive statistics for the groups are shown below. Compute LSD and draw a matrix to show which groups differ significantly from one another.

Group	Mean (M)
Daily	2.6
Every other day	3.8
Every third day	5.5
Weekly	7.2

Exercise 11.13: Using Data Analysis Programs: Within-Subjects ANOVA

A researcher replicated the weigh-in study described in exercise 11.12 in a geographic region that is known for its high rate of obesity and examined the effect of weighing every day (1), every other day (2), every third day (3), or once a week (4) on participants' confidence that they could lose weight. The output for this study is found below.

Descriptive Statistics

	Mean	Std. Deviation	N
daily	2.8750	1.24642	8
every other day	3.0000	1.30931	8
every third day	4.0000	1.06904	8
weekly	6.5000	1.60357	8

Mauchly's Test of Sphericity[a]

Measure: weighin

Within Subjects Effect	Mauchly's W	Approx. Chi-Square	df	Sig.	Epsilon[b]		
					Greenhouse-Geisser	Huynh-Feldt	Lower-bound
factor1	.534	3.587	5	.615	.698	1.000	.333

Tests the null hypothesis that the error covariance matrix of the orthonormalized transformed dependent variables is proportional to an identity matrix.
a. Design: Intercept Within Subjects Design: factor1
b. May be used to adjust the degrees of freedom for the averaged tests of significance. Corrected tests are displayed in the Tests of Within-Subjects Effects table.

Tests of Within-Subjects Effects

Measure: weighin

Source		Type III Sum of Squares	df	Mean Square	F	Sig.	Partial Eta Squared
factor1	Sphericity Assumed	67.844	3	22.615	21.679	.000	.756
	Greenhouse-Geisser	67.844	2.095	32.376	21.679	.000	.756
	Huynh-Feldt	67.844	3.000	22.615	21.679	.000	.756
	Lower-bound	67.844	1.000	67.844	21.679	.002	.756
Error (factor1)	Sphericity Assumed	21.906	21	1.043			
	Greenhouse-Geisser	21.906	14.668	1.493			
	Huynh-Feldt	21.906	21.000	1.043			
	Lower-bound	21.906	7.000	3.129			

Pairwise Comparisons

					95% Confidence Interval for Difference[b]	
(I) factor1	(J) factor1	Mean Difference (I-J)	Std. Error	Sig.[b]	Lower Bound	Upper Bound
1	2	−.125	.441	1.000	−1.727	1.477
	3	−1.125	.479	.308	−2.868	.618
	4	−3.625*	.420	.000	−5.152	−2.098
2	1	.125	.441	1.000	−1.477	1.727
	3	−1.000	.423	.299	−2.536	.536
	4	−3.500*	.567	.003	−5.561	−1.439
3	1	1.125	.479	.308	−.618	2.868
	2	1.000	.423	.299	−.536	2.536
	4	−2.500*	.681	.048	−4.977	−.023
4	1	3.625*	.420	.000	2.098	5.152
	2	3.500*	.567	.003	1.439	5.561
	3	2.500*	.681	.048	.023	4.977

Based on estimated marginal means
*. The mean difference is significant at the .05 level.
b. Adjustment for multiple comparisons: Bonferroni.

1. Fill in the blanks: F (_____, _____) = _____, p _____ _____.

2. Timing of weigh-ins accounted for _____% of the variance in confidence.

3. Write a Results section for this study, using APA format and including all needed information.

_____

_____

_____

_____

_____

_____

4. Interpret the results as you would in a Discussion section. Include one limitation and one way to address the limitation.

_____

_____

_____

_____

_____

Exercise 11.14: The Big Picture: Selecting Analyses and Interpreting Results for Dependent-Groups Designs

1. Identify the flaw(s) in each item below **and** correct it(them).

    a. Your classmate solicits participants who believe that they experience strong test anxiety and has them watch a video on human causes of global warming and then take a test on the material. She then has them participate in a meditation designed to relax students and to have them focus on their strengths as a student. The students then watch a video on additional causes of global warming and take a test on that material. She finds that the students score significantly higher on the second test and concludes that the intervention significantly reduces test anxiety.

    _____

    _____

    _____

    _____

    b. A social service director offers clients the option to attend a 6-week job training course or a 6-week life skills course. Of the 50 clients contacted, 34 agree to participate in the courses. After matching the participating clients on depression, the director assigns one of each matched pair to the course taught on the night most convenient for them. Six clients drop out of the courses over the 6 weeks (4 from job training and 2 from life skills). At the end of the 6-week period, the remaining matched clients report significantly less depression after taking the life skills course than the job skills course, $t(10) = 3.65, p < .05, d = .20$. The director concludes on the basis of these findings that the agency will now require all clients to attend the life skills course because attendance in the course causes a reduction in depression.

_____

_____

_____

_____

_____

c. A psychologist is hired to try to increase the productivity of employees at a call center. He decides to test the effect of different types of appreciation on increasing productivity. He matches the employees at the call center on extraversion and randomly assigns one of each group to one of three types of appreciation (a weekly free meal provided at work, an extra hour during one lunch each week, or a free movie pass each week). The study runs for one month, after which productivity of each employee in the study is measured. The researcher finds no difference in the productivity of the groups $F(2, 38) = 1.58, p = .16, \eta_{partial}^2 = .20$. The researcher concludes that different types of appreciation do not increase productivity.

_____

_____

_____

_____

_____

2. For the following studies, name the type of design and the characteristics that define the design, the appropriate statistical analyses, and the appropriate interpretation. We have completed some of this for you.

Study	Design	Characteristics	Inferential Statistic and Effect Size	Interpretation
Does alcohol positively impact video game performance? Young adults matched on the amount of time they report playing video games and randomly assigned to drink either 12 oz. of water or 12 oz. of alcohol. Game scores are recorded after the participants play a video game for 30 minutes.	Dependent two matched groups, experiment	Matched pairs 1 IV on a nominal scale with random assignment of pairs to manipulated condition DV on ratio scale	Dependent-samples t test, Point biserial correlation or Cohen's d as effect size Confidence interval	Causation
Is relationship status (married, in a committed relationship, not in a committed relationship) related to satisfaction with life? Participants are matched on age and income.		Preexisting multiple groups matched on relevant variable Predictor variable is nominal scale Outcome is interval scale	One-way within-subjects ANOVA, η^2 *partial* as effect size. If F is statistically significant, post hoc tests with correction for possibility of increased Type I error	
Do children attend more to an educational video with very frequent, somewhat frequent, or no gesturing by the narrator? Students are randomly assigned to the viewing order of the three videos and their direct gaze is measured.	Dependent multiple-groups experiment, repeated measures			
Is there a difference in the hopefulness of a class of graduating high school seniors who are randomly assigned to take an introduction to college class and a class who is randomly assigned to take a life after high school class? Students are matched on high school GPA and family income.			Dependent-samples t test, Point biserial correlation or Cohen's d as effect size Confidence interval	

(*Continued*)

(Continued)

Are sports fans more likely to attend to ads promoting beer, cars, food, or technology? Patrons at a sports bar are observed as prerecorded ads are shown during a pro football game. The percentage of the relevant ads they watch is recorded.		Multiple conditions (4) are manipulated Participants are exposed to all conditions but not randomly assigned to their order IV is nominal DV is ratio		Correlation
Do older adults (75 years+) exercise more on a sunny day than on a rainy day? Adults meeting the age criterion in assisted living are asked on a sunny day how long they exercised and asked the same question on a rainy day.	Dependent two groups, repeated measures			

YOUR RESEARCH

1. In the "Your Research" exercise in Chapter 10 of this study guide, you selected either a simple experiment or a multiple-group design. Restate the hypothesis for the design you chose.

   _____

   _____

2. Is it possible to use a dependent-groups design, either matching or repeated measures, to test this hypothesis? _____ If no, explain why not.

   _____

   _____

   If yes, answer the following:

   a. Which would be a better design, matching or repeated measures? Explain.

   _____

   _____

   b. Briefly describe the procedures you would follow for the design you chose.

   _____

   _____

c. What inferential statistic would you use to test your hypothesis? Explain.

_____

_____

d. What would be the disadvantages of this design over an independent-groups design?

_____

_____

IBM® SPSS® DATA ANALYSIS AND INTERPRETATION

Conducting a Dependent-Samples *t* Test

You compute a dependent-samples (or matched-pairs) *t* test when you are examining differences between two related groups. The IV (if you have an experiment) or grouping variable (predictor, if you have a correlational design) is the related variable, and the DV for an experiment (or outcome, for correlation) is the measured variable.

Assumptions of the Dependent-Samples *t* Test

1. Two groups that are related due to matching or repeated measures

2. Because the two groups are related, the *n* of the groups is always equal

3. IV (or grouping variable) is nominal and dichotomous

4. DV (or outcome variable) is interval or ratio

5. DV is normally distributed

A Test by Any Other Name . . .

- SPSS calls this test a *paired-samples t test,* but this name should only be used in a report if you had matched (paired) samples.

- If you have a repeated-measures design, you could use the term *repeated-measures* t *test.*

- *Dependent-samples* t *test* is a more general term that can apply to either matched or repeated-measures designs.

Data Entry for Dependent Designs

In general, each row in the data table represents one participant. The exception is matched groups, in which each row represents one matched pair.

	Independent Groups (20 participants)		vs.	Dependent Groups (10 pairs *or* 10 participants)	

	IVgroups	DVscores
1	1.00	1.00
2	1.00	1.00
3	1.00	2.00
4	1.00	2.00
5	1.00	3.00
6	1.00	3.00
7	1.00	3.00
8	1.00	4.00
9	1.00	7.00
10	1.00	7.00
11	2.00	2.00
12	2.00	2.00
13	2.00	2.00
14	2.00	2.00
15	2.00	3.00
16	2.00	3.00
17	2.00	7.00
18	2.00	7.00
19	2.00	8.00
20	2.00	8.00

	Scores in Group 1	Scores in Group 2
1	1.00	2.00
2	1.00	2.00
3	2.00	2.00
4	2.00	2.00
5	3.00	3.00
6	3.00	3.00
7	3.00	7.00
8	4.00	7.00
9	7.00	8.00
10	7.00	8.00
11		
12		
13		
14		

When you enter data for a dependent groups design, you must enter the data for each group in a separate column.

Conducting a Dependent-Samples *t* Test

Repeated Measures Example

A researcher is interested in how the environment impacts problem-solving skills. He has two conditions: a peaceful environment (quiet with a few people reading quietly) and a stressful environment (with loud noises and lots of people scurrying about).

Each participant experiences both environments and completes a problem-solving test while in each environment. The researcher randomly assigned participants to sequence so that some experience the stressful situation first while others experience the nonstressful environment first.

Data Entry

The variable view would look like this:

	Name	Type	Width	Decimals	Label	Values	Missing	Columns	
1	ID	Numeric	8	2	ID number for participants	None	None	8	▤
2	peaceful	Numeric	8	2	problem solving in peaceful environment	None	None	8	▤
3	stressful	Numeric	8	2	problem solving in stressful environment	None	None	8	▤

The data view would look like this:

	ID	peaceful	stressful
1	1.00	8.00	7.00
2	2.00	6.00	6.00
3	3.00	7.00	6.00
4	4.00	5.00	5.00
5	5.00	9.00	8.00
6	6.00	7.00	7.00
7	7.00	6.00	5.00
8	8.00	8.00	7.00
9	9.00	5.00	4.00
10	10.00	7.00	8.00
11	11.00	8.00	8.00
12	12.00	7.00	6.00

In a repeated-measures design, each row represents one participant.

In this example, each participant has a unique ID number, a problem-solving score in the peaceful environment, and a problem-solving score in the stressful environment.

On the Menu Bar, Click

Analyze → Compare Means → Paired-samples *t* test

Use the same steps for matched groups and repeated measures.

1. Send each group you are comparing to the "Paired Variables" box.

2. Click "OK."

OUTPUT

Paired Samples Statistics

		Mean	N	Std. Deviation	Std. Error Mean
Pair 1	peaceful	6.9167	12	1.24011	.35799
	stressful	6.4167	12	1.31137	.37856

The first table provides descriptive information for each of your groups.

Paired Samples Correlations

		N	Correlation	Sig.
Pair 1	peaceful & stressful	12	.862	.000

Paired Samples Test

		Paired Differences							
					95% Confidence Interval of the Difference				
		Mean	Std. Deviation	Std. Error Mean	Lower	Upper	t	df	Sig. (2-tailed)
Pair 1	peaceful - stressful	.50000	.67420	.19462	.07163	.92837	2.569	11	.026

The third table shows the results for the paired-samples t test.

From this example, we would report $t(11) = 2.57$, $p = .03$.

Effect Size

SPSS does not compute an effect size for a dependent-samples t test. You can compute Cohen's d using the following formula:

$$d = \frac{M_1 - M_2}{\sqrt{SD_1^2 + SD_2^2 / 2}}$$

Or you can use the online calculator that is available at http://www.uccs.edu/~lbecker/

- If you use the online calculator, be sure to only use the first box calculator that asks for means (Ms) and standard deviations (SDs).

- If you choose to report r_{pb}^2 as an effect size, be sure to square the correlation that the calculator produces.

Writing Up Results

The write up is very similar to an independent-samples t test (see Chapter 10). However, you should be sure your language is consistent with your dependent design, either matched-groups or repeated-measures.

Also, you do not need to worry about Levene's test.
Include the following in your report:

- The type of analysis you conducted and the variables examined

- The mean and standard deviation for each group. You might also calculate and report the confidence intervals for the means (see Chapter 6)

- The *t* value, *df*, *p* value, and effect size. For example: $t(11) = 2.57, p = .03, d = 0.39$

- A statement about whether or not the difference was statistically significant

Conducting a One-Way Within-Samples ANOVA

This analysis is similar to the dependent-samples *t* test, except it allows you to examine the difference between three or more dependent groups.

- SPSS calls the analysis *repeated measures ANOVA;* you can use this term to describe analyses for a repeated-measures design.

- Use the term *matched groups ANOVA* when you used matching.

- You can use the term *dependent-designs ANOVA* or *within-subjects ANOVA* for either design.

Assumptions for the One-Way Within-Samples ANOVA

1. Groups are dependent (matched or repeated measures)

2. IV or predictor has three or more levels or groups

3. DV or outcome is interval or ratio scale of measurement

4. DV or outcome is normally distributed

5. Sphericity in variances of the differences between pairs of groups

Overview of the One-Way Within-Samples ANOVA

- This ANOVA analysis will give you an *F* like the independent-designs ANOVA, but this ANOVA is calculated as follows:

F = Between group differences (MS_A) $\div$ Within group differences minus the variability associated with individuals (MS_{AxS})

- When you report an *F* statistic, you need to report two types of *df:*

Between-groups (treatment) df_A = Number of groups (k) − 1

Within-groups (interaction error) df_{AxS} = *df* for groups times the number of participants per condition minus one or $(k-1)(k_{ps}-1)$

- You also need to report the effect size. Eta (η) is a correlation coefficient used to describe the magnitude of a relationship containing two or more levels. Partial eta^2 ($\eta^2_{partial}$) is the effect size used with a dependent ANOVA and reflects the proportion of variance in the test variable (DV) accounted for by the grouping variable (IV), with the error unique to individuals removed.

- If you find a statistically significant F, you will need to run post hoc tests analyses to determine which groups differ.

Conducting a One-Way Within-Subjects ANOVA

Matched-Groups Example

A researcher investigates the impact of Internet use on college students' impulsivity scores. Impulsivity is measured by the Continuous Performance Task, which is an individually administered test that requires the participant to attend to and discriminate among stimuli. Higher scores indicate higher impulsivity. Students are matched on their ability to identify identical objects from a set of similar objects. All students agree to spend a day (8 hours) in the research lab. One group is given unlimited Internet access, another group is allowed access for 3 hours, and the third group is given no access.

Data Entry

	matched group	unlimited	threehours	nointernet
1	1.00	7.00	6.00	6.00
2	2.00	5.00	5.00	3.00
3	3.00	6.00	5.00	6.00
4	4.00	7.00	7.00	5.00
5	5.00	5.00	4.00	5.00
6	6.00	5.00	6.00	5.00
7	7.00	5.00	4.00	4.00
8	8.00	7.00	7.00	5.00
9	9.00	9.00	8.00	6.00
10	10.00	4.00	4.00	4.00
11	11.00	7.00	7.00	6.00
12	12.00	6.00	7.00	6.00
13	13.00	7.00	6.00	7.00
14	14.00	5.00	5.00	6.00
15	15.00	8.00	7.00	6.00

In a matched-groups design, each row represents one matched group.

In this example, each matched group has a unique ID number, and then impulsivity scores for each matched participant in the unlimited, three hour, and no internet access conditions.

On the Menu Bar, click

Analyze → General Linear Model → Repeated Measures

Use the same steps for matched groups and repeated measures.

Optional: change "factor1" to the name of your independent or predictor variable (e.g., "internet" in this example).

1. Enter the number of levels for the IV or predictor (in this example, we have three levels).

2. Click "Add."

3. Click "Define."

4. Send each of your variables to "Within-Subjects Variables."

5. Click "Options."

6. Move your factor to "Display means."

7. ☑ Select "Compare main effects."

8. Click arrow under "Confidence interval adjustment" and click on "Bonferroni" or another post hoc choice.

9. ☑ Select "Descriptive statistics" and "Estimates of effect size."

10. Click "Continue" and then "OK" to run analyses.

OUTPUT (abbreviated)

We will only look at the following tables in the output:

- "Descriptive Statistics"
- "Mauchly's Test of Sphericity"
- "Tests of Within-Subjects Effects"
- "Pairwise Comparisons"

Descriptive Statistics

	Mean	Std. Deviation	N
unlimited	6.2000	1.37321	15
threehours	5.8667	1.30201	15
nointernet	5.3333	1.04654	15

> The "Descriptives Statistics" table displays the mean and standard deviation for each level of your factor (IV or predictor).

Mauchly's Test of Sphericity[a]

Measure: MEASURE_1							
Within Subjects Effect	Mauchly's W	Approx. Chi-Square	df	Sig.	Epsilon[b]		
					Greenhouse-Geisser	Huynh-Feldt	Lower-bound
factor1	.735	4.002	2	.135	.791	.874	.500

Tests the null hypothesis that the error covariance matrix of the orthonormalized transformed dependent variables is proportional to an identity matrix.
a. Design: Intercept Within Subjects Design: factor1
b. May be used to adjust the degrees of freedom for the averaged tests of significance. Corrected tests are displayed in the Tests of Within-Subjects Effects table.

> Like Levene's test, Mauchley's test of sphericity tests an assumption, and we hope that the test is NOT statistically significant. In this example, Mauchley's test of sphericity is not statistically significant ($p \geq .05$) and we can assume sphericity.
>
> If Mauchley's test of sphericity fails (i.e., it is statistically significant at $p < .05$), you would use an alternative test such as Greenhouse-Geisser or Huynh-Feldt in the "Tests of Within-Subjects Effects" table.

Tests of Within-Subjects Effects

		Type III Sum of Squares	df	Mean Square	F	Sig.	Partial Eta Squared
				Measure: MEASURE_1			
Source							
factor1	Sphericity Assumed	5.733	2	2.867	5.375	.011	.277
	Greenhouse-Geisser	5.733	1.581	3.626	5.375	.018	.277
	Huynh-Feldt	5.733	1.749	3.279	5.375	.014	.277
	Lower-bound	5.733	1.000	5.733	5.375	.036	.277
Error (factor1)	Sphericity Assumed	14.933	28	.533			
	Greenhouse-Geisser	14.933	22.135	.675			
	Huynh-Feldt	14.933	24.480	.610			
	Lower-bound	14.933	14.000	1.067			

> Use the "Sphericity Assumed" results when Mauchley's test is not statistically significant.
>
> In this example, $F(2, 28) = 5.38$, $p = .01$, $\eta^2_{partial} = .28$.
>
> Because we have a statistically significant F, we must report the post hoc test results.

Pairwise Comparisons

					95% Confidence Interval for Difference[b]	
					Measure: MEASURE_1	
(I) factor1	(J) factor1	Mean Difference (I-J)	Std. Error	Sig.[b]	Lower Bound	Upper Bound
1	2	.333	.187	.288	-.175	.841
	3	.867*	.291	.030	.077	1.656
2	1	-.333	.187	.288	-.841	.175
	3	.533	.307	.311	-.300	1.366
3	1	-.867*	.291	.030	-1.656	-.077
	2	-.533	.307	.311	-1.366	.300

> The "Pairwise Comparisons" table depicts the results of the post hoc tests. We only report these comparisons if our F was statistically significant.
>
> In this example, we used a Bonferroni correction that accounts for the increased chance of a Type I error due to computing multiple comparisons. Here we find the corrected p values for all our comparisons:
>
> - (1) unlimited access vs. (2) 3-hour access: $p = .29$
> - (1) unlimited access vs. (3) no access: $p = .03$
> - (2) 3-hour access vs. (3) no access: $p = .31$

Writing Up Results

The write-up is very similar to a one-way between-samples ANOVA (see Chapter 10). However, you should be sure your language is consistent with your dependent design, either matched-groups or repeated-measures.

Include the following:

- The type of analysis you conducted and the variables examined

- The mean and standard deviation for each group (or report in a table). You might also calculate and report the confidence intervals for the means (see Chapter 6)

- The results of the F test and the effect size (e.g., $F(2, 28) = 5.38, p = .01$, $\eta^2_{partial} = .28$)

- If the F was statistically significant, identify the type of post hoc tests you ran (e.g., a Bonferroni correction). Report the results of all the pairwise comparisons, including the p values

Practice Exercise 1

A researcher interested in dating violence matches participants on their Attitudes toward Women scale (AWS). Participants read a scenario describing violence (a slap during an argument) between a dating couple. Matched pairs are randomly assigned to a scenario in which the perpetrator of the violence is a male or a female. All participants rate the violence of the act (a slap) after reading the scenario (10 = *extremely violent*). The data are shown below:

Male Perpetrator	Female Perpetrator
9	8
8	9
8	7
7	6
8	8
7	6
6	5
6	4
5	5
5	4

1. What is the design of this study (be specific)? _____

   _____

2. What is the IV? _____ DV? _____

3. State a directional alternative hypothesis for the study.

   _____

4. Compute (by hand or using SPSS) all the appropriate statistics to test your hypothesis.

5. Are the findings significant? _____ How do you know?

   _____

6. State and interpret the effect size. _____

7. Describe the Results using APA format.

   _____

   _____

   _____

   _____

   _____

   _____

8. Interpret the results as you would in a Discussion section. Include one limitation and one way to address the limitation.

   _____

   _____

   _____

   _____

   _____

   _____

Practice Exercise 2

Research has found that physicians often ignore complaints in older patients that they take seriously in younger patients. In an effort to reduce this prejudice before it becomes too ingrained, a researcher designs a study to have fourth-year medical students see videos of 10 patients (who are really actors) a month apart. In one sequence of the 10 videos, an actor is made up to look about 70 and talks about being retired, and in the other sequence of the 10 videos, the same actor is depicted as his own age (30). The actor presents similar complaints in each video. Students are randomly assigned to the order of viewing these two sequences of videos a month apart. After viewing each of the videos, the students list the questions they would ask the patient, their diagnosis of the complaint(s), and their rating for the health of the "patient" on a 15-point scale, with higher scores representing better health. The researcher is interested in comparing the responses to the same complaints for the different "age" patient. The data for these videos are below:

Older patient	Younger patient
9.00	14.00
12.00	15.00
9.00	10.00
11.00	11.00
14.00	15.00
10.00	8.00
9.00	10.00
8.00	8.00
12.00	14.00
11.00	15.00
11.00	8.00
9.00	10.00
5.00	9.00
13.00	12.00
10.00	12.00

1. State a directional alternative hypothesis for the study.

   _____

2. Compute the statistics needed to test your hypothesis.

3. Are your findings significant? _____ Explain your answer.

   _____

4. What is the probability of a Type I error? _____ Type II error?

   _____

5. What potential problem(s) do you identify in the study design?

_____

_____

_____

_____

6. Write a few sentences describing the findings as you would in a Results section.

_____

_____

_____

_____

_____

_____

7. Interpret the findings (what are the implications?).

_____

_____

_____

_____

8. What do you suggest for future researchers to improve upon the study?

_____

_____

_____

Practice Exercise 3

A researcher examines the effects of different types of advertisements on persuasiveness (in terms of buying a product). She matches a sample of 40 young adults on sense of self as a consumer. One student in each matched group is randomly assigned to rate 10 advertisements that depict people as sex-objects (erotic ads), people in traditional gender roles (traditional ads), people in nontraditional gender roles (progressive ads), or product-oriented with no humans in the ad (control ads). Participants rate the full-page color advertisements from several magazines on a variety of characteristics, such as color, layout, attractiveness, and persuasiveness, to distract the students from the true purpose of the experiment. The researcher is only interested in the 20-point persuasiveness scale (1 = *not at all persuasive* to 20 = *very persuasive*). The results are presented below:

Erotic	Trad	Non-Trad	Product
15.00	13.00	17.00	15.00
14.00	14.00	16.00	17.00
12.00	12.00	18.00	15.00
16.00	14.00	19.00	15.00
15.00	15.00	17.00	15.00
17.00	16.00	19.00	13.00
14.00	14.00	18.00	14.00
13.00	13.00	17.00	16.00
14.00	13.00	16.00	17.00
16.00	15.00	18.00	16.00

1. What is the design of this study (be specific)? _____

2. What is the IV? _____ DV? _____

3. Compute (by hand or using SPSS) all the appropriate statistics to test your hypothesis.

4. Are the findings significant? _____ How do you know?

   _____

5. State and interpret the effect size. _____

6. Describe the Results using APA format.

   _____

   _____

   _____

   _____

   _____

   _____

7. Interpret the results as you would in a Discussion section. Include one limitation and one way to address the limitation.

_____

_____

_____

_____

_____

_____

Practice Exercise 4

A researcher who was examining the effect of different schedules of verbal reinforcement on correct answers in a vocabulary test randomly assigns the 4-year-olds to the order of reinforcement conditions and records the number of correct responses for each condition. Scores for each condition are below:

Reinforce only correct answers (C)	Reinforce all answers (B)	No Reinforce (N)
8	7	7
7	5	5
6	5	6
6	5	6
7	4	5
6	6	7
8	5	6
7	6	6
5	5	7
6	6	5

1. How many participants are in this study? _____

2. Enter the data into SPSS (or another statistical package) and calculate all of the appropriate statistics.

3. Describe the results using APA format as in a Results section.

_____

_____

_____

_____

_____

_____

4. Interpret the results as you would in a Discussion section. Include one limitation and one way to address the limitation.

_____

_____

_____

_____

_____

_____

Additional Practice

If you want additional practice with dependent-samples *t* tests and one-way within-subjects ANOVAs, open one of the databases found in the Web Resources, find databases online, or ask your professor for practice datasets. Identify variables that can serve as IV (predictor) and DV (outcome) for correlational, quasi-experimental, or experimental studies. Check your answers by comparing them with a classmate or study group members, or check with your instructor.

Factorial Designs

12

CHAPTER SUMMARY

Examining the impact of one variable on another might provide an incomplete picture, and often it is important to understand the interaction of multiple variables. Chapter 12 begins by introducing basic concepts in factorial designs, including the different types of factorials, factorial notation, and the difference between main effects and interaction effects. Next is a discussion of the rationale for factorial designs, with an emphasis on the benefits of examining complex relationships and controlling extraneous or confounding variables.

The second part of the chapter focuses on 2 × 2 designs. The chapter includes information on how to graph these designs and provides examples of different graphs with and without interaction effects. Strategies for articulating interaction hypotheses are provided, with three typical interaction patterns outlined along with example graphs demonstrating each pattern. The chapter provides details on how to analyze independent-groups designs using both formulas and a computer program (i.e., SPSS). The chapter also provides an overview of independent designs with more than two factors or with a nominal outcome or dependent variable, dependent-groups factorial designs, and mixed designs. The chapter ends by suggesting that the factorial design allows one to think more critically about the relationship among variables and therefore avoid overly simple explanations.

LEARNING OUTCOMES

After reading and reviewing Chapter 12, you should understand

- Basic concepts in factorial designs
- Rationale for conducting factorial designs
- How to hypothesize and interpret main effects and interaction effects
- How to analyze independent-groups factorial designs
- The basics of dependent-groups and mixed factorial designs

Exercise 12.1: Basic Concepts in Factorial Design (Review)

1. A _____ is a general name for a predictor or independent variable.

2. A factorial design that includes manipulation and random assignment for all the factors is called _____.

3. A design that includes manipulation and random assignment for at least one factor and no manipulation or random assignment for at least one factor is called _____.

4. The most simple factorial design is the _____ × _____, that has _____ factors, each with _____ levels.

5. A 3 × 5 factorial design has _____ factors, the first with _____ levels and the second with _____ levels.

6. A 2 × 2 × 2 factorial design has _____ factors, each with _____ levels.

7. A _____ is a comparison of one level of a factor across a level of another factor.

8. A 2 × 2 has _____ cells, and a 2 × 2 × 2 has _____ cells.

9. In a simple or multiple-group experiment, the effect of the independent variable (IV) on the dependent variable (DV) is a(n) _____ effect.

10. In a factorial experiment, there are at least two _____ effects and at least one _____ effect.

11. Write a definition for an interaction effect, using your own words:

    _____

12. In an interaction effect, the _____ is a factor that changes the strength or direction of the relationship between another factor and the outcome (or DV).

Exercise 12.2: Basic Concepts in Factorial Design (Application)

Use the following variables to create specific types of factorial designs:

Non-Experimental Variables	Experimental IVs
gender (male, female)	facial expression (smile, frown)
religion (religious, spiritual, or neither)	sexism (not sexist, hostile, benevolent)
year in college (1st, 2nd, 3rd, 4th)	

Example: A 2 × 3 correlational factorial: gender × religion

1. A 3 × 4 correlational factorial: _____ × _____

2. A 2 × 3 experimental factorial: _____ × _____

3. A 4 × 3 hybrid factorial: _____ × _____

4. A 2 × 3 hybrid factorial: _____ × _____ OR _____ × _____

5. A 2 × 4 × 2 hybrid factorial: _____ × _____ _____ × _____

Exercise 12.3: Rationale for Factorial Designs (Application)

1. Research suggests that parents' salary strongly predicts the salary their child will eventually earn. However, there are many examples of individuals from poor backgrounds who go on to have high salaries and also of individuals from wealthy backgrounds who go on to have low salaries. Explain how a factorial design might help us understand this complex relationship.

    _____

    _____

2. A researcher wants to examine how childhood experiences with police officers impact adult participants' current feelings about police. The researcher wants to increase power and is considering limiting the population to only African American participants. What is an alternative strategy the researcher might use?

    _____

    _____

3. A researcher wants to conduct an experiment to examine the effect of reading versus watching the news on anxiety. To increase internal validity, the researcher decides that the news story will be the same one about crime. However, the researcher realizes that this will limit external validity in that it will be unclear whether results are generalizable to other news stories, such as those about accidents. Make a case for using a factorial design instead.

_____

_____

_____

4. A classmate collected data for a simple experiment but did not find a statistically significant effect. The classmate is now considering examining how participant characteristics such as gender and age might have impacted the relationship between the IV and DV. Under what conditions might this be a good strategy? When might this be a bad strategy?

_____

_____

_____

Exercise 12.4: 2 × 2 Designs (Application)

1. Identify which of the following are main effects, and which one is an interaction:

   a. _____ Checking social media within an hour of going to bed will negatively impact the quantity and quality of sleep.

   b. _____ Drinking tea before going to sleep will improve the quantity and quality of sleep compared to drinking water.

   c. _____ Distractions will impede performance on the math test but will improve performance on a creativity test, and the opposite effect will occur in a distraction-free environment.

   d. _____ Compared to a placebo, taking medicine to go to sleep will increase the quantity of sleep but decrease the quality of sleep.

   e. _____ Both television viewing and social media use prior to bedtime will decrease the quality of sleep.

2. For the interaction you identified above, identify:

   a. Factor 1: _____; levels: _____

   b. Factor 2: _____; levels: _____

   c. Outcome/DV: _____

3. Which of the following graphs best fit the interaction: _____

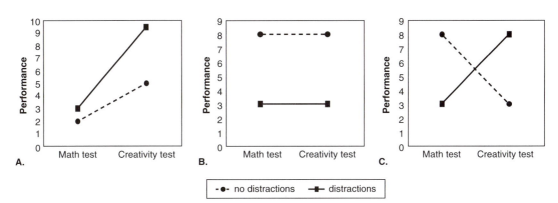

A.   **B.**   **C.**

-•- no distractions   -■- distractions

Exercise 12.5: 2 × 2 Tables and Graphs (Application)

1. Graph the results of a study on happiness:

		Pet	
		none	cat
Age	50–64	4	7
	65–80	4	7

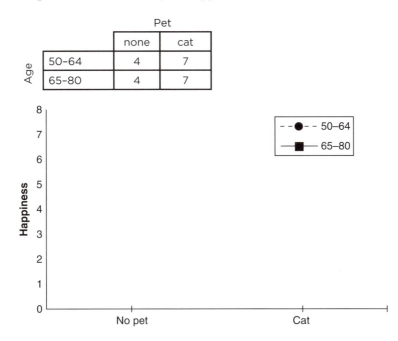

--•-- 50–64
--■-- 65–80

2. Does the steepness and direction of the lines in the graph indicate

    a. A main effect for pet? _____

    b. A main effect for age? _____

    c. An interaction? _____

3. Graph the results of a study on income:

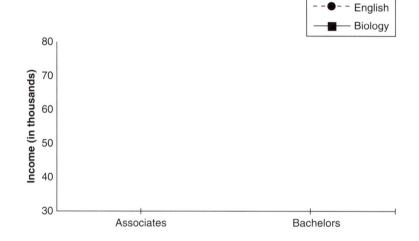

		Degree	
		Associates	Bachelors
Major	English	40,000	55,000
	Biology	50,000	77,000

4. Does the steepness and direction of the lines in the graph indicate

    a. A main effect for degree? _____

    b. A main effect for major? _____

    c. An interaction? _____

5. Graph the results of a study on quiz scores:

		Current Grade in Class	
		A or B	C or less
Study Session	Attended	9.5	8
	Did not attend	7.5	6

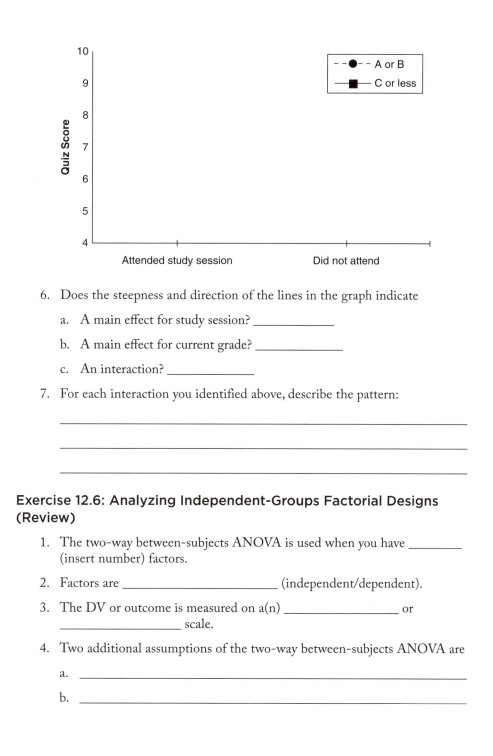

6. Does the steepness and direction of the lines in the graph indicate

    a. A main effect for study session? _____

    b. A main effect for current grade? _____

    c. An interaction? _____

7. For each interaction you identified above, describe the pattern:

    _____

    _____

    _____

Exercise 12.6: Analyzing Independent-Groups Factorial Designs (Review)

1. The two-way between-subjects ANOVA is used when you have _____ (insert number) factors.

2. Factors are _____ (independent/dependent).

3. The DV or outcome is measured on a(n) _____ or _____ scale.

4. Two additional assumptions of the two-way between-subjects ANOVA are

    a. _____

    b. _____

5. A researcher examines how race of a suspect and race of a victim impact ratings of seriousness of a crime.

   a. The _____ is the average ratings of seriousness of a crime for the entire sample.

   b. _____ are the means used to examine the main effect for race of suspect and the main effect for race of victim.

   c. _____ are the means used to examine the interaction.

Exercise 12.7: Formulas and Calculations: Two-Way Between-Subjects ANOVA (Application)

A researcher conducts a 2×2 factorial with 80 participants and equal numbers in all four cells.

1. Fill in the missing information in the ANOVA summary table:

Tests of Between-Subjects Effects				
Source	Sum of Squares	df	Mean Square	F
Factor 1	137.813	$k_{B1} - 1 = $ _____	$SS_{B1}/df_{B1} = $ _____	MS_{B1}/MS_w = _____
Factor 2	2.113	$k_{B2} - 1 = $ _____	$SS_{B2}/df_{B2} = $ _____	MS_{B2}/MS_w = _____
Interaction	25.313	$(df_{B1})(df_{B2})$ = _____	$SS_{B1 \times B2}/df_{B1 \times B2}$ = _____	$MS_{B1 \times B2}/MS_w$ = _____
Error	197.750	$C(n - 1) = $ _____	$SS_w/df_w = $ _____	
Total	362.988	$N - 1 = $ _____		

2. Look at Appendix C.8 to determine whether the F value for the main effects and interaction meet the criteria for statistical significance at $p < .05$.

	Is the F statistically significant at $p < .05$?
Main effect for factor 1	
Main effect for factor 2	
Interaction effect	

3. Compute the effect size ($\eta^2_{partial}$) for each main effect and the interaction using the formula $\eta^2_{partial} = SS_B/(SS_B + SS_w)$.

	$\eta^2_{partial}$
Main effect for factor 1	
Main effect for factor 2	
Interaction effect	

Exercise 12.8: Using Data Analysis Programs: Two-Way Between-Subjects ANOVA (Application)

A researcher hypothesizes that ADHD symptoms will exacerbate the distracting impact of a cell phone ringing during a lecture. Abbreviated SPSS output appears below:

Descriptive Statistics (Dependent Variable: Exam Score)			
Condition: ADHD Symptoms	Mean	Std. Deviation	N
No cell ring			
Low ADHD symptoms	6.8400	.85049	25
High ADHD symptoms	6.8000	1.19024	25
Total	6.8200	1.02400	50
Ringing cell phone			
Low ADHD symptoms	6.4000	1.19024	25
High ADHD symptoms	5.8800	1.09240	25
Total	6.1400	1.16075	50
Total			
Low ADHD symptoms	6.6200	1.04764	50
High ADHD symptoms	6.3400	1.22241	50
Total	6.4800	1.14133	100

Test of Between-Subjects Effects (Dependent Variable: Exam Score)						
Source	Type III Sum of Squares	df	Mean Square	F	Sig.	Partial Eta Squared
Corrected Model	14.960[a]	3	4.987	4.199	.008	.116
Intercept	4199.040	1	4199.040	3536.034	.000	.974
Condition	11.560	1	11.560	9.735	.002	.092
ADHD	1.960	1	1.960	1.651	.202	.017
Condition * ADHD	1.440	1	1.440	1.213	.274	.013
Error	114.000	96	1.187			
Total	4328.000	100				
Corrected Total	128.960	99				

Use these results to fill in the blanks below. Round your answers to two decimal places, except when important information for the p value would be lost with rounding (e.g., $p = .004$ or $p = .045$).

1. The grand mean = _____

2. The group means for ADHD symptoms: low = _____; high = _____

3. The group means for cell phone condition: no ring = _____; ring = _____

4. The cell means:

   a. low ADHD and no ring: _____; high ADHD and no ring: _____ _____

   b. low ADHD and ring: _____; high ADHD and ring: _____

5. Fill in the blanks for the inferential statistics:

   a. Main effect for ADHD symptoms: F(_____, _____) = _____, p = _____

   b. Main effect for ring condition: F(_____, _____) = _____, p = _____

   c. ADHD × condition interaction: F(_____, _____) = _____, p = _____

6. a. Is the main effect for ADHD symptoms statistically significant? _____

   b. Is the main effect for ring condition statistically significant? _____

   c. Is the interaction statistically significant? _____

7. Fill in the blanks for the effect sizes:

   a. ADHD symptoms accounted for _____% of the variance in exam scores ($\eta^2_{partial}$ = _____).

   b. Ring condition accounted for _____% of the variance in exam scores ($\eta^2_{partial}$ = _____).

   c. The interaction accounted for _____% of the variance in exam scores ($\eta^2_{partial}$ = _____).

Exercise 12.9: The Big Picture: Embracing Complexity

Indicate which of these tests you should use to analyze the following designs:

   a. chi-square test of independence

   b. two-way between-subjects ANOVA

c. two-way within-subjects ANOVA

d. mixed ANOVA

1. A factorial design with one matched variable and one between-subjects variable, and an outcome measured on an interval scale: _____

2. An independent-groups experiment with two IVs and a ratio DV: _____

3. An independent-groups experiment with two IVs and a nominal DV: _____

4. A repeated-measures experiment with two IVs and an interval DV: _____

5. A study on the relationship between political orientation (liberal or conservative), marital status (married, cohabitating, or single), and a rating scale assessing attitudes toward same-sex marriage: _____

6. A study on the relationship between political orientation (liberal or conservative), marital status (married, cohabitating, or single), and voting history (voted in last national election or did not vote): _____

7. A drug trial in which participants are randomly assigned to take either a sugar pill or an antidepressant medication. They rate their level of depression at the start of the trial (pretest) and after taking their assigned pill for six weeks (posttest):_____

YOUR RESEARCH

Develop an interaction hypothesis for a 2 × 2 experimental or hybrid factorial design.

1. State a hypothesis for a simple experiment on your topic (with one IV, with two levels, and one DV). This should be based on past research on your topic.

   _____

   _____

2. Go back to the research on your topic to decide between these two options:

   1. Option 1 (experimental factorial): Does research suggest that the IV will impact the DV under all conditions? If not, find at least one research article that suggests that a second IV will moderate the effect.

   2. Option 2 (hybrid factorial): Does research suggest that the IV will impact the DV for all participants? If not, find at least one research article that suggests that a participant characteristic, such as gender, age, or personality, will moderate the effect.

3. Based on the option you chose and the research article(s), develop an interaction hypothesis that suggests one of the following:

   a. A certain condition (option 1) or participant characteristic (option 2) will strengthen or weaken the effect you stated in your simple experiment hypothesis.

   b. The simple experiment hypothesis you stated only occurs under a certain condition or for certain participants.

   c. The direction (e.g., positive or negative) of the effect of your IV on your DV depends on a certain condition or participant characteristic.

   _____

   _____

4. Graph your hypothesized interaction.

IBM® SPSS® DATA ANALYSIS AND INTERPRETATION

Analyzing Factorial Designs

- To analyze an independent-groups factorial with an interval or ratio outcome variable/DV, follow directions for the two-way between-subjects ANOVA provided in the next section.

- To analyze an independent-groups factorial with a nominal outcome variable or DV, follow directions for the chi-square test of independence. (See Chapter 13 of this study guide.)

- To analyze either a dependent-groups or mixed factorial design with an interval or ratio outcome variable/DV, build on the directions for the one-way within-subjects ANOVA (See Chapter 11 of this study guide) by adding at least one within-subjects or between-subjects factor.

The Two-Way Between-Subjects ANOVA

Data Entry

At minimum, you need three variables: (1) Factor 1; (2) Factor 2; (3) Outcome/DV

Example: Below is fictional data for 20 pregnant women who participated in a 2×2 hybrid design in which they were randomly assigned to have different magazines available in their doctor's waiting room (nature vs. family) and whether or not they have been pregnant before (no vs. yes). Fear of delivery is the DV and measured on an interval scale.

	IV conditions:	
	Nature Magazines	**Family Magazines**
History: **Never been pregnant before**	5 4 5 3 4	2 3 3 4 2
Has been pregnant	3 5 4 5 3	8 6 7 6 8

In the example dataset that follows, we have entered these variables in SPSS:

- "magazine" coded as 1 = *nature magazines*, 2 = *family magazines*

- "history" coded as 1 = *never been pregnant*, 2 = *has been pregnant*

- "fear" scored on an interval scale.

	magazine	history	fear
1	1.00	.00	5.00
2	1.00	.00	4.00
3	1.00	.00	5.00
4	1.00	.00	3.00
5	1.00	.00	4.00
6	1.00	1.00	3.00
7	1.00	1.00	5.00
8	1.00	1.00	4.00
9	1.00	1.00	5.00
10	1.00	1.00	3.00
11	2.00	.00	2.00
12	2.00	.00	3.00
13	2.00	.00	3.00
14	2.00	.00	4.00
15	2.00	.00	2.00
16	2.00	1.00	8.00
17	2.00	1.00	6.00
18	2.00	1.00	7.00
19	2.00	1.00	6.00
20	2.00	1.00	8.00

Conducting a Two-Way Between-Subjects ANOVA

On the Menu Bar, click **Analyze → General Linear Model → Univariate**

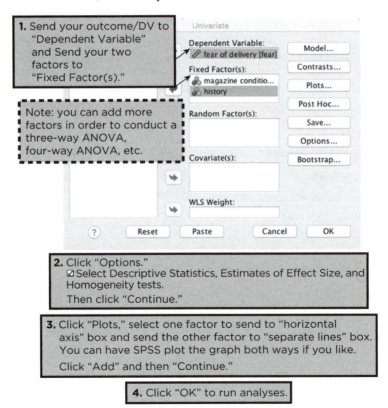

1. Send your outcome/DV to "Dependent Variable" and Send your two factors to "Fixed Factor(s)."

Note: you can add more factors in order to conduct a three-way ANOVA, four-way ANOVA, etc.

2. Click "Options."
☑ Select Descriptive Statistics, Estimates of Effect Size, and Homogeneity tests.
Then click "Continue."

3. Click "Plots," select one factor to send to "horizontal axis" box and send the other factor to "separate lines" box. You can have SPSS plot the graph both ways if you like.
Click "Add" and then "Continue."

4. Click "OK" to run analyses.

OUTPUT (abbreviated)

Descriptive Statistics

cell means

group means for Factor 1

group means for Factor 2

grand mean

Dependent Variable: fear of delivery				
magazine condition	history	Mean	Std. Deviation	N
nature magazine	never been pregnant	4.2000	.83666	5
	has been pregnant	4.0000	1.00000	5
	Total	4.1000	.87560	10
family magazine	never been pregnant	2.8000	.83666	5
	has been pregnant	7.0000	1.00000	5
	Total	4.9000	2.37814	10
Total	never been pregnant	3.5000	1.08012	10
	has been pregnant	5.5000	1.84089	10
	Total	4.5000	1.79179	20

Levene's Test of Equality of Error Variances[a]

Dependent Variable: fear of delivery			
F	df1	df2	Sig.
.220	3	16	.881
Tests the null hypothesis that the error variance of the dependent variable is equal across groups.			

[a]. Design: Intercept + magazine + history + magazine * history

In this example, Levene's is not statistically significant. If it was, check that the outcome/DV is normally distributed and check for outliers. A significant Levene's may occur when there is a statistically significant interaction effect.

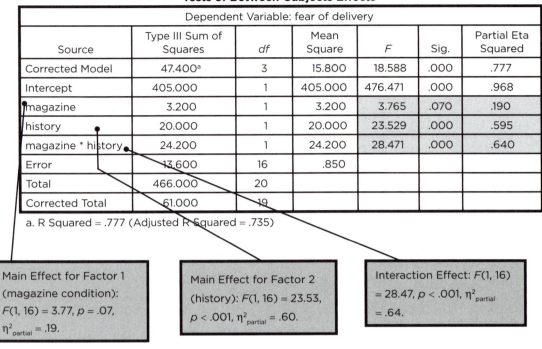

Tests of Between-Subjects Effects

Source	Type III Sum of Squares	df	Mean Square	F	Sig.	Partial Eta Squared
Corrected Model	47.400[a]	3	15.800	18.588	.000	.777
Intercept	405.000	1	405.000	476.471	.000	.968
magazine	3.200	1	3.200	3.765	.070	.190
history	20.000	1	20.000	23.529	.000	.595
magazine * history	24.200	1	24.200	28.471	.000	.640
Error	13.600	16	.850			
Total	466.000	20				
Corrected Total	61.000	19				

a. R Squared = .777 (Adjusted R Squared = .735)

Main Effect for Factor 1 (magazine condition): $F(1, 16) = 3.77$, $p = .07$, $\eta^2_{partial} = .19$.

Main Effect for Factor 2 (history): $F(1, 16) = 23.53$, $p < .001$, $\eta^2_{partial} = .60$.

Interaction Effect: $F(1, 16) = 28.47$, $p < .001$, $\eta^2_{partial} = .64$.

Writing up Results

Include the following:

- The type of analysis and the variables examined
- For each main effect: the means, standard deviations, and results from the *F* test (including *F, df, p, and* $\eta^2_{partial}$)
- The results of the interaction:
  - If *not statistically significant,* simply report that and the *F, df, p, and* $\eta^2_{partial}$
  - If *statistically significant,* you should report the results as well as an explanation of the interaction, with the cell means. A table is a good way to report the cell means and standard deviations. (Tables are placed after the References in an APA-style report.)

Note: Ask your professor whether you should report confidence intervals for your means. If so, see Chapter 6 of this study guide for directions on calculating and reporting confidence intervals.

Example

Results

A 2 (history of pregnancy) × 2 (magazine type) between-subjects ANOVA was conducted to examine factors that impact a pregnant women's fear of delivery. There was no significant difference in fear levels for women who were given family-oriented magazines vs. nature magazines ($M = 4.90$, $SD = 2.38$ vs. $M = 4.10$, $SD = 0.88$), $F(1, 16) = 3.77$, $p = .07$, $\eta^2_{partial} = .19$. Women who had never been pregnant ($M = 3.50$, $SD = 1.08$) had lower levels of fear than women who had been pregnant ($M = 5.50$, $SD = 1.84$). The relationship between history and fear of delivery was strong and statistically significant, $F(1, 16) = 23.53$, $p < .001$, $\eta^2_{partial} = .60$.

The main effects were qualified by a statistically significant interaction effect, $F(1, 16) = 28.47$, $p < .001$, which accounted for 64% of the variance in fear. Women who had never been pregnant reported much lower fears about their upcoming delivery when exposed to family magazines than when exposed to nature magazines. The opposite effect was found for women who had been pregnant in the past. These women reported much higher fears when exposed to family magazines rather than nature magazines (see Table 1).

Table 1

Fear as Function of Pregnancy History and Magazine Group

	Family Magazines		Nature Magazines	
	M	*SD*	*M*	*SD*
History of Pregnancy				
Never been pregnant	2.80	0.84	4.20	0.84
Has been pregnant	7.00	1.00	4.00	1.00

You might also want to include a graph to demonstrate a significant interaction. **Don't cut and paste from the output;** rather, create a graph using MSWord or data processing software such as Excel.

In an APA-style research report, Figures appear after Tables.

Figure 1 Interaction Between Magazine Condition and Pregnancy History

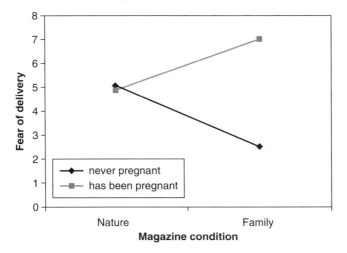

Practice Exercise 1

Following are results based on a factorial experiment that examined the effect of posture and forgetfulness on ratings of independence of an older adult. Use this information to fill in the tables below.

Posture conditions did not result in a statistically significant difference in independence ratings (good posture $M = 3.46$ $SD = 0.89$ vs. poor posture $M = 3.30$, $SD = 0.88$), $F(1, 214) = 1.69$, $p = .36$, $\eta^2_{partial} = .01$. Likewise, the man who forgot his keys ($M = 3.32$ $SD = 0.89$) was not rated as significantly less independent than the man who remembered his keys ($M = 3.43$ $SD = 0.88$), $F(1, 214) = 0.85$, $p = .20$, $\eta^2_{partial} = .004$. However, there was a significant posture by forgetting interaction, $F(1, 214) = 6.84$, $p = .01$. Results revealed that the man with poor posture who forgot his keys was rated the least independent ($M = 3.09$ $SD = 0.90$), whereas the man with good posture who forgot his keys was rated the most independent ($M = 3.55$ $SD = 0.83$). The man with poor posture who remembered his keys was rated more positively ($M = 3.51$ $SD = 0.81$) than the man with good posture who remembered his keys ($M = 3.35$ $SD = 0.96$). It should be noted that the interaction only accounted for 3% of the variance in independence.

Descriptive Statistics

Posture condition	forget condition	Mean	Std. Deviation	N
1.00 good posture	1.00 no forgetting			51
	2.00 forgot keys			56
	Total			107
2.00 poor posture	1.00 no forgetting			55
	2.00 forgot keys			56
	Total			111
Total	1.00 no forgetting			106
	2.00 forgot keys			112
	Total	3.38	.888	218

Tests of Between-Subjects Effects

Source	Type III Sum of Squares	df	Mean Square	F	Sig.	Partial Eta Squared
Corrected Model	7.371(a)	3	2.457	3.210	.024	.043
Intercept	2481.255	1	2481.255	3241.978	.000	.938
Posture	1.292	1	1.292			
Forget	.654	1	.654			
Posture * forget	5.237	1	5.237			
Error	163.785	214	.765			
Total	2656.000	218				
Corrected Total	171.156	217				

Dependent Variable: how independent?

a. R Squared = .043 (Adjusted R Squared = .030)

Practice Exercise 2

A teacher has heard that adding a humorous cartoon to an exam might ease tension and even raise scores. She wonders whether adding an inspirational quote might also have a positive effect and possibly strengthen the effect of a cartoon. She creates four different versions of an extra-credit quiz and randomly assigns students to condition. The quiz results for each condition are as follows:

Inspirational Quote

Humorous Cartoon		no quote	quote
no cartoon		5	6
		3	5
		4	4
		8	4
		6	7
cartoon		6	4
		7	3
		9	6
		6	6
		9	2

1. Using SPSS, enter the data and calculate a between-subjects two-way ANOVA. Alternatively or additionally, calculate these statistics by hand by following the directions in Chapter 12 of the textbook.

2. Write a Results section and put the cell means and standard deviations in a Table.

_____

_____

_____

_____

_____

_____

_____

_____

_____

_____

Table 1

The Effect of Humor and Inspirational Quotes on Quiz Scores

	No Inspirational Quote		Inspirational Quote	
	M	*SD*	*M*	*SD*
No Humorous Cartoon	_____	_____	_____	_____
Humorous Cartoon	_____	_____	_____	_____

3. Interpret your results as you would in a Discussion section.

_____

_____

_____

_____

_____

Practice Exercise 3

Go to https://edge.sagepub.com/adams2e. Click on "Datasets" and open the file called "Reminiscence Study":

- Read over the description of the datasets (reminiscence description.pdf)

- Download the compiled dataset (reminiscence compiled dataset.sav)

1. Calculate a between-subjects two-way ANOVA to determine whether college students tend to positively anticipate the future more than those who are not in college, and whether this relationship is moderated by gender.

2. Repeat with "savoring the moment" as the outcome variable.

3. Write a Results section that summarizes both these analyses.

_____

_____

_____

_____

_____

_____

_____

_____

_____

_____

Nonparametric Statistics

13

CHAPTER SUMMARY

Nonparametric statistics are used with nominal or ordinal data, or when the data violate the assumptions required for parametric statistics. Chapter 13 outlines the key differences between nonparametric and parametric statistics and then provides information about when to use the various nonparametric tests.

Because chi-square analyses and Spearman's rho are relatively common tests in the social sciences, the chapter details the computations for these tests and also provides examples of how to conduct these analyses using a data analysis program. For the other nonparametric tests, the computations are included in Appendix D rather than in the chapter. The chapter focuses on selecting the appropriate nonparametric test based on the type of data (nominal vs. ordinal) and design (independent vs. dependent groups).

REVIEW AND APPLICATION OF KEY CONCEPTS FROM CHAPTER 13

Exercise 13.1: Parametric and Nonparametric Tests (Review)

1. Statistics that are used to analyze interval or ratio data, and that are assumed to have a normal distribution and have similar variance among groups, are called _____.

2. Statistics that are used to analyze nominal or ordinal data and are used when the assumptions of parametric statistics are violated are called _____ _____.

LEARNING OUTCOMES

After reading and reviewing Chapter 13, you should understand

- The differences between parametric and nonparametric tests

- When to compute different nonparametric tests

- How to compute chi-square goodness of fit and chi-square test for independence (tests for nominal data)

- The appropriate analyses for independent- and dependent-groups designs with nominal data

- How to compute Spearman's rank order correlation coefficient for ordinal data

- The appropriate analyses for independent- and dependent-groups designs with ordinal data

3. Fill in the chart below:

Parametric	Nonparametric
Interval or ratio data	
	Distribution free
Tests for interactions	
	Small samples or pilot studies
Complicated computations	
	Violates homogeneity of variance
Powerful	

Exercise 13.2: Nonparametric Tests for Nominal Data (Review)

1. We use a chi-square goodness of fit test to compare observed frequencies to expected or known frequencies when we have _____ data.

2. A chi-square goodness of fit compares _____ frequencies with _____ frequencies.

3. The statistic used to analyze the relationship between two nominal variables is _____, with the statistical notation _____.

Exercise 13.3: Formulas and Calculations: Chi-Square Goodness of Fit (Review and Application)

1. The frequencies in each category the researcher counts are the _____ _____ frequencies and are symbolized by _____.

2. The count we expect in each category is called the _____ _____ frequency and is symbolized by _____.

3. We determine the expected frequency by dividing the _____ _____ by the _____. The formula for the expected frequency is $E =$ _____.

4. When we expect twice as many in one category or group, we add _____ _____ to k.

5. The assumptions for a chi-square goodness of fit include the following:

    a. _____

    b. _____

    c. _____

    d. _____

6. In a chi-square goodness of fit, we determine the degrees of freedom by
   _____ _____.

7. A researcher is studying whether people in different age groups (18–30, 31–45, 46–60, 60+) were equally likely to vote in the last election. He computes chi-square goodness of fit and finds $\chi^2(3, N = 400) = 5.35$.

   a. The null hypothesis for this study is
      H_0: _____

      _____

   b. The alternative hypothesis for this study is
      H_a: _____

      _____

   c. In this study $df =$ _____.

   d. What is the minimum number of voters that should be included in the sample? _____

   e. How many voters were in the sample? _____

   f. He should have completed a chi-square with _____
      _____ (equal/unequal) expected values.

   g. The critical χ^2 for $p < .05$ value = _____.

   h. Did the researcher find statistical significance? _____ How do you know?

      _____

8. A researcher wants to know whether residents who use a new park match the percentage of different ethnicities in the county, which is 20% African American, 60% Caucasian, 20% Hispanic/Latino.

   a. Should the researcher compute a chi-square goodness of fit test with equal or unequal frequencies? _____

   b. In this study, $k =$ _____ because _____
      _____.

   c. The null hypothesis for this study is
      H_0: _____

      _____

   d. The alternative hypothesis for this study is
      H_a: _____

      _____

e. The $df =$ _____ and the critical χ^2 value = _____.

f. If the researcher finds $\chi^2(2, N = 125) = 7.33$, did he find statistical significance? _____

g. What can you conclude about the use of the park by different ethnicities?

_____

9. Is there a favorite snack among elementary school students? Students select from among three snacks (healthy, moderately healthy, junk food).

Healthy	Moderately Healthy	Junk Food
10	20	30

a. State your null hypothesis.
H_0: _____

_____

b. State an alternative hypothesis.
H_a: _____

_____

c. For this study: $N =$ _____; $k =$ _____; $E =$ _____

d. Calculate a chi-square goodness of fit test.

e. Can you reject the null hypothesis? _____ Why or why not?

_____

f. What is the probability of a Type I error? _____ Type II error? _____

g. Write a Results section for your findings. Use APA format and include the variable measured and type of statistical test, observed and expected frequencies, whether the observed frequencies deviated from the expected frequencies, and results of the chi-square test.

_____

_____

_____

_____

_____

_____

h. Write a Discussion section for your findings. Include the findings, interpretation/explanation/implication of the findings, and possible next studies.

_____

_____

_____

_____

_____

_____

Exercise 13.4: Using Data Analysis Programs: Chi-Square Goodness of Fit (Application)

Suppose a sport studies researcher decides to test whether birth months of adolescents playing soccer in the Olympic Development Program in the United States demonstrate the Relative Age Effect (which states that people born earlier in the year are more likely to be selected for competitive sports teams). She records the birth months of a sample of 50 adolescents and divides the birth months into quartiles (1 = *Jan–Mar*, 2 = *Apr–Jun*, etc.). She then computes a chi-square goodness of fit test for equal frequencies and the following output results.

Birth Quartile

	Observed N	Expected N	Residual
1.00	21	12.5	8.5
2.00	14	12.5	1.5
3.00	10	12.5	-2.5
4.00	5	12.5	-7.5
Total	50		

Test Statistics

	Birth Quartile
Chi-Square	10.960[a]
df	3
Asymp. Sig.	.012

[a] 0 cells (0.0%) have expected frequencies less than 5. The minimum expected cell frequency is 12.5.

1. Did the research conduct a chi-square test for equal or unequal frequencies? _____ How do you know?

_____

2. Is the result of the analysis significant? _____ Explain how you know.

   _____

3. What is the probability of a Type I error? _____ Type II error?

   _____

4. Did the researcher find support for the Relative Age Effect? _____
   Explain your answer.

   _____

   _____

5. Write a few sentences that you think the researcher should include in her
   Discussion section.

   _____

   _____

   _____

6. Name at least one limitation that the researcher could mention and a future
   study that could address this limitation.

   _____

   _____

   _____

7. What recommendation might the researcher make to coaches of high
   school soccer teams (or principals of high schools)?

   _____

   _____

   _____

Exercise 13.5: Formulas and Calculations: Chi-Square Test for Independence (Review and Application)

1. When we examine the relationship between two nominal variables, the table
   that summarizes the data is called a _____.

2. The chi-square test compares _____ and _____
   values.

3. A chi-square test requires that the minimum expected value be at least ___.

4. Answer questions 4a–4e using the information in the following study: Is developmental status (adolescence vs. emerging adult) related to unhealthy dieting among females? Tenth-grade and college senior females who self-report that they are dieting describe their diet practice as moderate (e.g. exercise, balanced diet, reduced fats), unhealthful (e.g., skipping meals, eating only one food a day), or dangerous (e.g., fasting, vomiting, using laxatives).

   a. These data can be summarized in a ___ × ___ contingency table.

   b. The minimum sample size for this study is _____.

   c. The appropriate statistic to analyze these data is _____.

   d. The appropriate effect size statistic for these data is _____ because _____.

   e. The df = _____.

5. Answer questions 5a–5d using the information in the following question: Is race (African American/Caucasian) related to having been stopped for a traffic violation in the last month (yes/no)?

   a. This is a _____ × _____ contingency table.

   b. The appropriate effect size statistics for this analysis is _____.

   c. The df = _____.

   d. Suppose the researcher found χ^2 = 5.62. Look at Appendix C.7 in the textbook. Is this relationship significant at $p < .05$? _____. Explain.

Exercise 13.6: Using Data Analysis Programs: Chi-Square Test for Independence (Application):

Answer the following questions according to the output:

Immigrant Status * Employment Crosstabulation

			Employment			Total
			Unemployed	Part time	Full time	
Immigrant Status	No	Count	6	4	15	25
		Expected Count	5.0	6.0	14.0	25.0
	Yes	Count	4	8	13	25
		Expected Count	5.0	6.0	14.0	25.0
Total		Count	10	12	28	50
		Expected Count	10.0	12.0	28.0	50.0

Chi-Square Tests

	Value	df	Asymptotic Significance (2-sided)
Pearson Chi-Square	1.876[a]	2	.391
Likelihood Ratio	1.905	2	.386
Linear-by-Linear Association	.000	1	1.000
N of Valid Cases	50		

a. 0 cells (0.0%) have expected count less than 5. The minimum expected count is 5.00.

Symmetric Measures

		Value	Approximate Significance
Nominal by Nominal	Phi	.194	.391
	Cramer's V	.194	.391
N of Valid Cases		50	

1. These data represent a ___ × ____ contingency table.

2. Name the two variables being correlated. _____

3. How many participants were in this study? _____

4. Is the relationship statistically significant? _____ How do you know?

_____

5. The effect size is _____ (name the exact value). You interpret this as meaning _____.
The effect size is _____ (strong/moderate/weak).

6. There is a possibility of a Type _____ error.

7. Describe these findings as you might in a Results section.

_____

_____

_____

8. Interpret the meaning of the findings, possible flaws, and next studies as you might in a Discussion section.

_____

_____

_____

Exercise 13.7: Formulas and Calculations: Spearman's rho (Review and Application)

1. _____, with the statistical notation _____ is the appropriate correlation statistic to analyze a relationship between two ordinal variables.

2. Spearman's rho values can vary from _____ to _____, just like the _____ correlation coefficient, and it is interpreted similarly.

3. As part of a larger study about employment at a small company, a researcher explored the relationship between employees' job satisfaction and the number of sick days taken over the last year. Employees ($N = 24$) were ranked from most satisfied to least satisfied with their job and ranked in terms of number of sick days taken. The analysis showed $r_s = .36$.

   a. Is the relationship between the ranks significant at $p < .05$ for a two-tailed test? (Hint: see Appendix C.8) _____ Explain.

   _____

   b. Is the relationship between the ranks significant at $p < .05$ for a one-tailed test? _____ Explain.

   _____

Exercise 13.8: Using Data Analysis Programs: Spearman's rho (Application)

Answer the following questions given the output.

Correlations

			Prematurity	Language Skills
Spearman's rho	Prematurity	Correlation Coefficient	1.000	-.582*
		Sig. (2-tailed)	.	.023
		N	15	15
	Language Skills	Correlation Coefficient	-.582*	1.000
		Sig. (2-tailed)	.023	.
		N	15	15

*Correlation is significant at the 0.05 level (2-tailed).

1. What statistic was computed? _____

2. What variables were correlated? _____

3. How many participants were in the study? _____

4. Is the correlation statistically significant? _____

5. What is the probability of a Type I error? _____ Type II error? _____

6. Describe the relationship between the two variables as you would in a Results section, using APA format.

_____

_____

_____

Exercise 13.9: The Big Picture: Selecting Parametric vs. Nonparametric Tests

Fill in the blanks with the appropriate parametric or nonparametric test

Design	Parametric Test	Nonparametric Test
Correlation/No groups		
Two independent groups		
Two related groups (matching or repeated measures)		
Multiple independent groups		
Multiple related groups		

YOUR RESEARCH

Select a primary research article on your topic.

1. Look through the entire Method and Results section to identify any nonparametric statistics from this chapter. List any that you found and explain how the authors used them. (It is possible that the authors did not use nonparametric statistics. If this is the case, try searching through other articles on your topic.)

_____

_____

_____

_____

_____

_____

2. List up to three other inferential statistics that you recognize from other chapters and explain how the authors used them.

_____

_____

_____

_____

_____

_____

IBM® SPSS® DATA ANALYSIS AND INTERPRETATION

Conducting a Chi-Square Goodness of Fit

On the Menu Bar, click

Analyze → Nonparametric Test → Legacy Dialog → Chi-Square

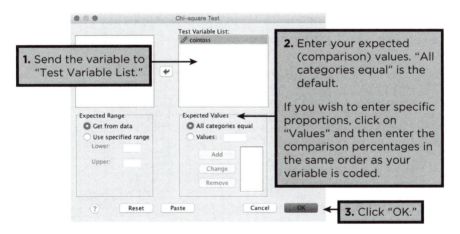

OUTPUT

Chi-Square Test

Frequencies

cointoss

	Observed N	Expected N	Residual
heads	18	15.0	3.0
tails	12	15.0	-3.0
Total	30		

The first table provides the observed and expected values and total *N*.

Test Statistics

	cointoss
Chi-Square	1.200[a]
df	1
Asymp. Sig.	.273

> The second table provides the χ^2, *df*, and *p* value.
>
> In this example, the χ^2 is not statistically significant and we would report $\chi^2(1, N = 30)$ $= 1.20, p = .27$.

Conducting a Chi-Square Test for Independence

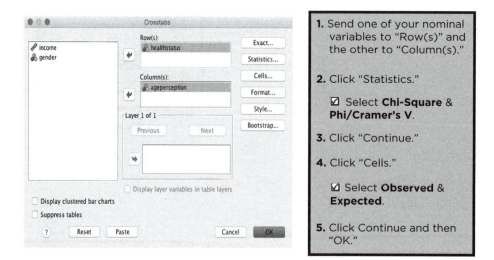

	healthstatus	ageperception
1	1.00	1.00
2	1.00	1.00
3	1.00	3.00
4	1.00	2.00
5	2.00	2.00
6	1.00	2.00
7	1.00	3.00

Data Entry

Enter the two variables into SPSS as independent codes.

In this example, Health status is coded as 1 = *healthy*, 2 = *unhealthy*.

Perception of one's aging process relative to chronological age coded as 1 = *younger*, 2 = *equal*, 3 = *older*.

To calculate chi-square test for independence, click on the Menu Bar

Analyze → Descriptive Statistics → Crosstabs

1. Send one of your nominal variables to "Row(s)" and the other to "Column(s)."

2. Click "Statistics."

   ☑ Select **Chi-Square** & **Phi/Cramer's V**.

3. Click "Continue."

4. Click "Cells."

   ☑ Select **Observed** & **Expected**.

5. Click Continue and then "OK."

OUTPUT (abbreviated)

Health Orig * Aging Perception Crosstabulation

			Aging Perception			Total
			younger	equal	older	
Health Orig	healthy	Count	4	8	1	13
		Expected Count	2.6	6.5	3.9	13.0
	unhealthy	Count	0	2	5	7
		Expected Count	1.4	3.5	2.1	7.0
Total		Count	4	10	6	20
		Expected Count	4.0	10.0	6.0	20.0

Chi-Square Tests

	Value	df	Asymptotic Significance (2-sided)
Pearson Chi-Square	9.304[a]	2	.010
Likelihood Ratio	10.483	2	.005
Linear-by-Linear Association	7.879	1	.005
N of Valid Cases	20		

We use the Pearson Chi-Square and would report:

$\chi^2(2, N = 20) = 9.30, p = .01$.

A statistically significant χ^2 means that our observed values were significantly different than the expected values.

[a]5 cells (83.3%) have expected count less than 5. The minimum expected count is 1.40.

Symmetric Measures

		Value	Approximate Significance
Nominal by Nominal	Phi	.682	.010
	Cramer's V	.682	.010
N of Valid Cases		20	

Square the phi or V to find the proportion of variance accounted for. In this example, we square .68 and find $V^2 = .46$, or 46% of the variance accounted for.

Writing Up Results

- Explain the analysis conducted and variables examined.

- Explain whether there was a significant relationship or effect.

- Report the results of the chi-square test for independence (e.g., $\chi^2(2, N = 20) = 0.28, p = .60$).

- Report the appropriate effect size statistic or proportion of variance accounted for (e.g., $\phi^2 = .02$).

- Explain the results by referring to the count or frequency of the groups (in the text or in a table).

Example

Results

Results of a chi-square test for independence revealed that reports of health had a statistically significant relationship with, and accounted for a large amount of the variance in, age perceptions. Participants view those who are healthy as their correct age ($n = 8$) or as younger ($n = 4$) more than those who are unhealthy ($n = 0$ and $n = 0$, respectively). Participants guess older ages for those who are unhealthy ($n = 5$) more than for those who are healthy ($n = 1$), $\chi^2(2, N = 20) = 9.30$, $p = .01$, $V^2 = .46$.

Calculating a Spearman's rho Correlation (r_s)

Spearman's rho is used to examine the relationship between two ordinal variables. After entering your data, follow the same commands as for a Pearson's r (see Study Guide Chapter 8) except click "Spearman."

Correlations

			Ranking by Supervisor A	Ranking by Supervisor B
Spearman's rho	Ranking by Supervisor A	Correlation Coefficient	1.000	.587*
		Sig. (2-tailed)	.	.045
		N	12	12
	Ranking by Supervisor B	Correlation Coefficient	.587*	1.000
		Sig. (2-tailed)	.045	.
		N	12	12

The output in SPSS will look the same as for Pearson's r and is interpreted similarly.

Here $r_s = .587$, $p = .045$, meaning the correlation between the rankings of the supervisors is statistically significant.

$r_s^2 = .34$, meaning that 34% of the variance in one ranking is accounted for by the other ranking.

*Correlation is significant at the 0.05 level (2-tailed).

Practice Exercise 1

Go to https://edge.sagepub.com/adams2e. Click on "Datasets" and open the file called "Game of Thrones." Here you will find two files:

- Description of the Game of Thrones dataset (.pdf)
- The dataset (.sav)

Read over the description of the Game of Thrones dataset, paying special attention to how variables are named and coded.

1. There has been much publicity about the major role of female characters in the television series *Game of Thrones*. But in the first season, was the ratio of males to females greater than what would be expected by chance?

   a. What inferential statistic would you use to answer this question?

   b. Using SPSS, calculate the statistic you identified.

   c. Write a sentence summarizing the results as you would in a Results section.

2. There has been much talk about how many characters have been killed on the show. For those characters that started the first season, are more of them dead or alive by the end of Season 6?

   a. What inferential statistic would you use to answer this question?

   b. Using SPSS, calculate the statistic you identified.

   c. Write a sentence summarizing the results as you would in a Results section.

Practice Exercise 2

An administrator at University Prestige wants to know whether gender is independent of status for full-time faculty at the institution. He finds the following data:

Status

Gender	Assistant Professor	Associate Professor	Full Professor
Male	10	20	30
Female	30	15	10
Other	3	2	0

1. State the alternative hypothesis for the study.

   _____

2. What is the appropriate statistic to test this relationship? _____

   _____

3. What is the appropriate test for the effect size? _____

   _____

4. Compute the statistic and effect size. Write a couple of sentences describing your findings as you would in a Results section.

_____

_____

_____

5. Interpret the results for the administrator.

_____

_____

_____

Practice Exercise 3

Two judges for a poetry contest were asked to rank the 10 finalists' poems from 1 = best to 10 = least good. Their rankings are below:

Judge 1	1	2	3	4	5	6	7	8	9	10
Judge 2	4	7	3	1	9	2	10	8	5	6

1. What is the appropriate statistic to compute? _____

2. Compute the statistic with SPSS, by hand, or both, and write a few sentences describing your finding and its implications.

_____

_____

Focusing on the Individual

CASE STUDIES AND SINGLE *N* DESIGNS

(14)

CHAPTER SUMMARY

Previous chapters have focused on sample-based studies. The primary goal of sample-based studies is to extrapolate results to the population from which the sample was drawn, but it is not clear whether the results from such studies will be relevant or helpful to a specific individual. Chapter 14 outlines two alternatives to sample-based designs: the case study and the single *N* design. The case study is typically qualitative, whereas the single *N* design is quantitative. Effective use of each of these designs is discussed, along with the strengths and limitations of each. The chapter ends with a discussion of when to choose a sample, case study, or single *N* design.

REVIEW AND APPLICATION OF KEY CONCEPTS FROM CHAPTER 14

Exercise 14.1: Samples Versus Individuals (Review and Application)

1. Sample-based studies help us to determine whether a pattern or relationship found in the sample is likely to exist in the _____.

2. Sample-based studies cannot determine whether a pattern or relationship found in the sample is likely to exist in _____.

3. Sample-based evaluations of the Drug Abuse Resistance Education (DARE) program consistently show that it is ineffective. In other words, these studies suggest that it does not reduce the use of alcohol and drugs among children and adolescents. Explain why school administrators

LEARNING OUTCOMES

After reading and reviewing Chapter 14, you should understand

- Strengths and limitations of using sample-based studies

- What the case study is, how it is conducted, and its strengths and limitations

- What the single *N* study is, how to plan and conduct different types of single *N* designs, and the strengths and limitations of the different designs

- How to choose between a case study and single *N* design

should take such results seriously and look for alternative programs with demonstrated effectiveness.

_____

_____

_____

_____

4. After explaining the results of sample-based studies that suggest DARE is ineffective, you hear from one parent who tells you that DARE helped her child stay away from drugs. Explain how it is possible that DARE might have helped this child, even though sample-based studies suggest it is ineffective.

_____

_____

_____

_____

5. Provide an alternative explanation for why someone might believe that DARE was effective for a child, even though the program might not have caused a change in the child's behavior. (This is a review question about the criteria for causality. See Chapter 9 if you need a refresher.)

_____

_____

_____

_____

Exercise 14.2: Case Studies (Review)

1. Explain the strengths of the case study. _____

_____

_____

2. One should choose a case for a case study because that case is

a. _____

b. _____

c. _____

3. _____ uses several individual cases in order to build a theory.

4. _____ uses several individual cases within a group organization to understand the overall group or organization.

5. What are the limitations of the case study?

   a. _____

   b. _____

   c. _____

Exercise 14.3: Single *N* Designs (Review)

1. Does a single *N* design use qualitative or quantitative measures?

   _____

2. The goal of the single *N* design is to find a _____ relationship, but this type of design is best categorized as a _____ because there is no random assignment to condition.

3. A study that involves several single *N* studies is called a

   _____.

4. In the baseline phase, the _____ variable is measured without any manipulation.

5. The _____ is the ideal baseline that has no trend and little variability.

6. The baseline phase is also called phase _____.

7. The manipulation phase is called phase _____.

8. _____ is the simplest single *N* design.

9. A design with more than one manipulation is called a _____

   _____.

10. Three manipulations would be designated as _____, _____,
    and _____.

11. A single *N* design that includes a return to baseline is called a

    _____.

12. The simplest reversal design is the _____ design.

13. A _____ introduces the manipulation at different points across different _____,
    _____, or _____.

14. The primary way to analyze a single *N* design is _____, which involves comparing the baseline and manipulation phases. (Keep in mind there are more complex statistical analyses that can be used that you might learn in advanced courses.)

15. Why is a stable baseline important in a single *N* design?

_____

_____

Exercise 14.4: Stability of the Baseline (Application)

1. Client A keeps track of how many cigarettes she smokes over a 10-day period and finds the following results: 18, 20, 19, 20, 21, 18, 19, 20, 21, 20. Is this a stable baseline? Explain.

_____

2. Client B keeps track of how many cigarettes he smokes and finds the following results: 2, 5, 10, 7, 1, 0, 5, 8, 12, 9. Is this a stable baseline? Explain.

_____

3. Client C keeps track of how many cigarettes she smokes and finds the following results: 0, 3, 5, 7, 9, 11, 13, 15, 17, 19. Is this a stable baseline? Explain.

_____

4. Client D keeps track of how many cigarettes he smokes and finds the following results: 22, 20, 20, 16, 17, 15, 16, 16, 14, 12. Is this a stable baseline? Explain.

_____

5. If you wanted to implement and evaluate an intervention to help these clients reduce the amount they smoked, which *two* clients would be most ready to begin the manipulation phase? Explain.

_____

_____

_____

_____

_____

_____

Exercise 14.5: Single *N* Designs (Application)

1. A yoga student consistently meditated 10 minutes each day for 5 days. In order to increase the meditation time, the student tries to add nature sounds to the routine and is able to meditate for 14 minutes that day, 13 minutes the next day, and 15 minutes the following 3 days.

   a. Graph these results.

   b. Is there sufficient evidence to say that the intervention was effective? Explain.

   _____

   _____

   c. The yoga student is considering adding a return-to-baseline phase (ABA design).

      i. If the intervention is effective, what would the student expect to see? Graph an example ABA design (make up data for the second baseline):

ii. If the intervention is *not* effective, what would the student expect to see? Graph an example ABA design (make up data for the second baseline):

2. An individual is trying to drink less cola and wonders whether a simple note to himself saying, "Drink water, not cola!" will help. He conducts a multiple-baseline across settings to test the effectiveness of the note and finds the following:

Day:	1	2	3	4	5	6	7	8	9	10	11	12
Number of sodas drunk at home	Baseline:				Intervention:							
	4	5	4	4	3	2	1	1	2	3	2	1
Number of sodas drunk at work	Baseline:								Intervention:			
	6	6	7	6	7	7	5	6	7	6	7	7

a. Graph these data:

b. How would you interpret these results?

_____

_____

3. How would you interpret the following results from a multiple-manipulation design testing the effectiveness of two interventions designed to decrease procrastination?

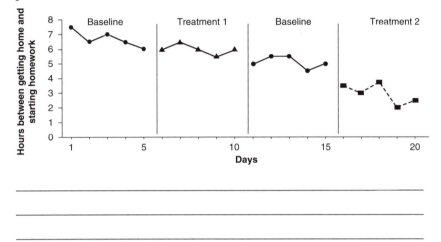

_____

_____

_____

Exercise 14.6: Return to Baseline Only When It Is Ethically Appropriate (Application)

1. If an AB design suggests that an individual spent more time meditating during the intervention stage than the baseline, would it be ethically appropriate to add a return-to-baseline phase? Explain.

_____

_____

_____

2. If an AB design suggests that an individual smoked less during the intervention stage than the baseline, would it be ethically appropriate to add a return-to-baseline phase? Explain.

_____

_____

_____

3. If an AB design suggests that an individual consistently drove while intoxicated during the baseline but stopped during the intervention, would it be ethically appropriate to add a return-to-baseline phase? Explain.

_____

_____

Exercise 14.7: Strengths and Limitations of Single *N* Designs (Review)

1. What are the unique strengths of single *N* designs?

   a. _____

   b. _____

   c. _____

2. Single *N* designs require one to be _____ in both measurement and implementation of the manipulation.

3. As with case studies, an advantage of single *N* designs is _____

   _____.

4. a. As with case studies, a limitation of single *N* designs is

      _____.

   b. However, single *N* designs have an advantage in this area in that the quantitative assessments are more _____.

Exercise 14.8: The Big Picture: Choosing Between a Sample, Case Study, or Single *N* Design (Application)

Identify which would be the best design for the following questions. Explain.

1. To determine whether a drug use treatment program is likely to be effective for a population.

   _____

2. To determine whether a drug use treatment program is effective for an individual.

   _____

3. To determine the process by which your high school principal decided which programs were beneficial for students and evaluated the cost/benefit ratio of implementing the program.

   _____

4. To understand how the director of the film *Moonlight* felt about winning the 2017 Academy Award for Best Picture after *La La Land* was first mistakenly given the award.

    _____

5. To understand how viewers felt when the film *Moonlight* was awarded the 2017 Academy Award for Best Picture after *La La Land* was first mistakenly given the award and whether reactions varied based on gender, age, or race.

    _____

6. To determine whether turning off your Internet access at home increases or decreases the amount of time you study.

    _____

YOUR RESEARCH

Is a Case Study or Single *N* Design a Good Choice for Your Topic?

1. Does your topic cover a unique phenomenon? Or do you have a reason to gain in-depth information about one individual or a handful of individuals?

   - If your answer is no to either of these questions, stop here. You should stick with one of the sample-based studies discussed in previous chapters.

   - If your answer is yes to either of these questions, answer questions 2 and 3.

2. Which is a better choice for your topic, a case study or single *N* design? Explain.

   _____

   _____

   _____

   _____

   _____

   _____

3. If you chose the case study method, explain whether or not an embedded case study or using grounded theory would be part of your methodology.

OR, if you chose the single N design, identify the specific design (AB, reversal, multiple baseline, multiple manipulation) you would use and why.

_____

_____

_____

_____

_____

_____

How to Decide?

CHOOSING A RESEARCH DESIGN AND SELECTING THE CORRECT ANALYSIS

CHAPTER SUMMARY

Chapter 15 is a review chapter, which means you can take stock of all that you have learned and focus on some key takeaway points about research methods and analyses. The first part of the chapter includes information about the decision-making process involved in choosing a research design. As always, you are reminded to base your study on past research, to consider internal and external validity, and to determine whether your goal is to describe, predict, or explain. Additionally, you should consider whether or not you will examine groups, and if so, you will need to decide the number of groups, whether to conduct an independent- or dependent-groups design, and whether or not to conduct a factorial design.

The second part of the chapter focuses on selecting the appropriate statistical analyses. The focus is on selecting analyses based on the type of data collected. The tables and figures in the chapter can help guide your decision-making process for any current or future research project. Remember that a single research study might contain different designs and different analyses, and the chapter highlights two examples from the research to illustrate this point.

We hope you take a moment to savor all that you have learned about research methods. We also hope that you will take these lessons with you as you move on to new challenges and opportunities.

LEARNING OUTCOMES

After reading and reviewing Chapter 15, you should understand

- How to choose a research design
- How to select the appropriate statistical analysis based on your data
- How to be a critical consumer and producer of research

REVIEW AND APPLICATION OF
KEY CONCEPTS FROM CHAPTER 15

Exercise 15.1: Choosing a Research Design (Review)

1. Once you choose a topic, you should then _____
    _____.

2. Descriptive and correlational designs generally have better
    _____ validity and quasi-experiments and experiments
    have better _____ validity.

3. Experiments have better _____ validity than
    quasi-experiments, but quasi-experiments generally have better
    _____ validity than experiments.

4. Fill in the name of the design:

    a. _____ designs are used to describe.

    b. _____ designs are used to predict.

    c. _____ designs are used to explain.

5. _____ designs may or may not examine groups, but
    _____ and _____
    designs always examine groups.

6. If you have a group design, you need to determine whether your groups will
    be _____ or _____.

7. Dependent group designs are _____ and _____.

8. Two reasons to choose a factorial design are

    a. _____

    b. _____

Exercise 15.2: Choosing a Research Design (Application)

1. Using Figure 15.1 in the textbook, decide whether a descriptive,
    correlational, or experimental design would be the best way to help answer
    each of the following questions:

    a. How much fast food do Americans eat?

    _____

b. Do married individuals eat more or less fast food than single individuals?

_____

c. Has television viewing increased, decreased, or stayed the same over the last 10 years? _____

d. Can watching comedies on television decrease depression? _____

_____

e. Does binge-watching a television series in one night versus watching the series over several weeks have an effect on anxiety?_____

f. Is there a relationship between age and binge-watching television? _____

_____

2. For the correlational designs above, identify the one(s) that

a. Will definitely examine groups: _____

b. May or may not examine groups: _____

_____

3. For the question, "Does binge watching a television series in one night versus watching the series over several weeks have an effect on anxiety?" what are some reasons for expanding from the current two-group design to a multiple-groups design?

_____

_____

4. Look at Figure 15.2 in the textbook to answer the following:

a. For the question, "Can watching comedies on television decrease depression?" explain why you might choose

i. an independent-groups design

_____

_____

ii. a dependent, matched-groups design

_____

_____

iii. a dependent, repeated-measures design

_____

_____

b. For the question, "Do married individuals eat more fast food than single individuals?" two out of the three designs in Figure 15.2 are possible choices.

   i. Which two are they and why?

   _____

   _____

   ii. Explain how you would decide between these two choices.

   _____

   _____

   _____

   _____

Exercise 15.3: Selecting Your Statistical Analyses (Application)

1. Use Figure 15.4 in the textbook to help identify the appropriate statistical analyses for each of the following questions:

   a. How much fast food do Americans eat? _____
   _____

   b. Do married individuals eat more or less fast food than single individuals?

      i. No matching: _____

      ii. Individuals matched on socioeconomic status: _____
      _____

   c. Does the amount of fast food eaten by married vs. single individuals depend on whether the individual is male or female?

      i. No matching: _____

      ii. Individuals matched on socioeconomic status: _____
      _____

   d. Does binge-watching a television series in one night versus watching the series over several weeks have an effect on anxiety?

      i. Independent groups design: _____

      ii. Dependent groups design: _____

   e. Are there differences in mood after watching a comedy, drama, or horror movie?

      i. Independent groups design: _____

      ii. Dependent groups design: _____

2. Identify three to five inferential statistics that you covered in your class. Come up with research questions that you could test with each statistic. We have provided an example for you to get you started, but this table is designed to help you review inferential statistics important in your class. We expect that your professor may have skipped or glossed over some of the statistics in this textbook.

Inferential statistic	A question that can be tested
Independent-samples *t* test	Are critical thinking skills better among those who have completed a research methods course than among those who have not yet completed such a course?

Exercise 15.4: Summary of Key Statistics (Review)

In the first column below, list all the inferential statistics you have learned in your course. Then fill in the rest of the table. Try this first without looking at Table 15.1 in your textbook, but then use that table to check your answers.

Inferential Statistic	When to use?	Effect size?	Post hoc?

(Continued)

(Continued)

YOUR RESEARCH

1. After reading past research on your topic, what are the primary questions that deserve further investigation?

   _____

   _____

   _____

   Choose one of these that interests you the most, you believe you could objectively study, and you could carry out given your time and resource limitations. Put an asterisk (*) next to the question or questions you chose.

2. Use Figure 15.1 of the textbook to help determine what type of research design you might use to help answer the research question you chose. Note your decision here.

   _____

   _____

3. If you are evaluating groups, use Figure 15.2 in the textbook to help you decide whether your groups should be independent or matched or whether you should use repeated measures. Note your decision here.

   _____

   _____

4. Does it make sense to do a factorial design? Why or why not?

   _____

   _____

5. What inferential statistic would you use to help answer the question? Explain.

   _____

   _____

Answers to Odd-Numbered Questions and Data Analysis Practices

(Instructors have access to the complete answer keys.)

CHAPTER 1

Exercise 1.1

There are no right or wrong answers. Rather, the goal is for you to practice thinking critically and thinking like a researcher.

Exercise 1.2

1. nonmaleficence

3. anonymity

5. informed consent; debriefing

7. deception; debriefing

Exercise 1.3

1. The ethical principle of nonmaleficence was violated because the experiment harmed the participants (or you might have framed this as a violation of beneficence). Additionally, the study violated the principle of respect (which is named slightly differently across the different ethics codes, e.g., APA names this "respect for people's rights and dignity" whereas AAA names this "responsibility to people").

3. a. How does this research advance disciplinary knowledge and how might it benefit individuals or society? A study must have some merit for it to be ethical.

   b. Will the researcher interact with individuals on the social media site or will it be purely observational? If it is a completely unobtrusive observation of an open social media site, the researcher does not need to obtain informed consent or debrief participants. However, if the researcher plans to interact with those on the social media site, then informed consent and debriefing are likely required.

c. If the researcher interacts with individuals, will there be deception? For example, will the researcher pretend to be someone that he or she is not? If deception is used, the researcher must be sure to avoid causing emotional distress and debrief as soon as possible.

d. How does the researcher plan to handle data? The social media site is anonymous, but the members might still reveal personal or identifying information that the researcher must keep confidential.

5. a. Deception is the primary ethical issue in this study, and the participants might experience emotional distress if they were to find out that the researcher was actually a woman who lied to obtain personal information from the clients. Moreover, the clients had not agreed to be part of a research study (there was no informed consent), and a therapy group would be considered a private space.

b. It is unlikely that an IRB would approve this study because the risks to participants are not justified by the benefits.

c. Although there is still some deception, the researcher in this case is in a public space and is not interacting with participants. If the researcher can demonstrate that the deception is justified and she maintains the confidentiality of those she observes, this study is ethically acceptable.

Exercise 1.4

1. The steps in the scientific method are

- Step 1: Identify a topic
- Step 2: Find, read, and evaluate past research
- Step 3: Refine topic and develop a hypothesis
- Step 4: Design the study
- Step 5: Carry out the study
- Step 6: Analyze the data
- Step 7: Communicate results

3. experimental

5. correlational

7. independent; assigned; dependent

Exercise 1.5

1. The following studies can be examined with an experiment:

b. Can political campaigns raise more money using negative campaign ads?

c. Are attractive people perceived as more or less intelligent than not-so-attractive people?

h. Can daily statements of gratitude improve one's well-being?

Note that technically, *e* could be made into an experiment, but it would not be ethical to expose someone to violence if it is expected to increase heart disease.

3. a. Do student athletes study more or less than nonathletes?
   Correlational

   d. How do individuals perceive their local police department?
   Descriptive

   e. Does exposure to violence increase risk of heart disease?
   Correlational

   f. Are people who take a lot of "selfies" narcissistic?
   Correlational

   g. Is humanity becoming more or less violent?
   Descriptive

Exercise 1.6

Student 1: This is plagiarism. Student 1 correctly cited the source and thus credited Cash and Whittingham (2010) for the ideas. However, because he or she copied the excerpt word for word and did not use quotation marks, the student is passing Cash and Whittingham's words off as his or her own.

Student 3: This is plagiarism. Student 3 used quotation marks for the phrases that belong to Cash and Whittingham (2010) but did not credit those authors for the words or the ideas by including a citation.

Exercise 1.7

1. No. A single study can never prove a result. A single study can only examine one part of a population in a very specific way, so it remains unclear whether the results will hold true for other participants, methods, and settings.

3. If research consistently finds that mindfulness training is an effective stress-reduction strategy, we could say with some confidence that there is a good chance that mindfulness training will work.

5. Science helps us understand a phenomenon when multiple studies find similar results, and then the process of science can help us to identify and help answer increasingly complex and in-depth questions about that phenomenon.

CHAPTER 2

Exercise 2.1

1. scholarly

3. secondary

5. primary; scholarly

Exercise 2.2

1. True

3. peer review

5. conference presentations; unpublished manuscripts

Exercise 2.3

1. a. popular   b. primary

3. a. scholarly   b. primary

5. a. The first (by Ansari) and fourth (by Lewandowski)

    b. The second (by Eastwick)

    c. The third (by Hitsch)

Exercise 2.4

1. a. Sara Staats, Julie M. Hupp, and Anna Hagley

    b. 2008

    c. *The Journal of Psychology: Interdisciplinary and Applied*

    d. 142

    e. pp. 357–372

    f. primary

3. 494

5. 66

Exercise 2.5

1. Title; Authors; Abstract; Introduction; Method; Results; Discussion; References

3. Method

5. Results; Discussion

7. Discussion

9. Introduction

Exercise 2.6

1. "Practice makes perfect: Improving students' skills in understanding and avoiding plagiarism with a themed methods course."

3. Primary

5. Plagiarism has been a long-standing issue among college students, and one reason for this might be that students do not fully understand what plagiarism is.

7. Explain the purpose of the current study and provide the hypothesis.

9. Answer should reflect that the researchers found that compared to the control group, those in the plagiarism-themed course were better able to identify and avoid plagiarism and appeared to have a better understanding of why avoiding plagiarism is important.

Exercise 2.7

1. a. Foster (2013)

   b. (Estow et al., 2011)

   c. Kurzban and Weeden (2005)

   d. Li et al. (2013)

   e. (Buss & Schmitt, 1993)

3.

Many of us like to believe that "beauty comes from within" and that that inner beauty is more important than physical beauty. However, research suggests that physical attractiveness is the single most important factor that impacts our desire to date someone (Kurzban & Weeden, 2005; Li et al., 2013). An early cross cultural survey conducted by Buss ~~&~~**and** Schmitt **(1993)** found that across the world physical attractiveness of one's partner was more important for men than it was for women ~~(1993)~~. A more recent meta-analysis found that gender differences only occur in ratings of ideal romantic partners and ratings of hypothetical target. Both men and women generally find physical attractiveness equally important in actual face-to-face interactions (Eastwick, Luchies, Finkel, & Hunt, 2014). Moreover, although we might all desire an attractive partner, we tend to wind up with someone who matches our levei of physical attractiveness (Miller, (2010). Thus our stated preferences do not fully predict our actual dating behaviors (Eastwick~~, Luchies, Finkel, & Hunt,~~ **et al.,** 2014).

Exercise 2.8

1. Finding, reading, and evaluating past research helps to identify the current state of knowledge in an area and helps to identify questions that should be examined by future research in order to progress scientific understanding.

CHAPTER 3

Exercise 3.1

1. reliability

3. reliability

5. reliability

7. validity

Exercise 3.2

1. construct

3. quantitative

5. true (absolute) zero

7. ratio

9. ordinal

Exercise 3.3

1. questionnaire

   a. stem; response

   b. scale score

   c. open-ended; closed-ended

   d. open-ended

   e. closed-ended

   f. forced-choice

   g. open-ended; closed-ended

   h. For example: How much time do you spend on your cell phone each day?
   _____

   i. For example: What is the most frequent activity you complete on your cell phone? (check one)

Texting _____   Calls _____   Facebook _____   Games _____

j.

Format	Advantage	Limitation
Open-ended format	Allows participants to state their own ideas/views; doesn't limit participants to researchers' preconceived responses	Interpretation can be time-consuming and difficult Comparison of responses can be difficult
Closed-ended format	Easier to compile, analyze, and compare across participants/ groups	Response choices may not represent participants' view

3. physiological measures

    a. For example, a person's blood pressure, heart rate, respiration rate, GSR, etc.

    b. the equipment required is not available to them, or the equipment or assessment may require advanced training.

Exercise 3.4

1. interrater reliability

3. Cronbach's alpha

5. even; odd

7. test-retest

Exercise 3.5

1. face validity; construct validity

3. divergent validity

5. predictive validity

7.

Measurement Reliability	Measurement Validity

I. Internal consistency
   A. Cronbach's alpha (α)
   B. Split-half reliability
II. Test-retest reliability
III. Alternate forms reliability
IV. Interrater reliability
	I. Face validity
	II. Construct validity
	   A. Content validity
	   B. Convergent validity
	   C. Divergent validity
	   D. Criterion validity
	      i. Concurrent validity
	      ii. Predictive validity

Exercise 3.6

1. Test-retest is the only type of measurement reliability that can assess a single-item measure. The political scientist should have people respond to the item once and then again some time later (e.g., a week later). Then she should correlate the scores on the two responses for all of her sample.

3. a. Cronbach's alpha (α) to assess internal consistency. After any needed recoding of items in the 5-item scale, Cronbach's could be computed on the non-altered items and the recoded one. If $\alpha < .70$, the output should be reviewed to scc if omitting an item or two will increase α to meet the .70 criteria.

    Split-half reliability: The scores on the even and odd items could be correlated to check for internal consistency.

    Test-retest: The anxiety scale could be administered to the same sample at different times.

    The researcher should not try to assess interrater reliability as he is assessing a scale and not observing behaviors. He also can't check alternate forms reliability unless he has two different (but comparable) forms of the anxiety scale.

    b. The content validity of the anxiety scale could be assessed by asking mental health professionals to evaluate the items on the scale and/or by reviewing published scholarly articles on anxiety or comparing items to the DSM-5.

    He could also assess convergent validity by comparing scores on his measure to a measure of anxiety or stress with established reliability and validity; divergent validity by comparing scores to a scale not measuring anxiety (maybe a measure of life satisfaction); concurrent validity to a measure of current insomnia; predictive validity to health problems six months later.

Exercise 3.7

1. reliability

3. internal; external

5. internal validity; external validity

7. External validity

Exercise 3.8

1. literal

3. study

5. External

Exercise 3.9

1. internal consistency

3. reliable

Chapter 3: IBM® SPSS® Practice Exercises

Practice Exercise 1

1. Enter data for the Academic Honesty Dataset.

2. Recode #2 and #3 in the questionnaire so that higher scores represent stronger values for academic honesty.

3. a. Reliability: alpha (α) = .83

   b. Decision: The scale shows solid internal consistency as the Cronbach's value is greater than .70.

4. Total scores are shown below (in order of participant ID number):
   22.00
   12.00
   19.00
   21.00
   20.00
   21.00
   12.00
   14.00
   17.00
   10.00

CHAPTER 4

Exercise 4.1

1. prevalence

3. prevalence

5. trend

7. trend

Exercise 4.2

1. These questions can be tested with a descriptive study: 1, 3, 4, 6, 7, 8.

   Question 2 cannot be tested with a descriptive study because the question requires examining a relationship between age and popularity of the show (this could be examined with a correlational study).

   Question 5 cannot be tested with a descriptive study because the question requires an examination of a causal relationship between killing a character and anxiety (this could be examined with an experiment).

   Question 9 cannot be examined with any research study (at least not until 200 years have passed).

Exercise 4.3

1. Study

3. pilot study

5. as

7. internal; less

Exercise 4.4

1. survey research (or surveys)

3. overt; covert

5. confederate

7. narrative

9. rating scale

11. Archival

13.

Description of Bias	Name of Bias	How to Reduce (list strategies)
Observers focus on behaviors or interpretations that support their expectations.	Observer bias	1. blind observers 2. multiple observers 3. training of observers 4. The more structured the observation, the less room for bias
Interviewers provide verbal or nonverbal cues that impact the participants' responses.	Interviewer bias	1. training of interviewer(s) 2. The more structured the interview, the less room for bias
Participants respond based on what they think is socially acceptable or how the want to be perceived.	Social desirability bias	1. anonymity (easiest for questionnaires) 2. neutrally worded questions 3. Include questions to test for validity of participants' responses

Exercise 4.5

1. Survey

   a. Advantage: The main advantage of a survey is that you can obtain student opinions and attitudes that you could not observe. Disadvantage: The main disadvantage is that surveys are subject to the social desirability bias, in that the students might want to appear to have more or less team spirit based on how they want to appear, what they think is the socially appropriate answer, or what they think you want to hear.

   b. You may have chosen either an interview or questionnaire. If you chose an interview, you could obtain more detailed responses and participants might be more likely to carefully consider the questions. A semi-structured interview would allow you to ask follow-up questions. If you chose a questionnaire, you could have many participants, the questionnaire could be anonymous (to reduce the social desirability bias), and administration would be easy.

3. Archival Research

   a. If your college keeps track of game attendance or purchases of team paraphernalia, that could be useful information to tell you how popular the team is.

b. Attendance records might be public, or you might need to talk with the coaches or school administration. Attendance would not answer questions about how people view the team, and like observations, you would not know why people attended or not. Unlike observations, you would not know how those who attended acted at the game. Perhaps they were enthusiastically rooting for the team, or perhaps they were disinterested or even hostile. Buying team paraphernalia does not necessarily tell you why students attended a game: they may buy t-shirts, hats, etc. because they support the college/university rather than the team or because they needed the item.

Exercise 4.6

1. population

3. sample

5. probability sampling (or random sampling); random selection

Exercise 4.7

Identify the specific type of probability or nonprobability sampling described.

Description	Probability Sampling	Nonprobability Sampling
Uses random selection? (yes or no)	YES	NO
Most basic method	simple random sampling	convenience sampling
Sample proportions of a key characteristic match population proportions	stratified random sampling	quota sampling
Identify clusters instead of individuals within population	cluster sampling	---------
Sample represents extremes within a population	------------	maximum variation sampling
Participants recruit others	------------	snowball sampling

Exercise 4.8

1. *Game of Thrones* interview:

   a. Randomly select a sample from the list of characters. You could do this by writing all the character names on separate pieces of paper, mixing them up, and then randomly selecting the sample. Or, you could transfer the list to a program such as SPSS and use the program to select your sample. Once you have your sample, you will need to try to interview the entire sample. Keep track of and attempt to reduce the nonresponse bias.

b. Stratified random sampling; create separate lists for males and females, determine what proportion of your population is male vs. female, then randomly select from each of those lists in proportions equal to that in the population. For example, if 60% of Game of Thrones actors are male and 40% are female, then you should select a number of male actors that represents 60% of the total sample and 40% of the random sample should be female. Once you have identified your sample, you will need to try to interview the entire sample. Keep track of and attempt to reduce the nonresponse bias.

c. Minimum sample size:
    i. 97
    ii. 44

Exercise 4.9

1. The main advantage of using nonprobability sampling is that it is a lot easier and less time-consuming than probability sampling. If you are trying to interview actors, it is unlikely that you'll have access to everyone equally. In other words, you might identify a random sample of the actors but then not be able to actually interview those people in your sample. In probability sampling, you can't just include those who are willing to be interviewed. Additionally, sample size estimates from Exercise 4.8 suggest that you would need a pretty large proportion of the population in order for probability sampling to yield a representative sample, and it might be unrealistic for you to interview that many actors even if you did have access to them.

    With nonprobability sampling you could interview those who are willing, and you could even ask the actors you interviewed to help you reach other actors from the show (as in snowball sampling).

3. Snowball sampling would start out like convenience sampling, but you would also ask the actors you interviewed to help you recruit other actors for your study.

5. Maximum variation sampling; You would identify the extremes you are examining and then try to get at least one participant who meets each criterion (so one star actor, and one unknown extra, and someone who played a character that was killed and another who played a character that lived, etc.).

Exercise 4.10

1. descriptive

3. experimental

Chapter 4: IBM® SPSS® Practice Exercises

3. a. Check your new dataset to make sure there are 44 cases.

   b. ii. The median is 2.
      iii. Create a new variable so that values 1 through 2 = 1 (low) and values 3 through 6 = 2 (high). You should have 75 in the low category and 54 in the high category.

   d. Check your new datasets to make sure one contains 26 cases, all coded as low number of seasons, and the other contains 18 cases, all coded as a high number of seasons.

CHAPTER 5

Exercise 5.1

1. coding *or* numerical coding (numerical coding involves categorizing and numbering, whereas coding just involves categorizing)

3. central tendency

5. variability

7. frequency or percentage (answer can be in either order)

9. z score

Exercise 5.2

1. $f_{online} = 7; f_{store} = 11; f_{catalog} = 2$

3. mode; store

Exercise 5.3

1. 40%

3. 10

5. 6

Exercise 5.4

1. mean; 2

3. bimodal

5. skewed

7. median; observed minimum and maximum OR range

9. Split the sample into two normally distributed distributions and report the mean and standard deviation of each distribution; report both modes.

Exercise 5.5

1. a.

Hours (Predicted)	f
1	1
2	3
3	5
4	2
5	1

b.

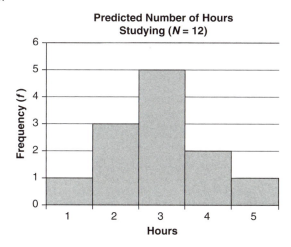

c. Yes

d. The mean is the best measure of central tendency for normally distributed data. To calculate by hand, add up all the scores and then divide by N:

$M = (1 + 2 + 2 + 2 + 3 + 3 + 3 + 3 + 3 + 4 + 4 + 5)/12$
$M = 2.92$

e. The standard deviation is the best measure for normally distributed data. To calculate by hand, use the following formula:

$$SD = \sqrt{\frac{\sum(X - M)^2}{N - 1}}$$

First calculate the squared difference $(X - M)^2$ for each score, and then multiply it by the frequency of each score:

hours (X)	f	X − M	(X − M)²	(X − M)² × f
1	1	1 − 2.92 = −1.92	3.6864	3.6864 × 1 − 3.6864
2	3	2 − 2.92 = −0.92	0.8464	0.8464 × 3 = 2.5392
3	5	3 − 2.92 = 0.08	0.0064	0.0064 × 5 = 0.32
4	2	4 − 2.92 = 1.08	1.1664	1.1664 × 2 = 2.3328
5	1	5 − 2.92 = 2.08	4.3264	4.3264 × 1 = 4.3264

Calculate the sum of the squared differences by adding all the numbers in the last column.

$$\sum(X - M)^2 = 3.6864 + 2.5392 + 0.32 + 2.3328 + 4.3264 = 13.2048$$

Next, divide the sum of the squared differences $\left[\sum(X - M)^2\right]$ by one less our sample size $(N - 1)$.

$13.2048/11 = 1.2004$

Finally, take the square root of that number.

$SD = \sqrt{1.2004} = 1.10$ (rounded)

Exercise 5.6

1. A z score is a score standardized to standard deviations from the mean of the distribution. A z score helps us evaluate individual scores within a distribution. We can quickly see how far any score deviated from the mean. For example, a z score of 1 indicates a score that is one standard deviation above the mean, and a z score of −3.2 indicates a score that is 3.2 standard deviations below the mean.

3. A percentage is based on actual scores, so that a 95% indicates that the student correctly answered 95% of the exam questions. On the other hand, a percentile is relative to all the scores in the distribution. Scoring in the 95th percentile indicates that the student did better than 95% of the other students. On an easy exam, that might mean that the student scored nearly 100%, or on a tougher exam, that might mean the student scored only 60%. The percentiles depend on how well everyone else did.

Exercise 5.7

1. Include five of the following: data entry errors, coder errors, participants' misunderstanding a question or not reporting accurate information, not using reliable measures, not using valid measures, conducting inappropriate statistics, reporting inappropriate or incorrect statistics.

Chapter 5: IBM® SPSS® Practice Exercises

Practice Exercise 1

1. The authors report the Cronbach's alpha for the Research Methods Attitude Scale. Cronbach's alpha is an indicator of internal consistency. They created a total score using three items, which resulted in a very strong alpha of .88.

2. The only type of construct validity that can be gleaned from the information is content validity. Content validity can be evaluated by examining the three questions that make up the Research Methods Attitude Scale. In this case, the three items (*Research Methods is a good learning experience, I am afraid of Research Methods* [recoded], *I look forward to Research Methods*) appear to assess the intended content. The items were related to feedback provided by students in previous research methods courses.

3. Answers will vary. Check to make sure your paragraph is grammatically correct, concise, and reports statistics using correct APA format.

Practice Exercise 3

3. a. The question ("responseC") is measured on a nominal scale, so you should run a frequency command in SPSS but not request any additional statistics.

    b. Select if "youfreq" = 0

    Then run a frequency command in SPSS for "responseC"

    c. Select all
    Split file (compare groups by "status")
    Then run a frequency command in SPSS for "responseC"

    d. Below is an example. Your write-up should contain similar information.

Results

Participants were asked if students who plagiarized should be allowed to redo the assignment. Only 39 of the 152 participants (26%) endorsed this policy, with the majority indicating that this was not an appropriate response. Endorsement was even lower among the 91 participants who reported they had never plagiarized ($n = 21$; 23%). We also compared those who were currently undergraduates ($n = 102$) to those who were not ($n = 50$). The proportion of undergraduates in our sample who endorsed a redo policy was slightly higher compared to those who were not undergraduates (27% vs. 22%), but overall both groups disagreed with allowing plagiarism offenders to redo an assignment.

CHAPTER 6

Exercise 6.1

1. Inferential

3. Mu (μ)

5.

Descriptive	Inferential
sample	**population**
statistic	parameter
mean (*M*)	**mu (μ)**
standard deviation (*SD*)	sigma (σ)

7. Hypothesis testing

Exercise 6.2

1. alternative

3. reject

5. reject; have

7. chance alone; do not

9. more; there is a smaller region of rejection in each tail of the sampling distribution (because the region of rejection is divided and half of it is in each tail)

11. critical

13. Type I; *p* value

15. probability

17. power

Exercise 6.3

1. null

3. alternative; directional

5. First you name a percentage occurring for all households, say 30%. You would then draw a sample of 50 (or whatever *N* you select) households

and compute the mean percentage of income spent on housing for each sample. You would repeat this process of drawing a sample of 50 households and computing their mean percentage of income many times. You would then have a distribution of means of percentage of income that should vary around a mean of 30%. This distribution of means is the sampling distribution for your study.

7. a. State the null hypothesis. H_0: Males and females will not differ in how often they bully their classmates.

   b. State the alternative hypothesis. In this case, a one-tailed (directional) hypothesis is appropriate. H_a: Males will bully their classmates more often than females.

   c. Determine the sampling distribution and criterion level. The sampling distribution is determined by the null hypothesis, so there should be a mean of zero difference between the frequency of bullying by the two genders. This would be determined by drawing multiple samples (of the same size) of students who report how often they have bullied and comparing the male and female means. You would typically select .05 as the criterion level.

   d. Collect information about frequency of bullying from a sample of male and female students and compute statistics to compare their responses.

   e. Compare your results to the sampling distribution, which has a mean difference of 0 (no difference in frequency of bullying between males and females).

   f. Decide whether to reject or retain your null hypothesis.

   g. Consider the possibility of a Type I error (if you rejected the null) or a Type II error (if you retained the null).

9. a. yes because $p < .05$

   b. reject

   c. probability of Type I = .04; no probability of Type II

   d. i.   use $p < .01$ as the criterion level
       ii. use a two-tailed rather than one-tailed test

11. The second study with more participants is likely to have more power.

   a. The mean of bullying for the larger sample size is likely to better represent the population mean.

   b. The sample with just 4th graders is more homogeneous than the K–5 sample and so error is decreased.

Exercise 6.4

1. effect size

3. practical significance

5. percentage of variability accounted for

Exercise 6.5

1. a. weak

   b. strong

   c. moderate

   d. strong

   e. weak

   f. moderate

   g. weak

3. a. yes

   b. Although the exam mean for the second-year students is higher than the mean for the first-year students, there is a great deal of overlap in the confidence intervals. First years' interval ranged from 71.70 to 78.88, while the second years' ranged from 74.11 to 86.55, suggesting the two distributions could represent the same population.

   c. Scores for first-years were in the C range, whereas the average score for second-years was a low B, and the confidence interval ranged from a mid-C to a mid-B. Although we would not want to make too much of these differences, it appears that there is a practical difference in grades between first and second years.

Exercise 6.6

1. a. Statistical significance reports the probability of obtaining a result by chance alone, given the sampling distribution defined by the null hypothesis. It provides some confidence that rarely would we get our results if there was no difference in the population.

   b. Effect size provides the magnitude of an effect. This tells us how strong the impact of our variable is, which helps us to judge whether our variable has a noticeable impact.

   c. Confidence intervals help us to see the range of expected values for the population value, given our results. If the range is large, it is not very helpful in identifying the population value, but a small confidence interval suggests our data are representative of the population value.

d. Practical significance is an interpretation of the usefulness of our findings in everyday life. We would like our findings to have implications outside of the laboratory and to help us better understand, explain, and predict behavior.

3. a. The p value = .003 and tells you that the results of your recycling study would occur only .3% of the time if there were no difference between the convenience group and flyer group. You would interpret it as meaning you found a significant difference in the amount of material recycled by the two groups.

b. The effect size is moderate to strong (very close to the accepted cutoff of 25% for a strong effect). You would be confident that making recycling convenient increases the amount of material recycled.

c. You are confident that 95% of the time the population value for recycling for the convenience group would be between 20.25 and 29.75 pounds, while for the flyer group it would be between 6.50 and 13.50 pounds. Because there is no overlap in the expected population means for the two groups, you are confident that they represent different populations.

d. The convenience group had a mean of 25 pounds of recycled material, while the flyer group recycled a mean of 10 pounds. If the 15-pound difference represented only one month, that would suggest quite a large difference in recycling over a year, one that could make a large difference in land fill size and in reuse of materials. If the difference was over a year, the practical significance is much less.

5. a. The first study had statistically significant results; the p value was .003, which is less than .05.

b. The first study had a stronger effect size, with a moderate to strong effect size (22% of the variance accounted for). The second one had a weak effect size (Cohen's d = .25).

c. The first study has more practical significance as the difference between the means for the two groups is noticeable *and* the variability is relatively small, suggesting that the measure of recycling amount is a reliable one. Although the means for recycling were the same for the two groups, in the second study there is much more variability in the scores, so we are not sure that we have a reliable measure. Remember that practical significance is a matter of interpretation, so different researchers may interpret the same data somewhat differently.

Chapter 6: IBM® SPSS® Practice Exercises

1. You should have two variables, one for the tip percentage and one for the waiter (coded as 1 and 2).

2. Tip percentage is a ratio variable, and you therefore should have requested a skewness statistic along with descriptive statistics such as the mean and standard deviation.

3. To compare the two waiters, first split the file by waiter. Then calculate the same descriptive statistics you did for question 2.

4. Turn off the split file and then calculate the confidence interval for the full sample using the one-sample t test command. Then split file by waiter and run the one-sample t test command again.

5. Answers will vary. Following are some guidelines and an example:

   - The distribution for the full sample met the criteria for a normal distribution and therefore, at minimum, you would report the mean and standard deviation for tip percentage ($M = .18$, $SD = .05$).

   - The distributions for each waiter met the criteria for a normal curve, and therefore, at minimum, you should report the means and standard deviations for each waiter. The first waiter earned a mean tip percentage of .17 ($SD = .04$), and the second waiter earned a mean tip percentage of .19 ($SD = .06$).

   - The 95% confidence interval for the entire sample is .15 to .20. For the first waiter it is .14 to .20, and for the second waiter it is .14 to .23. Considering how much overlap exists between these two confidence intervals, it appears that the two waiters fared about equally well.

Results

Results indicated that on average, the waiters earned a tip percentage of .18 ($SD = .05$), 95% CI [.15, .20]. One waiter earned a slightly higher percentage ($M = .19$, $SD = .06$), 95% CI [.14, .23] than the other ($M = .17$, $SD = .06$), 95% CI [.14, .20]. However, the overlap of the confidence intervals suggests that the waiters are likely to earn similar tip percentages.

6. One waiter received tips that were on average 2% more of a customer's bill than the other waiter. That could be a trivial or a meaningful amount of money, depending on the actual bill and how many total customers the waiters had (e.g., a 2% tip difference from a $5 bill would only be 10 cents, but for a $500 bill it would be $10, which would add up if the waiters had many customers throughout the evening). It would be helpful to know the actual amount of money that the waiters took home in addition to the tip percentages to better determine the practical significance.

CHAPTER 7

Exercise 7.1

1. one-sample *t* test

3. nominal

Exercise 7.2

1. null

3. directional alternative

5.

A Results section should include
1. **Variables analyzed and their descriptive statistics**
2. Type of statistical test(s)
3. **Results of test, effect size, confidence interval**
A Discussion section should include
1. **Major findings and whether they support the hypothesis**
2. Interpretation of findings, including how they fit with previous research
3. **Practical significance or implications**
4. Possible limitations of the study
5. **Appropriate next research to address limitations/flaws or next steps**

Exercise 7.3

1. a. one-sample *t* test

   b. Directional because you are predicting that fathers will talk more than the national average and not just a different amount of time.

   c. H_a: Fathers who have completed a parenting class will spend more time talking to their toddlers than the national average for fathers.

3. A one-sample *t* test requires that data are measured on an interval or ratio scale, but choice of candidates in an election is measured on a nominal scale.

Exercise 7.4

1. standard error of the means

3.

Statistic	Symbol
sample mean	M
population mean	μ
standard deviation	SD
sample size	N

5. critical

Exercise 7.5

1. 24

3. a. 2.145

   b. yes

   c. The obtained/calculated t value is greater than the critical t value.

   d. 15

   e. Fathers who participated in a parenting class talked significantly more to their toddlers than the national average time for fathers.

5. a. The percentage of trips during which your classmates use their cell phones while driving does not differ from the national average for using cell phones while driving.

   b. Directional: Students use their cell phones while driving less often than the national average. Nondirectional: Students' use of their cell phones while driving is different from the national average.

   c. The question stated in the study description states a direction (significantly less use), so the directional alternative hypothesis is more appropriate.

   d. $t = \dfrac{M - \mu}{SD\sqrt{N}} = \dfrac{.52 - .60}{.10\sqrt{25}} = \dfrac{.08}{.10(5)} = -.16$

   e. No; the critical t value for $df = 24$ for a two-tailed test at $p < .05 = 2.060$, which is larger than the calculated t value.

   f. zero; some probability of Type II error

   g. $d = \dfrac{M - \mu}{SD} = \dfrac{.52 - .60}{.10} = \dfrac{.08}{.10} = .80$

h. Your answer should follow APA format for reporting the variable measured, descriptive statistics, and statistical test and results. Include all of the information requested.

i. The results (significance and effect size) should be stated without listing the statistics. State whether you supported your hypothesis. Include all of the other information requested.

Exercise 7.6

1. effect size

3. a. eta squared

   b. 15% of the variability in calories consumed is accounted for by the group (obese 5-year-olds); moderate

Exercise 7.7

1. confidence interval

3. You are 95% confident that the difference between your sample mean and the population mean falls between 3.30 and 5.70 minutes.

Exercise 7.8

Be sure to follow the format your instructor prefers. Write clearly and succinctly.

1. Center and bold the heading "Results." Report the variable measured (general science knowledge) and descriptive statistics (M and SD), state the mean is higher than the national average, type of statistical test (one-sample t test), and outcome [significant difference, $t(15) = 2.34$, $p = .033$]. In addition, report one of the effect sizes (eta square or Cohen's d). If your instructor prefers, you may report the 95% confidence interval for the mean-mu difference.

Exercise 7.9

1. one-sample t test

3. one-sample t test

5. chi-square goodness of fit

7. one-sample t test

Chapter 7: IBM® SPSS® Practice Exercise

1. You should have calculated a one-sample *t* test.

   ### *T* Test

One-Sample Statistics				
	N	Mean	Std. Deviation	Std. Error Mean
percentage with cell	25	.4420	.22247	.04449

One-Sample Test						
	Test Value = .60					
					95% Confidence Interval of the Difference	
	t	*df*	Sig. (2-tailed)	Mean Difference	Lower	Upper
percentage with cell	−3.551	24	.002	−.15800	−.2498	−.0662

2. Yes. The sample average of .44 (*SD* = .22) was less than the national average of .60, and the *p* value from the one-sample *t* test (*p* = .002) met the criteria for statistical significance of *p* < .05.

3. The chance of a Type I error is .2%, and because we rejected the null there is no chance of a Type II error.

4. *d* = .72

5. The sample average was 16% less than the national average, which suggests that the sample might be less prone to accidents caused by cell phone use. However, an average of 44% (or almost half) of the students still reported using their cell phone while driving, which is a risky behavior.

6. Answers will vary. Following is an example.

Results

We calculated a one-sample *t* test to test the hypothesis that a college sample would use their cell phones while driving less than the national average of 60%. The sample average (*M* = .44, *SD* = .22) was significantly lower, *t*(24) = −3.55, *p* = .002, *d* = .72.

7. Should include the following:

- Review of major findings
- Interpretation of findings, including how they fit with previous research
- Discuss implications/practical significance of findings
- Possible limitations of the study
- Suggest possible future studies

CHAPTER 8

Exercise 8.1

1. correlational

3.

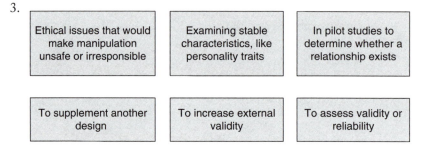

5. a. ceiling

   b. floor

Exercise 8.2

1. correlational; unethical

3. You are correct in suggesting a correlational design as you would not want to impose risk-taking behaviors on the sample. That would be unethical.

5. No; a correlational design is strengthened by variables with established validity. The ratings of the supervisor could be affected by many variables, including that the supervisor is rating both characteristics for the workers. The 10-point range may also not be wide enough to establish a correlation.

7. ceiling; decrease

Exercise 8.3

1. Pearson's correlation coefficient (r)

3. positive

5. +1.0 and −1.0

7. scatterplot or scattergram

9. straight line with all the points on it; +1.0

Exercise 8.4

1. negative

3. math anxiety and statistics exam scores; −.63 is closer to the absolute value of 1.0 than .34, so the negative correlation is stronger than the positive one.

5. a. The graph depicts a positive correlation between salary and education, which appears to be strong.

   b. Pearson's r

Exercise 8.5

1. a. H_0: Health status and time exercising are not related.

   b. H_a: Health status is positively related to time spent exercising each week.

   c. 28

   d. No; Using a two-tailed test for 28 df, the critical r value = .36. The obtained r = .32, which is less than the critical value. The relationship is not significant.

Exercise 8.6

1. point-biserial correlation coefficient; r_{pb}

Exercise 8.7

1. a. Pearson's r

   b. related humor and disparaging humor

   c. yes; p = .02, which is less than .05

   d. r^2 = .02; The relationship between the two types of humor accounts for 2% of the variability; weak effect

   e. Answers will vary. Following is an example.

Results

A Pearson's correlation coefficient was computed to examine the relationship between related humor and disparaging humor that were used in the classroom. The relationship was significant, r = .15, p = .02. Two percent of the variability was accounted for by the relationship between the two variables.

(If we had the descriptive statistics [M, SD] for the two variables, we would also have included that information in the Results.)

   f. The hypothesis was supported, and a weak positive relationship was found between student ratings of professors' use of related and disparaging humor in the classroom. Although the relationship is not strong, the findings could suggest that professors who use humor may use more than one type, or students' interpretation of different types of humorous comments are related (similar). The effect size (r^2) is very weak and very little of the variability in the scores is accounted for, so you should not make too much of the relationship. You should incorporate evidence from past research to support your interpretation of the results.

3. a. point-biserial correlation or r_{pb}

    b. yes; p = .02, which is less than .05

    c. .02 or 2%; no chance of a Type II error because we would reject the null hypothesis

    d. Answers will vary. Following is an example.

Results

A point-biserial correlation coefficient was computed to explore the relationship between pet ownership (yes/no) and happiness. The result was significant, r_{pb} = −.42, p = .02, indicating that those who owned pets tended to be happier.

(If you had the frequency of owning/not owning pets and the *M*, *SD* for happiness, you would also include these statistics.)

    e. Elderly people who live independently should be encouraged to own pets, given the relationship between pet ownership and happiness. Of course, other factors will need to be considered: health of the elderly, allergies, financial status, size of pet, etc.

    f. For example: The relationship could be explained by the financial status of individuals (e.g., those who are more financially secure may be happier and are able to afford to own pets). Health status could also explain the relationship; those who are healthier are happier and feel able to own a pet.

Exercise 8.8

1. two; interval or ratio (in either order)

3. criterion

5. multiple regression; *R*

Exercise 8.9

1. *Y* predicted; *Y'*

3. slope; *Y*-intercept

5. change in *Y* with each unit of change in *X*; *b*

7. standard error of the estimate; $s_{y'}$

9. Coefficient of determination; r^2

Exercise 8.10

1. yes; $p = .025$, which is less than .05

3. 2.5% or .025; 0 (zero)

5. $Y' = 2.08X - 1.60$

7. Answers will vary. Following is an example.

Results

The relationship between ratings of the environment as an important political issue and the number of hours spent outside weekly was examined and showed a significant positive correlation, $r = .38$, $p = .02$. Views on the importance of the environment accounted for 14% of the variability in the number of hours spent outside.

A linear regression was computed using views on the importance of the environment to predict the number of hours spent outside and was significant, $F(1, 33) = 5.55$, $p = .02$. The regression equation ($Y' = 2.08X - 1.60$) showed that hours outside increased 2.08 for each unit that the rating of the importance of the environment increased. The standard error of the estimate was 4.16.

Exercise 8.11 Review of Different Correlational Statistics

1. Complete the following chart:

Correlational Statistics

Scale of Measurement	Correlational Analysis	Appropriate for What Design(s)?
Two interval/ratio variables	Pearson's correlation coefficient (r)	Correlational design
One dichotomous, one interval/ratio	Point-biserial correlation coefficient (r_{pb})	Correlational or experimental designs
Two nominal variables with two or more categories	Chi-square test for independence (χ^2)	Correlational or experimental designs
Two ordinal (ranked) variables	Spearman rho (r_s)	Correlational design

Chapter 8: IBM® SPSS® Practice Exercises

1. a. Minutes on Internet $M = 77.95$, $SD = 78.27$; Likelihood to find partner $M = 2.90$, $SD = 1.33$

    b. Pearson's r

c.

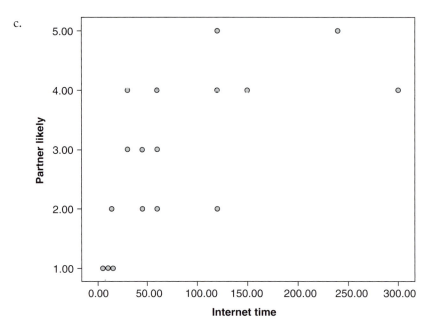

The graph suggests a positive relationship between time on the Internet and views about finding a romantic partner on the Internet.

d. H_0: Time on the Internet and views about finding a partner on the Internet are not related.

H_a: Time on the Internet will be positively related to views about finding a partner on the Internet.

e. $r = .639, p = .002$

f. yes, computed $p = .002$ which is $< .05$

g. $r^2 = .41$

h. Yes, the relationship between the variables is significant, so it is appropriate to compute a regression equation.

i. $Y' = .011X + 2.05$

j. $s_y = 1.05$ for a 5-point scale (predicting view about likelihood of finding a romantic partner on the Internet). This is 20% error on the scale, so it could be considered moderate.

k. $Y' = .011(90) + 2.05 = 3.04$

l. Include the descriptive statistics for the variables, the statistical test and results, state type of relationship, effect size, regression equation, and its meaning.

m. Include the major findings for the correlation and regression and your interpretation of the meanings (relative to past literature if you have it), implications and usefulness of the findings, possible flaws, and future studies to address them.

CHAPTER 9

Exercise 9.1

1. Causality, cause and effect, causation, causal relationship, causative factor, effect of one variable on another, one variable affects another

3. correlation; sequence; ruling out alternative explanations

5. confound

Exercise 9.2

1. Statistical regression

3. Selection

5. History

7. Maturation

Exercise 9.3

1.

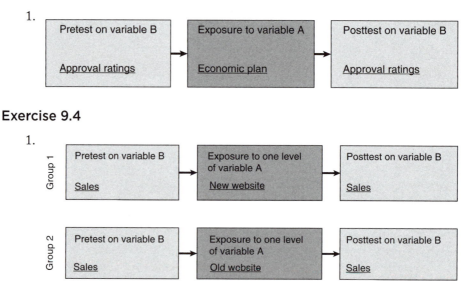

Exercise 9.4

1.

3. Testing would be a threat only in the design from question 1 that includes a pretest. This can be avoided by making the pretest exactly the same across the groups or by eliminating it altogether.

5. History is the threat to internal validity, and this is a problem because the groups are experiencing different events (other than exposure to different websites).

7. Instrumentation is the threat to internal validity, and this is a problem because it might be the differences in measures used rather than the websites that caused any observed difference in the groups.

Exercise 9.5

1. manipulation of an independent variable; measurement of the dependent variable; random assignment to IV condition (and may also note that control of extraneous variables is important)

3. independent; dependent

5. control

7. manipulation check

Exercise 9.6

1. independent; dependent

3.

Recruit participants
Prescreen for: <u>Ability to hear and understand language spoken in study (e.g. English), 18 or older (unless you have parental consent).</u>
Inform potential participants: <u>that they will listen to police instructions and then be asked follow-up questions, their participation is voluntary, they can withdraw at any time without penalty, and that their answers will be confidential.</u>

↓

Randomly assign participants to independent variable (IV) conditions
<u>Simple, stratified, or cluster random assignment.</u>
<u>If simple random assignment: flip a coin, pull numbers out of a hat; or do other random assignment procedure for each individual;</u>   <u>if stratified random assignment: divide sample into strata first (e.g., men and women), then flip coin, or do other random assignment procedure within each stratum;</u>   <u>if cluster random assignment: randomly assign each cluster to IV condition.</u>

IV condition (or level) 1:	**IV condition (or level) 2:**
<u>Officer repeats instructions</u>	<u>Officer includes listenability features</u>

Keep everything else constant (the same) across the two conditions
The officer should be the same in both conditions and deliver the instructions in the same tone of voice and with the same nonverbal gestures (consider taping the participants at about the same time of day and in the same room, give same greeting and instructions, use same DV measure.

↓

Measure Dependent Variable (DV)
DV: Comprehension of instructions; could operationally define by giving participants a comprehension test, or having participants repeat or carry out the instructions and code for accuracy.

Exercise 9.7

1. Hawthorne effect

3. experimenter expectancy effects

5. waitlist control

Exercise 9.8

1. You should not explicitly tell the participants that there are two different groups, and you could covertly randomly assign them to condition (e.g., don't flip a coin in front of them). You could also create a cover story so that the participants are not aware of the real purpose of the study, such as telling the participants you want them to focus on how well the officer delivers the instructions.

3. If you controlled the scope of the instructions, the room the participants were in, and so on to increase internal validity, you likely weakened the external validity. In this case, we would question the ecological validity (a type of external validity) because the police officer would not be giving real instructions in a real-life situation. In real-world situations, citizens might be more emotional or distracted than in a lab setting.

CHAPTER 10

Exercise 10.1

1. correlational; quasi-experimental; experiment

3. randomly assign participants to a group; manipulate an IV; imply causation

5. do not

7. manipulate an IV

9. do not

Exercise 10.2

1. correlational; predictor; outcome

3. Randomly assign households to recycling condition (each week vs. each month) *or* cluster households by blocks or streets and then randomly assign the housing clusters to recycling condition.

Exercise 10.3

1. independent-samples experiment

3. Yes; the requirements for an experiment were met and we can assume causation.

5. Use an existing valid and reliable measure of novel uses or creativity; rate the uses on more than one criterion (trait); have more than one person rate the generated uses of objects; record the session so that you don't miss any responses generated; collect both the creative uses names and the gestures that accompanied them.

7. Studies involving children require extra concern about ethics in terms of consent (both parents/guardian and child), establishing rapport with the child at the beginning of the study, being vigilant about each child's comfort level during the study (they may be less willing than an adult to say they are too stressed or want to stop), having the child leave the study feeling satisfied with her performance or not anxious or stressed by it.

Exercise 10.4

1. independent-samples *t* test

3. chance alone

Exercise 10.5

1. standard error of the difference between the means; SD_{x-x}

3. pooled variance; standard deviation; N

5. 0 (zero)

7. t_{crit}

9. homogeneity of variance

11. a. Simple experiment; There are two groups, participants are randomly assigned, an IV is manipulated, and its effect on a DV is measured.

    b. H_a: Students who take notes in longhand will retain more information from a lecture than those who take notes on a computer.

    c. For this study: IV = notetaking method; levels = longhand and computer notes; DV = short answer test scores
$df = 25$
$t_{crit} = 2.060$

    d. yes, $t_{obt} > t_{crit}$ OR the obtained t value is greater than the critical t value

    e. These results are not significant as $t_{obt} < t_{crit}$. In this case, $t_{crit} = 2.021$ for $p < .05$, two-tailed test.

Exercise 10.6

1. confidence interval

3. We are more satisfied with the first confidence interval (1.65, 4.80) as it represents a smaller range of possible mean differences. The second confidence interval suggests there is greater error in the ability of our study to represent the actual difference between the groups.

Exercise 10.7

1. point-biserial correlation squared; Cohen's d

3. Cohen's d; d

5. This is a strong effect size, with 50% of the variability in the DV accounted for by the IV.

Exercise 10.8

1. Practical significance is the usefulness of our findings or their implications for everyday life.

Exercise 10.9

1. a. Quasi-experimental; there is a manipulated variable (IV) and DV is measured (liking of class), but there is no random assignment to group/level.

    b. H_a: Students will like a class more when an instructor uses humor than when the instructor does not use humor.

    c. For this study: IV = humor in class; levels = humor vs. no humor; DV = liking of class.

    d. homogeneity of variance; Levene's test is significant; $p = .008$

    e. Because Levene's is significant, we use the second line of the t test output, and the p value is greater than .05 ($p = .052$) or not significant. We interpret the study as showing use of humor by instructors in the classroom has no impact on students' liking of a class. (If we had not violated the assumption of homogeneity of variance, we could have concluded that humor did have a significant effect on students' liking for a class based on the first line of output, $p = .046$.)

    f. $r_{pb}^2 = .19$

    g. $d = .86$

    h. Results should include the IV and DV, M, SD for each group, the type of statistical test (in this case, an independent-samples t test) and its results (use the values on the second line of the output), and the effect size (either r_{pb}^2 or d). Clarify with your instructor whether you need to include the confidence interval (found in the Independent Samples Test box of output). You should state that Levene's was significant (or that the assumption of homogeneity of variance was violated) and that a more stringent t test was used. Follow APA format in reporting your statistics.

    i. You can conclude that humor was not related to students' liking for a class. You might point out that the results were in the direction you expected but that students in the humor class showed much greater variability in their liking for the course. Perhaps that had to do with the type of humor or that students have very different views about what is humorous; thus, maybe some students did not interpret the instructor humor as such. Remember that the design is a quasi-experiment and you should not imply causation.

    j. An obvious flaw is the large difference in the variability of liking by the two groups. You could repeat the study, but first pilot what students find humorous before an instructor includes it in a class. This first step may decrease the variability in liking ratings when humor is used.

Exercise 10.10

1. multiple-groups design *or* multiple independent-groups design
3. correlational, quasi-experimental, experimental
5. more

Exercise 10.11

1. one-way analysis of variance *or* one-way ANOVA
3. between-group; within-group
5. within-group
7. error; treatment
9. treatment or between-group; error or within group
11. larger

Exercise 10.12

1. summary
3. sums of squares between groups
5. between
7. 1; $df_{\text{between}} + df_{\text{within}}$
9.

	Sum of Squares	df	Mean Square	F
Between Groups	43.844	**3**	**14.615**	**19.155**
Within Groups	**21.375**	28	**.763**	
Total	65.219	31		

11. a. 32
    b. 8
    c. yes; The *F* here is greater than the critical *F* of 2.95.
    d. Compute a post hoc test because F is significant and we want to know which of the 4 groups differ from one another.
    e. $k(k-1)/2 = 4(3)/2 = 12/2 = 6$

Exercise 10.13

1. a. dress styles; 4
    b. attractiveness
    c. less than .1%; zero
    d. business suit

e. khakis & vest

f. no; Levene's test was not significant ($p = .34$)

g. $\eta^2 = .67$; strong

h. jeans & polo vs. jeans & t shirt ($p = .03$);
   jeans & polo vs. business suit ($p < .001$);
   jeans & t shirt vs. business suit ($p = .004$);
   jeans & t shirt vs. khakis & vest ($p < .001$);
   business suit vs. jeans & polo ($p < .001$);
   business suit vs. khakis & vest ($p < .001$)

i. Answers will vary. Following is an example.

Results

A one-way ANOVA examined the effect of male clothing on ratings of attractiveness and was significant, $F(3, 28) = 19.16$, $p < .001$. Clothing type accounted for 67% of the variability in attractiveness ratings. An LSD post hoc test was performed and showed that all of the clothing types differed significantly from one another except khakis & vest ($M = 7.75$, $SD = .89$) vs. jeans & polo ($M = 7.00$, $SD = .76$; $p = .10$). Males dressed in a business suit ($M = 4.62$, $SD = 1.06$) were perceived as significantly less attractive than males in the other clothing—khakis & vest ($p < .001$); jeans & polo ($p < .001$); and jeans & t-shirt ($M = 6.00$, $SD = .76$; $p = .004$). In addition, males dressed in jeans & t-shirt were perceived as significantly less attractive than males dressed in khakis & vest ($p < .001$) and jeans & polo ($p = .03$).

j. Answers will vary. Following is an example.

Discussion

As expected, the clothing that males wear affects perceptions of their attractiveness. Males in a business suit, the most formal of the clothing styles, were perceived as significantly less attractive than males dressed in more casual attire. However, males wearing a t-shirt and jeans, the most casual dress style, were viewed as significantly less attractive than those wearing jeans and a polo or khakis and a vest. It appears that college students rate as less attractive those wearing clothing at the more extreme ends of the spectrum. They rated those wearing slightly casual (jeans and a polo) and slightly formal (khakis and vest) styles as more attractive. The effect of clothing was strong, accounting for almost two-thirds of the variability in attractiveness ratings. This suggests that college males who are interested in appearing attractive to their peers should select a middle-of-the-road attire, not too casual and not too formal. These findings may also be of interest to those who sell clothing as they develop new lines.

The results may be restricted to those who are in a casual environment (college classrooms) for many hours of the week. Future studies should examine similar ages of male targets and participants who are not in college as well as a variety of older ages before these findings can be generalized to the wider population.

Exercise 10.14

1. a. She is using nominal data (frequency of males and females), rather than interval or ratio data. She could change her measure to something interval or ratio or compute a different (appropriate) statistical test.

   b. There is no random assignment. He puts the first 25 into 1 group, etc. These people may be different from the others and that is why they scored better, not because of the time constraint. He should randomly assign participants to condition.

   c. She is retaining the null (saying there was no effect) but saying she may have committed a Type I error, which is impossible. There is no chance of a Type I, but there is a chance of a Type II.

Chapter 10: IBM® SPSS® PRACTICE EXERCISES

Practice Exercise 1

1. Quasi-experimental two independent-groups design

2. IV = type of continuing education (mindfulness or general leadership); DV = supervisor effectiveness

3. H_a: Supervisors who participate in mindfulness education will be rated as more effective than supervisors who participate in general leadership education.

4.

Group Statistics

	Mindfulness	N	Mean	Std. Deviation	Std. Error Mean
Leadership	Mindful	15	6.1333	1.12546	.29059
	Not mindful	15	5.0000	1.55839	.40237

Independent Samples Test

		Levene's Test for Equality of Variances		t-test for Equality of Means							
										95% Confidence Interval of the Difference	
		F	Sig.	t	df	Sig. (2-tailed)	Mean Difference	Std. Error Difference	Lower	Upper	
Leadership	Equal variances assumed	.830	.370	2.283	28	.030	1.13333	.49634	.11664	2.15003	
	Equal variances not assumed			2.283	25.481	.031	1.13333	.49634	.11209	2.15458	

Correlations

		Course	Effectiveness
Course	Pearson Correlation	1	−.396*
	Sig. (2-tailed)		.030
	N	30	30
Effectiveness	Pearson Correlation	−.396*	1
	Sig. (2-tailed)	.030	
	N	30	30

*Correlation is significant at the 0.05 level (2-tailed).

5. Yes, $p = .03$

6. $r_{pb}^2 = .16$; moderate strength; Cohen's $d = .83$; strong

7. Report the IV and DV and t test results, descriptive statistics for each group, effect size, confidence interval for the difference between the means.

8. Include whether your results were significant; whether they supported your hypothesis; if you know something about the topic, how it compares to past studies; the strength of the effect; the implications/practical significance; any flaws; and how future studies might address them.

Practice Exercise 3

1. Multiple independent-groups experiment

2. IV = type of ad; DV = likelihood of voting for the candidate

3.

Report

	Likelihood Vote		
Ad	Mean	N	Std. Deviation
rationale	55.8333	12	18.92969
berate	42.5000	12	17.90124
contrast	73.7500	12	18.23147
Total	57.3611	36	22.05468

ANOVA Table

		Sum of Squares	df	Mean Square	F	Sig.
Likelihood Vote * Ad	Between Groups (Combined)	5901.389	2	2950.694	8.754	.001
	Within Groups	11122.917	33	337.058		
	Total	17024.306	35			

Measures of Association

	Eta	Eta Squared
Likelihood Vote * Ad	.589	.347

Test of Homogeneity of Variances

Likelihood Vote			
Levene Statistic	df1	df2	Sig.
.046	2	33	.955

Multiple Comparisons

Dependent Variable: Likelihood Vote						
LSD						
		Mean Difference (I-J)	Std. Error	Sig.	95% Confidence Interval	
(I) Ad	(J) Ad				Lower Bound	Upper Bound
rationale	berate	13.33333	7.49509	.084	−1.9155	28.5822
	contrast	−17.91667*	7.49509	.023	−33.1655	−2.6678
berate	rationale	−13.33333	7.49509	.084	−28.5822	1.9155
	contrast	−31.25000*	7.49509	.000	−46.4989	−16.0011
contrast	rationale	17.91667*	7.49509	.023	2.6678	33.1655
	berate	31.25000*	7.49509	.000	16.0011	46.4989

*The mean difference is significant at the 0.05 level.

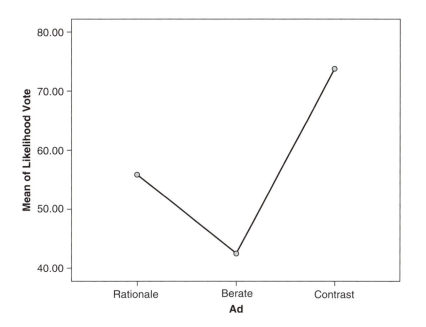

4. Yes, the ANOVA shows $p = .001$

5. $\eta^2 = .35$; type of ad has a strong effect on likelihood to vote for a candidate

6. Answers will vary. Following is an example.

Results

Registered voters reported how likely they were to vote for a candidate after viewing an ad that contrasted the candidate's and opponent's views ($M = 73.75$, $SD = 18.23$), described the candidate's rationale for their views ($M = 55.83$, $SD = 18.93$), or berated the opponent ($M = 42.50$, $SD = 17.90$). A one-way between-subjects ANOVA found that the likelihood of voting for the candidate significantly differed for the different ads, $F(2, 33) = 8.75$, $p = .001$, $\eta^2 = .35$. A Least Significant Difference post hoc test showed that voters who saw the contrasting views ad were significantly more likely to vote for the candidate than were the voters who saw the ad berating the opponent ($p < .001$) and the voters who saw the ad describing the candidate's rationale for views ($p = .02$). Voters who saw the berating ad and the candidate's rationale did not differ in their likelihood to vote for the candidate ($p = .08$).

7. Discussion should include a restatement of major findings and whether they supported your hypothesis, a comparison with past research, the strength of the results in terms of their implications/practical significance (e.g., what type of ads candidates may want to run), a discussion of possible flaws or limitations of the study (e.g., only three types of ads, only one candidate with gender, age, ethnicity, experience, etc.), possible future studies to expand on results or to correct flaws of the current study.

CHAPTER 11

Exercise 11.1

1. random assignment

3. more

Exercise 11.2

1. a variable that is correlated to the DV/outcome variable

3. in the preexisting groups and then analyze their scores on the outcome variable

5. correlated

Exercise 11.3

1. a. Age may not be an appropriate matching variable as it is unlikely to significantly correlate with English-language skills (older and younger participants are likely to possess a range of skills in English).

   b. Time studying English might be a better matching variable.

3.

Participant	AWS score	Participant	AWS score	Matched Pairs
1	25	18	25	1 – 18
5	21	16	23	5 – 16
2	18	15	20	2 – 15
8	16	14	17	8 – 14
6	15	17	15	6 – 17
4	14	13	14	4 – 13
3	12	12	13	3 – 12
7	11	19	7	7 – 19
9	6	20	6	9 – 20
10	5	11	5	10 – 11

Exercise 11.4

1. control; error

3. In repeated-measures design, participants experience all conditions of the study. In multiple-trials study, the participants experience the same condition multiple times.

5. order; sequence

7. fewer

Exercise 11.5

1. Carryover, boredom, or fatigue effects could result from back-to-back sessions for this age group. The researcher should spread out participation in the sessions, such as one session on one morning and one session the next morning.

3. No, repeated measures design should not be used when a permanent change results from participation. Once students learn how to do long division (even if partially), they cannot be a naïve participant for the second teaching method. The teacher should use a matched-pairs or independent-groups design.

Exercise 11.6

1. paired-samples (or within-subjects or dependent-samples) t test

3. between matched participants' scores (matched design) or differences between a participant's scores in the different conditions

Exercise 11.7

1. mean difference; M_D

3. smaller; the SD_D is the variability associated with mean differences (a sampling distribution), which is smaller than the variability for raw scores

5. a. 11

   b. 2.201

   c. yes; $t_{obt} > t_{crit}$

   d. $(SD_D)(-t_{crit}) + (M_D) \leq \mu_D \leq (SD_D)(+ t_{crit}) + (M_D) = .34(-2.201)$
      $+ .84 \leq \mu_D \leq .34(2.201) + .84 = -.74834 + .84 \leq \mu_D \leq .74834$
      $+ .84 = .09 \leq \mu_D \leq 1.59$

   e. $d = \dfrac{(M_1 - M_2)}{\sqrt{(SD_1^2 + SD_2^2) \div 2}} = \dfrac{7.92 - 7.08}{\sqrt{(1.56^2 + 1^2) \div 2}} = \dfrac{.84}{\sqrt{(2.43 + 1) \div 2}}$

   $= \dfrac{.84}{\sqrt{1.72}} = \dfrac{.84}{1.31} = .64$

   Moderate strength

   f. There is almost a 10% difference on the means for the multiple-choice quiz (7.9 vs. 7.0), a grade difference that students would notice. Plus there is moderate strength in terms of the effect of the type of presentation. These results suggest that the findings would have practical significance for students in their classes.

Exercise 11.8

1. a. repeated-measures experiment

    b. The participants are elderly, so the researcher should take special care that the participants are able to give consent for their participation, or the researcher must ask the participant's legal guardian for consent in addition to the agreement of the participant. The study should be explained in terms that the participant understands and in a form that is loud enough or in large print, if necessary. The person administering the word game should be sensitive to any signs that the participant is too fatigued, agitated, or upset by the process. The researcher should also ensure that the participant remains awake during the comedy viewing. The researcher should make clear verbally and by their behavior that the participant is not being judged on his or her performance during the word game or during the alertness measure. All other ethical considerations for an ethical study should be in effect (allowed to leave at any time, no sense of coercion, answer questions after the study, etc.).

    c. H_o: Alertness in the elderly will not differ after playing a word game or viewing a comedy segment.

       H_a: Alertness in the elderly will be greater after playing a word game than after viewing a comedy segment.

    d. 7

    e. 8; $df = N - 1$ and $df = 7$ plus the descriptive statistics table lists $N = 8$

    f. Yes, $p = .04$ which shows a significant difference

    g. Answers will vary. Following is an example.

Results

When elderly participants played a word game ($M = 14.50$, $SD = 5.29$), they scored higher on mental alertness than when they watched a comedy segment ($M = 13.00$, $SD = 4.66$). A within-subjects t test showed that the difference in alertness was significant, $t(7) = 2.51$, $p = .04$, $d = .30$. We are 95% confident that the mean difference for alertness falls between .09 and 2.91.

    h. Answers will vary. Following is an example.

Discussion

As predicted, the results showed that elderly adults (90 years or older) who play a word game are significantly more alert than when they watch a comedy segment for the same duration. The type of activity only had a small effect on alertness, so we cannot make too strong a claim advocating for participation in a mental activity rather than a passive activity. However, because we want the elderly to remain cognitively active, even a small increase in alertness can be beneficial, and the gain was easily achieved given that the word game lasted only 10 minutes.

Future studies should include a larger sample and elderly of varying cognitive levels to learn about the limits of the external validity of the findings. In addition, the duration of the two activities should be increased to determine whether longer cognitive stimulation produces a stronger effect in this population. In addition, other types of cognitive games should be studied to determine whether they produce the same effect.

Exercise 11.9

1. same

3. $k(k-1)$ where k = number of conditions

5. Partial

7. random partial

9. more; there are more orders to keep up with in the multiple-dependent groups designs

Exercise 11.10

1. 12

   a. complete

   b. partial

   c. BMI may be related to confidence in the ability to lose weight, as those who perceive they have less weight to lose may feel more confident than those who want to lose a lot of weight. Age seems unrelated to confidence in losing weight. Better matching variables might be how motivated the participants are to lose weight, whether participants were successful in losing weight before, or how much weight they want to lose, as these seem related to how confident a person might be that he or she can lose weight. (You may think of other appropriate matching variables.)

3. a. 6

   b. CBN BNC NCB CNB BCN NBC, children would then be assigned to one of these orders

   c. You would have each condition once in each order. You could use CBN BNC NCB or any other three sequences, as long as you meet the requirement for each condition once in each order.

Exercise 11.11

1. dependent-groups one way ANOVA; within-subjects one way ANOVA; repeated-measures one way ANOVA

3. sphericity

Exercise 11.12

1. between-group variance; within-group variance

3. sums of squares of subjects; SS_S; interaction sums of squares; SS_{AxS}

5. SS_A (sums of squares between conditions—treatment plus error variability) + SS_{AxS} (interaction sums of squares—error associated with participant by condition) + SS_S (sums of squares of subjects—error associated with individual participants)

7. partial eta square; $\eta^2_{partial}$

9. a. H_0: Weighing more frequently has no effect on confidence about losing weight
    H_a: State which groups will differ significantly in confidence about losing weight.

    b.

Source	SS	df	MS	F
Weighing (A)	24.60	3	8.20	4.10
Subject	72.72	36		
Interaction (A × S)	54	27	2	
Total	151.32	39		

    c. 4.60; not significant at $p < .01$, as $F_{obt} < F_{crit}$

    d. yes; $F_{obt} = 4.10$, which is greater than $F_{crit} = 2.96$ at $p < .05$

    e. $\eta^2_{partial} = SS_A/(SS_A + SS_{A \times S}) = 24.60/(24.60 + 54) = 24.60/78.60 = .31$. A strong effect size; frequency of weigh-ins accounts for 31% of the variability in confidence in losing weight.

    f. 6

    g. $LSD = \dfrac{t_{crit}}{MS_W} \sqrt{MS_W \left(\dfrac{1}{n_k} + \dfrac{1}{n_k} \right)} = 2.060\sqrt{2(1/10 + 1/10)}$

    $= 2.060\sqrt{2(.20)} = 2.060\sqrt{(.40)}$

    $= 2.060(.63) = 1.30$

	Daily	Every other day	Every third day	Weekly
Means	(2.6)	(3.8)	(5.5)	(7.2)
Daily	—	1.20	2.90*	–4.60*
Every other day	—	—	1.70*	3.40*
Every third day	—	—	—	1.70*
Weekly				

*$p < .05$

Exercise 11.13

1. $F(3, 21) = 21.68, p < .001$

3. Include descriptive statistics for confidence for the four groups; you may find it easier to present the M, SD for groups in a table; state the type of test (matched-groups one-way ANOVA) and the results (F, df, p) and the effect size ($\eta^2_{partial}$), state that the results are significant and that a post hoc test was computed using Bonferroni's correction. Describe the results of the post hoc test, noting the significance level for the groups that differed while also noting which group comparisons were not significant. Be sure to present the findings (and table, if you use one) in APA format.

Exercise 11.14

1. Possible flaws include the following:

   a. Your classmate didn't measure test anxiety; there is a possible order effect as she did not randomly assign the order of the two conditions; there could be carryover effects in terms of knowledge about global warming; you shouldn't use repeated measures when there is a risk of permanent change in DV (knowledge of global warming); it is better to use matched design that matches on test anxiety and randomly assign to condition.

   b. Many potential participants refused to attend either session and many clients dropped out of the study, so their matched partners also needed to be dropped, leaving very few of the original sample (22 of 50)—the results, then, do not represent the clients at the agency and the director should not generalize to everyone. This is a quasi-experimental design and you can't assume causation. The director should try to encourage broader participation and perhaps some incentive to finish the course so that there is less mortality and the results represent the agency clients. She should randomly assign matched pairs to the courses if she wants to be able to assume causation. In addition, the effect size is weak, suggesting the courses do not have much impact.

c. Extraversion may not be an appropriate matching variable (doesn't seem related to productivity). The researcher should consider using a matching variable related to productivity, such as past performance, satisfaction with work, length of time as an employee, income, etc. The effect size is moderate, suggesting that the methods of appreciation should be explored further.

Chapter 11: IBM® SPSS® Practice Exercises

Practice Exercise 1

1. Matched-pairs dependent design (experiment)

2. IV = gender of perpetrator; DV = violence

3. State whether you believe that males or females will be rated as more violent when they slap a dating partner.

4.

Paired Samples Statistics

		Mean	N	Std. Deviation	Std. Error Mean
Pair 1	male	6.9000	10	1.37032	.43333
	female	6.2000	10	1.75119	.55377

Paired Samples Test

		Paired Differences							
					95% Confidence Interval of the Difference				
		Mean	Std. Deviation	Std. Error Mean	Lower	Upper	t	df	Sig. (2-tailed)
Pair 1	male - female	.70000	.82327	.26034	.11107	1.28893	2.689	9	.025

5. yes, $p = .025$

6. $d = .44$, weak to moderate effect

7. See the examples for a Results section above and/or in the text. Your results should include descriptive statistics for violence ratings for the male and female perpetrators, state the type of test (matched-pairs *t* test or dependent samples *t* test) and the results (t, df, p) and the effect size (d), state that the results are significant, and the 95% confidence interval for the mean difference. Be sure to present the findings in APA format.

8. See the examples above and/or in the text. State the major findings and whether they supported your hypothesis, providing explanation of the implications and practical significance. (Remember that if you were writing a report from a study you had conducted, you would also compare your results to the findings of past studies.) If you did not find what you expected, you should explain why you think you obtained your results. Your discussion should make clear your interpretation of your findings and not just restate the findings. Note any flaw(s) in the study and how they might have influenced the results and how future studies could correct it/them. Finally, discuss how to further the topic of study (what are next studies to be conducted, what questions does your study raise, etc.).

Practice Exercise 3

1. multiple matched-groups design (experiment)

2. IV = type of ad; DV = persuasiveness

3.

Descriptive Statistics

	Mean	Std. Deviation	N
erotic	14.6000	1.50555	10
traditional	13.9000	1.19722	10
non-traditional	17.5000	1.08012	10
product	15.3000	1.25167	10

Mauchly's Test of Sphericity[a]

Measure: ad							
					Epsilon[b]		
Within Subjects Effect	Mauchly's W	Approx. Chi-Square	df	Sig.	Greenhouse-Geisser	Huynh-Feldt	Lower-bound
factor1	.280	9.837	5	.082	.596	.734	.333

Tests the null hypothesis that the error covariance matrix of the orthonormalized transformed dependent variables is proportional to an identity matrix.
[a] Design: Intercept Within Subjects Design: factor1
[b] May be used to adjust the degrees of freedom for the averaged tests of significance. Corrected tests are displayed in the Tests of Within-Subjects Effects table.

Tests of Within-Subjects Effects

Measure: ad

Source		Type III Sum of Squares	df	Mean Square	F	Sig.	Partial Eta Squared
factor1	Sphericity Assumed	72.875	3	24.292	15.663	.000	.635
	Greenhouse-Geisser	72.875	1.788	40.754	15.663	.000	.635
	Huynh-Feldt	72.875	2.202	33.092	15.663	.000	.635
	Lower-bound	72.875	1.000	72.875	15.663	.003	.635
Error (factor1)	Sphericity Assumed	41.875	27	1.551			
	Greenhouse-Geisser	41.875	16.094	2.602			
	Huynh-Feldt	41.875	19.820	2.113			
	Lower-bound	41.875	9.000	4.653			

Pairwise Comparisons

Measure: ad

(I) factor1	(J) factor1	Mean Difference (I–J)	Std. Error	Sig.[b]	95% Confidence Interval for Difference[b]	
					Lower Bound	Upper Bound
1	2	.700	.260	.149	−.176	1.576
	3	−2.900*	.433	.001	−4.358	−1.442
	4	−.700	.731	1.000	−3.159	1.759
2	1	−.700	.260	.149	−1.576	.176
	3	−3.600*	.400	.000	−4.946	−2.254
	4	−1.400	.653	.364	−3.597	.797
3	1	2.900*	.433	.001	1.442	4.358
	2	3.600*	.400	.000	2.254	4.946
	4	2.200	.696	.069	−.142	4.542
4	1	.700	.731	1.000	−1.759	3.159
	2	1.400	.653	.364	−.797	3.597
	3	−2.200	.696	.069	−4.542	.142

Based on estimated marginal means
* The mean difference is significant at the .05 level.
[b] Adjustment for multiple comparisons: Bonferroni.

4. yes; $p < .001$

5. $\eta^2_{partial} = .64$. This effect size is strong, indicating that 64% of the variability in persuasiveness ratings is accounted for by the type of ad.

6. See suggestions above or in the text for the information that is required for a one-way ANOVA.

7. See suggestions above or in the text for what is required in a Discussion section. Be sure to consider the interpretation of the post hoc tests and the implications for both those who design and those who view ads.

CHAPTER 12

Exercise 12.1

1. factor

3. a hybrid factorial design

5. 2; 3; 5

7. cell

9. main

11. Answers will vary but should explain that an interaction effect allows you to examine how the impact of one factor depends on levels of another factor.

Exercise 12.2

1. religion × year in college

3. year in college × sexism

5. gender × year in college × facial expression

Exercise 12.3

1. Answers will vary, but you should recommend looking at other factors (moderators) that might change the strength or direction of the relationship. Such factors might be education, mental health, physical health, personality, etc.

3. The researcher could examine different news story content (e.g., crime and accidents) in a factorial design to help control for the potential confound. Additionally, examining different news stories would allow for the examination of the complex relationship between news consumption (watching vs. reading) and anxiety.

Exercise 12.4

1. a. main effects

   b. main effects

   c. interaction

   d. main effects

   e. main effects

3. Graph C

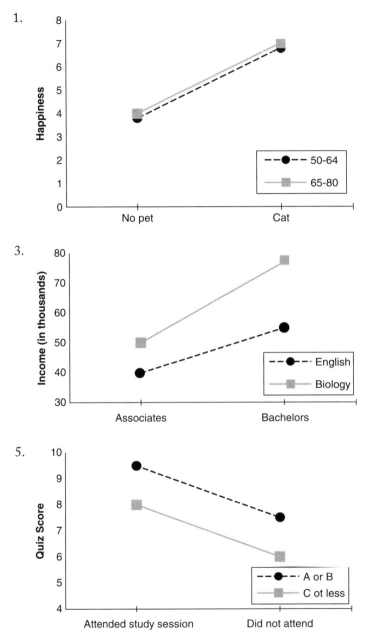

1.

3.

5.

7. The 2(degree) × 2(major) graph is the only one that depicts an interaction.

   The graph suggests that income increases with the more advanced degree, and this is especially evident for those who majored in biology.

Exercise 12.6

1. two

3. interval or ratio

5. a. grand mean

   b. group means

   c. cell means

Exercise 12.7

1.

Tests of Between-Subjects Effects				
Source	Sum of Squares	df	Mean Square	F
Factor 1	137.813	$k_{B1} - 1 = 1$	$SS_{B1}/df_{B1} = 137.813$	$MS_{B1}/MS_w = 52.96$
Factor 2	2.113	$k_{B2} - 1 = 1$	$SS_{B2}/df_{B2} = 2.113$	$MS_{B2}/MS_w = 0.81$
Interaction	25.313	$(df_{B1})(df_{B2}) = 1$	$SS_{B1 \times B2}/df_{B1 \times B2} = 25.313$	$MS_{B1 \times B2}/MS_w = 9.73$
Error	197.750	$C(n - 1) = 76$	$SS_w/df_w = 2.602$	
Total	362.988	$N - 1 = 79$		

3. Compute the effect size ($\eta^2_{partial}$) for each main effect and the interaction using the formula: $\eta^2_{partial} = SS_B/(SS_B + SS_w)$.

	$\eta^2_{partial}$
Main effect for factor 1	.41
Main effect for factor 2	.01
Interaction effect	.11

Exercise 12.8

1. 6.48

3. no ring = 6.82; ring = 6.14

5. a. Main effect for ADHD symptoms: $F(1, 96) = 1.65, p = .20$

   b. Main effect for ring condition: $F(1, 96) = 9.74, p = .002$

   c. ADHD × ring condition interaction: $F(1, 96) = 1.21, p = .27$

7. a. ADHD symptoms: 2%; $\eta^2_{partial} = .02$

   b. Ring condition: 9%; $\eta^2_{partial} = .09$

   c. Interaction: 1%; $\eta^2_{partial} = .01$

Exercise 12.9

1. d. mixed ANOVA

3. a. chi-square test of independence

5. b. two-way between-subjects ANOVA

7. d. mixed ANOVA

Chapter 12: IBM® SPSS® Practice Exercises

Practice Exercise 1

Descriptive Statistics

Posture condition	forget condition	Mean	Std. Deviation	N
1.00 good posture	1.00 no forgetting	3.35	0.96	51
	2.00 forgot keys	3.55	0.83	56
	Total	3.46	0.89	107
2.00 poor posture	1.00 no forgetting	3.51	0.81	55
	2.00 forgot keys	3.09	0.90	56
	Total	3.30	0.88	111
Total	1.00 no forgetting	3.43	0.88	106
	2.00 forgot keys	3.32	0.89	112
	Total	3.38	.888	218

Tests of Between-Subjects Effects

Dependent Variable: how independent?						
Source	Type III Sum of Squares	Df	Mean Square	F	Sig.	Partial Eta Squared
Corrected Model	7.371(a)	3	2.457	3.210	.024	.043
Intercept	2481.255	1	2481.255	3241.978	.000	.938
Posture	1.292	1	1.292	**1.69**	**.36**	**.01**
Forget	.654	1	.654	**0.85**	**.20**	**.004**
Posture * forget	5.237	1	5.237	**6.84**	**.01**	**.03**
Error	163.785	214	.765			
Total	2656.000	218				
Corrected Total	171.156	217				

a R Squared = .043 (Adjusted R Squared = .030)

Practice Exercise 3

1. Abbreviated SPSS Output. If you calculated the statistics by hand, you should have obtained similar results.

Dependent Variable: SBI Anticipate				
Is participant a college student?	gender of participant	Mean	Std. Deviation	N
yes	male	39.1176	7.06532	48
	female	39.8462	7.39736	52
	Total	39.4964	7.21264	100
no	male	41.8868	6.57694	53
	female	41.6154	8.63944	52
	Total	41.7524	7.63210	105
Total	male	40.5707	6.92001	101
	female	40.7308	8.05249	104
	Total	40.6519	7.49796	205

Tests of Between-Subjects Effects

Dependent Variable: SBI Anticipate						
Source	Type III Sum of Squares	Df	Mean Square	F	Sig.	Partial Eta Squared
Corrected Model	275.856[a]	3	91.952	1.651	.179	.024
Intercept	337694.745	1	337694.745	6064.257	.000	.968
collegestudent	263.522	1	263.522	4.732	.031	.023
gender	2.674	1	2.674	.048	.827	.000
collegestudent * gender	12.794	1	12.794	.230	.632	.001
Error	11192.903	201	55.686			
Total	350247.311	205				
Corrected Total	11468.759	204				

[a] R Squared = .024 (Adjusted R Squared = .009)

2. Abbreviated Output:

Dependent Variable: SBI Savor the Moment				
Is participant a college student?	gender of participant	Mean	Std. Deviation	N
yes	male	39.7083	7.44614	48
	female	40.3077	8.72126	52
	Total	40.0200	8.09911	100
no	male	40.5660	7.07789	53
	female	41.0096	7.87431	52
	Total	40.7857	7.45011	105
Total	male	40.1584	7.23150	101
	female	40.6587	8.27567	104
	Total	40.4122	7.76380	205

Tests of Between-Subjects Effects

Dependent Variable: SBI Savour the Moment						
Source	Type III Sum of Squares	Df	Mean Square	F	Sig.	Partial Eta Squared
Corrected Model	44.162[a]	3	14.721	.241	.867	.004
Intercept	334070.323	1	334070.323	5480.470	.000	.965
collegestudent	31.120	1	31.120	.511	.476	.003
gender	13.916	1	13.916	.228	.633	.001
collegestudent * gender	.310	1	.310	.005	.943	.000
Error	12252.258	201	60.957			
Total	347091.250	205				
Corrected Total	12296.420	204				

[a] R Squared = .004 (Adjusted R Squared = −.011)

3. Answers will vary. Following is an example. Add confidence intervals if your professor requires them.

Results

Two-way between-subjects ANOVAs were conducted to examine how college student status and gender predicted positive anticipation for the future and savoring the moment. College students had slightly lower positive anticipation scores ($M = 39.50$, $SD = 7.21$) than those who were not in college ($M = 41.75$, $SD = 7.63$). This difference was statistically significant, $F(1, 201) = 4.73$, $p = .03$, but the effect size was small, $\eta^2 = .02$. Savoring ability was about equal across these groups ($M_{college} = 40.02$, $SD = 8.10$ vs. $M_{nocollege} = 40.79$, $SD = 7.45$), $F(1, 201) = 0.51$, $p = .48$, $\eta^2 = .003$. Gender did not predict either anticipation ($M_{female} = 40.73$, $SD = 8.05$ vs. $M_{male} = 40.57$, $SD = 6.92$), $F(1, 210) = 0.05$, $p = .83$, $\eta^2 < .001$, nor savoring ($M_{female} = 40.66$, $SD = 8.28$ vs. , $M_{male} = 40.16$, $SD = 7.23$), $F(1, 210) = 0.23$, $p = .63$, $\eta^2 = .001$. Likewise, the interactions were not statistically significant for anticipation, $F(1, 210) = 0.23$, $p = .63$, $\eta^2 = .001$, or savoring the moment, $F(1, 210) = 0.005$, $p = .94$, $\eta^2 < .001$.

CHAPTER 13

Exercise 13.1

1. parametric statistics

3.

Parametric	Nonparametric
Interval or ratio data	**Nominal or ordinal data**
Raw data are normally distributed	Distribution free
Can test for interactions	**Can test for independence**
Minimum of 10/group	Small samples or pilot studies
Complicated computations	**Less complicated computations**
Homogeneity of variance	Violates homogeneity of variance
Powerful	**Less powerful**

Exercise 13.2

1. nominal

3. chi-square test for independence, χ^2

Exercise 13.3

1. observed; O

3. total count/number (N); number of categories/groups; N/k

5. a. nominal data

   b. independent groups

   c. minimum of 5 expected in each category

   d. every member belongs to only one category

7. a. The number of voters in each age group will be equal or will not deviate from normal.

   b. The number of voters in each age group will differ from expected (or normal).

   c. 3

   d. 20

   e. 400

   f. equal

   g. $\chi^2_{\text{crit}} = 7.81$

   h. no; the $t_{obt} < t_{crit}$ (5.35 < 7.81)

9. a. The frequency of children preferring the three types of snacks (healthy, moderately healthy, junk food) will not differ from normal.

    b. The frequency of children preferring the three types of snacks will differ from normal.

    c. 60; 3; 20

    d. $\chi^2 = \dfrac{\Sigma(O-E)^2}{E} = \dfrac{\Sigma(10-20)^2 + \Sigma(20-20)^2 + \Sigma(30-20)^2}{20} = \dfrac{200}{20} = 10$

    e. yes; $\chi^2_{obt} = 10.00 > \chi^2_{crit} = 5.99$

    f. 5%; zero

    g. Answers will vary. Following is an example.

Results

Young children ($N = 60$) selected the type of snack they preferred (healthy, moderately healthy, and junk food). A chi-square goodness of fit with equal frequencies (33.3%) was computed and showed that the preference for snacks differed from expected frequencies, $\chi^2(2, N = 60) = 10.00$. More children preferred junk food (30 or 50%) than expected, while fewer children preferred healthy snacks (10 or 16.7%) than expected. The number of children who preferred moderately healthy snacks (20 or 33.3%) was equal to the expected frequency.

    h. Answers will vary. Following is an example.

Discussion

More young children than expected preferred junk food, while fewer than expected preferred healthy snacks. The number preferring moderately healthy snacks fell in between. Three times as many children chose junk food as chose healthy snacks. This finding suggests that adults (parents, caregivers, teachers) who influence or determine the snacks of young children should be careful to limit children's snack choices in order to ensure that children eat a minimum of junk food. The current study does not provide information about whether the type of snack under each category influences children's snack choices. For instance, would children be more likely to choose fruits than vegetables when they are offered as a healthy snack? Future research should examine what types of food increase children's selection of healthy snacks. Given the attraction to junk food, those supervising young children should consider restricting access to such snacks and encouraging the selection of healthy snacks when such foods are only one of the choices offered.

Exercise 13.4

1. equal frequencies; in the first box of the output all of the Expected N's are the same (12.5).

3. 1.2%; zero

5. These results with adolescents participating in the Olympic Development Program in the U.S. are consistent with the Relative Age Effect (RAE). These results suggest that RAE generalizes to adolescents.

7. For example: the researcher might suggest that coaches/principals pay attention to birth months and allow high school students of all birth months similar opportunities to improve their skills, rather than focusing only on those already most highly skilled.

Exercise 13.5

1. contingency table

3. 5

5. a. 2×2

   b. phi squared (ϕ^2)

   c. 1

   d. yes; The obtained χ^2 is greater than the critical χ^2 in Table C.7 (5.62 > 3.84)

Exercise 13.6

1. 2×3

3. 50

5. $V^2 = .04$ (Cramer's V squared); Four percent of the variability in the relationship between immigrant status and employment status is accounted for; weak

7. Answers will vary. Following is an example.

Results

A chi-square test of independence was computed to investigate whether immigrant status and employment status were independent. The result was not significant, χ^2

$(2, N = 50) = 1.88$, $p = .39$, $V^2 = .04$. Employment status was similar for both groups, who were more likely to work full time ($N_{immigrants} = 13$; $N_{nonimmigrants} = 15$) than be unemployed ($N_{immigrants} = 4$; $N_{nonimmigrants} = 6$) or work part time ($N_{immigrants} = 8$; $N_{nonimmigrants} = 4$).

Exercise 13.7

1. Spearman's rho; r_s

3. a. no, the obtained $r_s = .36$ is less than the critical $r_s = .409$ for a two-tailed test at $p < .05$ (from Table C.8 in Appendix C)

   b. yes, the obtained r_s is greater than the critical $r_s = .343$ for a one-tailed test at $p < .05$

Exercise 13.8

1. r_s

3. 15

5. probability of a Type I error = 2.3%; no chance of a Type II because we reject the null hypothesis.

Exercise 13.9

Design	Parametric Test	Nonparametric Test
Correlation/No groups	Pearson's r	Ordinal data: Spearman's rho
Two independent groups	Independent-samples t test	Nominal data: Chi-square test of independence Ordinal data: Mann-Whitney U test with Rank Sums test
Two related groups (matching or repeated measures)	Related-samples t test	Nominal data: McNemar test Ordinal data: Wilcoxon T test
Multiple independent groups	One-way ANOVA for independent groups	Ordinal data: Kruskal-Wallis H test
Multiple related groups	One-way ANOVA for related or dependent groups	Nominal data: Cochran Q test Ordinal data: Friedman χ^2

Chapter 13: IBM® SPSS® Practice Exercises

Practice Exercise 1

1. a. You should have run a chi-square goodness of fit test.

b.

Chi-Square Test

Frequencies

Gender of character

	Observed N	Expected N	Residual
male	106	64.5	41.5
female	23	64.5	−41.5
Total	129		

Test Statistics

	Gender of character
Chi-Square	53.403[a]
df	1
Asymp. Sig.	.000

[a] 0 cells (0.0%) have expected frequencies less than 5. The minimum expected cell frequency is 64.5.

c. Results indicate that there were significantly more named male characters ($n = 106$) than female characters ($n = 23$), $\chi^2(1, N = 129) = 53.40, p < .001$.

2. a. Again, you should have run a chi-square goodness of fit test.

b.

Character's Status by End of Season 6

	Observed N	Expected N	Residual
alive	51	59.0	−8.0
dead	67	59.0	8.0
Total	118		

Test Statistics

	Gender of character
Chi-Square	2.169[a]
df	1
asymp. sig.	.141

a 0 cells (0.0%) have expected frequencies less than 5. The minimum expected cell frequency is 59.0.

c. Results indicate that although there were more first-season characters who were dead by the end of Season 6 ($n = 67$) than were alive ($n = 51$), the results were not statistically significant, $\chi^2(1, N = 118) = 2.17, p = .14$.

Practice Exercise 3

1. Spearman's rho (r_s)

2.

Correlations

			judge1	judge2
Spearman's rho	judge1	Correlation Coefficient	1.000	.297
		Sig. (2-tailed)	.	.405
		N	20	10
	judge2	Correlation Coefficient	.297	1.000
		Sig. (2-tailed)	.405	.
		N	10	10

State the variables analyzed and the test, $r_s = .279, p = .405$; note the relationship is not significant, suggesting that the two judges' views of quality of the poetry is not related. You would not be confident that you could determine the winner of the contest based on these findings.

CHAPTER 14

Exercise 14.1

1. population

3. Sample-based studies are used to make inferences about a population. School administrators need to consider their population of students, and if a program such as DARE consistently fails to show effectiveness in sample-based studies, then it is likely that it will likewise be ineffective for the population.

5. It is also possible that the parent is mistaken that DARE was effective for the child because the parent is mistaking correlation for causation. An alternative explanation is that something else prevented the child from using drugs, such as the child's disposition, positive parenting, or peer influence.

Exercise 14.2

1. Provides a holistic, qualitative, and in-depth perspective of a case. This is especially useful if you are examining a unique or rare phenomenon.

3. Grounded theory

5. (a) they often rely on anecdotal information; (b) they lack control, so you cannot determine causality; (c) details of a case study might be overly persuasive, so that the public ignores other information (consider the DARE example in Exercise 14.1).

Exercise 14.3

1. quantitative

3. small N design

5. stable baseline

7. B

9. multiple-manipulation design

11. reversal design

13. multiple-baseline; persons, settings, behaviors

15. A stable baseline serves as the best predictor of future behavior.

Exercise 14.4

1. Yes, there are no trends and very little variation.

3. No, there is an upward trend.

5. Client A, because she has a stable baseline. This means that you could predict that without the intervention, the client would smoke about 20 cigarettes a day. If the client smokes less than this during the intervention phase, you would have some evidence of the intervention's effectiveness. Also Client C, because the trend is going in the opposite direction to what you would expect from the intervention. If the trend is reversed or disrupted during the intervention phase, you would have some evidence of the intervention's effectiveness.

Exercise 14.5

1.

a.

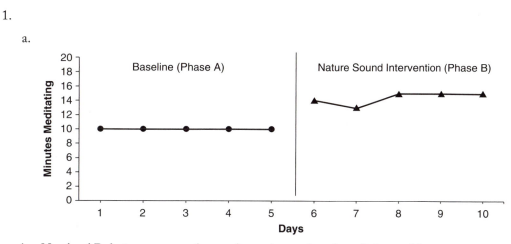

b. No. An AB design cannot rule out alternative explanations. It is possible that the intervention was effective, or it may be that something else caused the increase in meditation time, such as simply deciding to spend more time meditating.

c. i. The first baseline and intervention should be the same as in question 1a, the second baseline should show a similar pattern to the first baseline (with an average of about 10 minutes). For example,

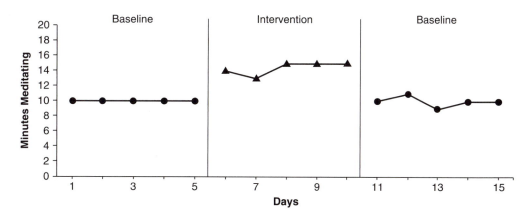

ii. If the intervention is not effective, the graph would show that the second baseline is similar to the intervention or continues to go up with practice (but no intervention). For example,

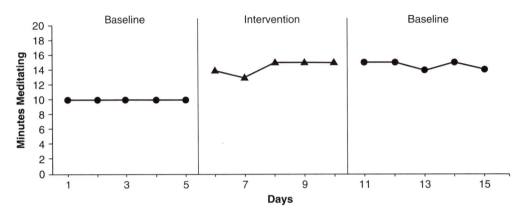

3. Procrastination seems to be on a downward trend overall, and it is difficult to tell whether the treatments had anything to do with this trend or whether there is an alternative explanation. Another baseline phase would be useful to evaluate the effectiveness of treatment 2.

Exercise 14.6

1. Yes, a return to baseline would be ethically appropriate. Although meditation may be a healthy behavior, it is unlikely that returning to the baseline level of meditation will have a severely negative impact on health or well-being.

3. No. Any single incident of driving under the influence could lead to injury or death for the individual and others.

Exercise 14.7

1. (a) Potential to find a cause and effect relationship; (b) can supplement randomized-group experiments; (c) flexibility of repeated assessment

3. they can examine a rare phenomenon

Exercise 14.8

1. Sample-based design because your goal is to make inferences to the population

3. Case study because you are focusing on past behavior of a single individual

5. Sample-based design because your goal is to make inferences to the population of viewers

CHAPTER 15

Exercise 15.1

1. refine it based on past research

3. internal; external

5. Correlational; experiments and quasi-experiments

7. matching; repeated measures

Exercise 15.2

1. a. Descriptive design

   b. Correlational design

   c. Descriptive design

   d. Experimental design

   e. Experimental design

   f. Correlational design

3. Research suggests there may be a nonlinear relationship and/or past research has already established the two-group effect, and you have reason to believe that adding a third or fourth group may lead to different results.

Exercise 15.3

1. a. descriptive statistics

   b. i. independent-samples t test
      ii. dependent-samples t test

   c. i. two-way between-subjects ANOVA
      ii. two-way mixed ANOVA

   d. i. independent-samples t test
      ii. dependent-samples t test

   e. i. one-way between-subjects ANOVA
      ii. one-way within-subjects ANOVA

Exercise 15.4

The inferential statistics you listed in the first column will vary based on what your course covered. Use Table 15.1 in the textbook to check your answers for the remaining columns.